Bed & Breakfast Homes Directory

Homes Away From Home

West Coast

6th Edition

6th Edition

Bed & Breakfast
Homes
Directory

Homes Away From Home
West Coast

by
Diane Knight

Graphics by Kevin McElvain
Maps by Joe McCabe
Editing by Suzy Blackaby
Introduction to British Columbia by Keith Ledbury

Edited by Suzy Blackaby
Cover design by Andrea Hendrick and Steve Penner
Front cover photo by Philip Gaulin
Back cover photo by Richard Shaffer

Typography by Document Design & Data, Felton, California

Printed and bound in U.S.A. by Publishers Press,
Salt Lake City, Utah

Library of Congress Catalog Card Number: 89-63313

ISBN 0-942902-06-8

In memory of
Leslie Lawrence Charles Hanelt

*If you reject the food, ignore
the customs, fear the religion,
and avoid the people, you
might better stay home. You
are like a pebble thrown into
the water; you become wet on the
surface, but you are never a
part of the water.*

—James A. Michener

CONTENTS

INTRODUCTION

This is perhaps the most satisfying edition of *BED & BREAKFAST HOMES DIRECTORY* yet to put together. At last, after expanding the territory covered with each new edition, this is the most geographically well-balanced version to date. The Pacific Northwest sections have been greatly enhanced, making it possible to travel the entire West Coast and inland regions with an adequate number of B&Bs to choose from in most areas. Six weeks of continuous travel throughout Oregon, Washington, and British Columbia last spring yielded many, many new discoveries that are certain to delight readers as they did me.

Some controversy has come to light in the past two years over the fact that some guidebook authors charge B&B owners to be listed.
To set the record straight, Knighttime Publications DOES charge a listing fee (for a two-year listing period) of two times the average double rate charged by the B&B. While this may seem on the surface to be a questionable policy, a deeper look should put readers' minds at ease.

Every effort is made to seek out and include only those B&Bs that meet our criteria of cleanliness, comfort, hospitality, and value. I am one of the bed and breakfast guidebook authors who actually visits, in person, each B&B and describes it from firsthand experience. The listing fee is accepted only after the B&B is visited and approved. Any B&B that is judged to be out of line in any of the above-mentioned areas is not included. Further, I do not list any B&B that I would not personally be pleased to stay in.

In addition to the expense of visiting every new B&B and occasionally re-visiting old ones, there are the substantial expenses of actual publication of *BED & BREAKFAST HOMES DIRECTORY*. On several fronts, it simply would not be possible to produce the book without the income derived from the listing fees.

Readers, be assured that you are my foremost concern. The integrity of this book must remain high so that you will continue to buy and use it, and so that I can continue to do the work I love. No compromises are made in its creation.

B&B hosts have agreed to honor published rates for our readers at least until the end of 1990. In order for these rates to be honored, be sure to mention that you found their B&B in the current edition of this book. Some hosts offer a special discount to readers, as noted; you must have a copy of this edition to obtain the reader discounts.

Your feedback regarding your experiences while using this book is strongly encouraged. Comments and suggestions — as well as inquiries about being listed as a B&B establishment in a future edition — should be addressed to me at P.O. Box 1597, Freedom, CA 95019.

As your travels take you to some of the places and people that have touched my heart, I wish you the joy of serendipity.

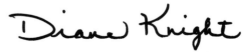

With this edition we are continuing the feature begun in 1988; that is, the addition of a listing of recommended restaurants for each geographic area covered in *BED & BREAKFAST HOMES DIRECTORY*. This is not intended to be a comprehensive listing of good restaurants, nor does it contain extensive information about each one. It offers some assistance in finding suitable places for lunch or dinner as you travel through unfamiliar territory. You will have to call or drop by the establishment that you're considering to find out more about it.

I have selected many of the restaurants from my own happy dining experiences. I must admit that part of my motivation in compiling the listings is the marvelous convenience of having at my fingertips the names, addresses, and phone numbers of an excellent assortment of wonderful restaurants spanning the U.S. and Canadian west coasts. I have found myself using the listings constantly since the last compilation. The Dining Highlights have been substantially revised and expanded in this edition.

In addition to choosing restaurants myself, I've also asked hosts to name those in their areas that they can recommend without hesitation. Each was personally selected by someone who has had firsthand knowledge of it over a period of time. Restaurants range from a simple taco stand in Santa Barbara to a world-class restaurant in Sooke, B.C., and prices vary accordingly. There was no charge to restaurants for a listing.

Criteria for selection were good quality ingredients, careful preparation, a pleasant atmosphere, and (most important), superior value. The majority of restaurants included are gems — really wonderful little places that tourists would be unlikely to discover on their own. While most offer good food at reasonable prices, some "splurge" restaurants are included — and judged to be well worth the cost.

Although most of the restaurants have proven track records, no guarantees are possible. Your feedback on these recommendations is encouraged.

ABOUT B&B IN PRIVATE HOMES

The B&Bs in this directory are, in most cases, strictly private homes, not commercial establishemnts. While some small, owner-occupied inns are also included, they are still the *homes* of the people who operate them. As a guest, remember to act with the same courtesy and consideration that you would expect of a guest in your own home.

Most *B&BHD* hosts don't consider themselves innkeepers. They are not in business full time — and therein lies some of the appeal of being treated "like family." There may be occasions when hosts can't accommodate you because they'll be on vacation, or because Great Aunt Martha from Omaha will be using the guest room.

In many cases, daily maid service and room service are not provided. This varies a great deal from one B&B to the next, but, generally, the smaller and less expensive accommodations do not offer such services. However, it is at this type of B&B that you are likely to encounter the spontaneous personal favor at just the right moment.

A number of B&B hosts will accept only cash or traveler's checks in payment for accommodations. Over time, though, more and more hosts are accepting credit cards. This information is now included in the second paragraph of each description for your convenience. Be sure to verify what forms of payment will be accepted *before* your visit.

When reserving accommodations in B&B homes, it is very important to agree upon your time of arrival with the host. There is always some flexibility, but arrival time should be discussed. If it appears that you will be later than planned, it is only considerate (and most appreciated) that you call and let your host know.

Room rates include at least a Continental breakfast. In many cases, the rate includes a full breakfast; in a few situations, there may be an extra charge (as noted) for a full breakfast. If anything more than a Continental breakfast is served, it is so stated in each listing.

Many hosts look forward to having guests join them for a family-style breakfast. In some cases — if the guest unit is totally separate and has cooking facilities — the host(s) will simply leave the ingredients for breakfast so that guests may prepare it at their leisure. There are hosts who will be glad to serve you breakfast in your room, or even in bed. Morning may find you at a table of your own, or perhaps you'll breakfast at a large table with other B&B guests. As in many aspects of B&B travel, the accent is on *variety*.

For each listing:

The first line tells either the name(s) of the host(s) or the name given to the B&B and the phone number to call for reservations.

The second line gives the mailing address of the B&B to use if you're writing for reservations.

The third line, in parentheses, indicates the general location of the B&B. You should get specific directions from your host.

Next you'll find a descriptive paragraph about the B&B. It often tells something about the unique qualities of the home itself, the setting, the host(s), points of interest in the area.

The second paragraph indicates whether there are indoor pets and gives the host(s) preferences, such as "no smoking" or "children welcome." These appear in a consistent sequence in each listing. They are given only if the host(s) have indicated a specific policy on the subject. The paragraph also lists facilities or features available to guests, such as "laundry" or "hot tub."

Available transportation is sometimes indicated, as well as the host(s) willingness to pick up guests at a nearby airport (largely for the benefit of private pilots).

The following code refers to the headings at the end of each description:

ROOM — Refers to a guest unit. The unit may be a room in the B&B home, an adjoining apartment, or a separate cottage near the home. Each letter (A, B,...) designates one guest unit, whether it has one, two, or more rooms.

BED — Number and type(s) of bed(s) given for each guest unit. This means total beds per unit.
T = twin, **D** = double, **Q** = queen, **K** = king

BATH — **Shd** means you'll share a bath with the host(s). **Shd*** means the bath is shared by other guests, if present. (You may have it all to yourself, especially midweek or off-season.) **Pvt** means the bath goes with the guest unit and is shared by no one else. It may be across the hall, but it is all yours.

ENTRANCE — **Main** indicates you'll use the main entrance of the home. **Sep** means there is a separate entrance for guests.

FLOOR	The floor of each guest room is indicated by number in most cases. **LL** means lower level, usually with steps down. **1G** means a ground level room, with no steps.
DAILY RATES	**S** refers to a single (one person); **D** refers to a double (two persons); **EP** refers to the rate charged for an extra person (above two) traveling with your party (generally, when there is an extra bed of some sort in the guest unit.) **Most of the rates quoted will have a local tax added; some stated rates *include* the tax.**

Example:

ROOM	BED	BATH	ENTRANCE	FLOOR	DAILY RATES S - D	(EP)
A	1K	Pvt	Main	2	$40-$45	($10)

Room (or unit) A has one king-sized bed, a private bath, uses the main entrance to the home, is on the second floor. One person will pay $40; two persons will pay $45; an extra person will pay $10.

AC = **A**ir **C**onditioning; **VCR** = Video Cassette Recorder; **AARP** = American Association of Retired Persons; **BART** = Bay Area Rapid Transit (in San Francisco Bay Area).

HOW TO ARRANGE A B&B VISIT

1. Try to plan your visit as far ahead as possible. This helps to ensure you'll get to stay at the B&B of your choice. Notify your host(s) immediately of any change in plans.

2. Call your host(s) for reservations before 9 p.m. Be sure to allow for the time difference if you're not on Pacific Time.

3. Carefully check details about the B&B you're considering before calling or writing. Confirm with your host anything that's not clear to you. Ask pertinent questions!

4. Check what form(s) of payment your host(s) will accept. Ask if a deposit is required.

5. Agree on time of arrival.

Hosts listed in BED & BREAKFAST HOMES DIRECTORY have agreed to honor rates stated in the directory until the end of 1990.

The information contained in these listings has been prepared with great care, but we cannot guarantee that it is complete or in all cases correct. It is the user's responsibility to verify important information when making arrangements.

North Coast

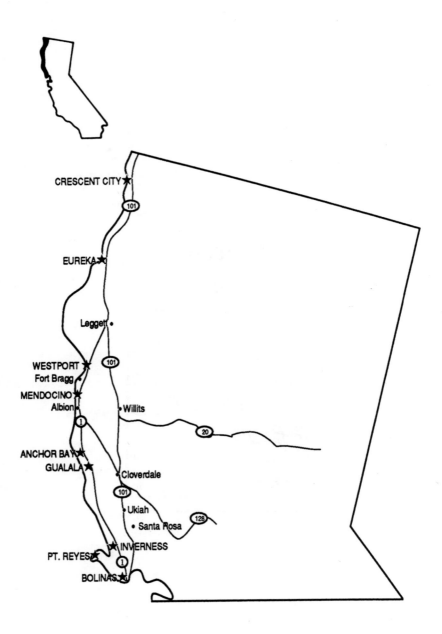

CRESCENT CITY ★
101

EUREKA ★

Leggett •

WESTPORT ★
Fort Bragg •
101

MENDOCINO ★
Albion •   • Willits
1
20

ANCHOR BAY ★
GUALALA ★
• Cloverdale
101

• Ukiah
128
• Santa Rosa

INVERNESS ★
PT. REYES ★
1
BOLINAS ★

Waves, woodlands, and wind-wafted fog work to encha
to the North Coast — the spell of nature is irresistible.
swept shores of the Sonoma and Mendocino County co
towering trees of the Redwood Highway, the scenery is
the exploring imagination.

The contrast of wood and wave is perhaps nowhere more dramatic
than at Point Reyes National Seashore. The steep cliffs, sighted some
400 hundred years ago by Sir Francis Drake, guard a peninsula of
dense forest, fern-filled canyons, and open pasture land. Beach aficio-
nados can choose between expansive sandy strands and futuristic
convolutions of rock. Tule elk, deer, sea lions, huge jack rabbits, and
hundreds of species of birds share the space with you; migrating whales
cruise by each winter.

From Bodega Bay north to Gualala, rolling hills spill into the sea,
where white foam swirls around imposing sea stacks. Here too, Fort
Ross — historic survivor of the nineteenth-century Russian presence in
California — sits high and dry on an isolated bluff. You can climb the
stairs of the restored stockade to watch the waves of the past wash up
below.

"Talk to me of Mendocino" goes the song, and indeed, nostalgia
has been known to overtake even the least sentimental in this trans-
posed bit of old New England. The town itself has sunk its sturdy roots
into a precarious-looking headland jutting into the sea and studiously
ignores the insistent pounding of the surf at its door. The nucleus of
a coastal community of artists and artisans, Mendocino offers an
abundance of galleries and shops housed in nineteenth-century buildings.

Seasoned wave-watchers recommend Mendocino Headlands State
Park for a show-stopping performance of water in motion, while from
Fort Bragg, wilderness devotees ride the "Skunks" (railway cars originally named for their pungent gas fumes) through forty miles of
redwood groves inaccessible by car.

A compelling symbol of California, the legendary redwoods rise in
original splendor along the Redwood Highway that stretches from
Leggett to Crescent City. It is hard not to think of these trees as the stuff
of myth. The hushed messages of their branches tell a story of
enduring grandeur. They are a discovery that never ages, and travelers
reaching the town of Eureka — meaning "I found it!" — can only add,
"You can't miss it."

Ed & Arlene Aaron   **(707) 884-3790**
P.O. Box 130, Gualala, CA 95445
(35001 Woodside Court, Anchor Bay)

The Aarons' redwood home is in perfect harmony with its surroundings. The forested setting allows great ocean views from all of the rooms. The living area has a fireplace, comfortable seating, and some beautiful work by local artists. It's just the place for relaxed conversation with the Aarons, people who truly enjoy having visitors. Ed, a retired veterinarian, will be glad to show you the exotic plants he raises. Arlene's special interests include Oriental cooking, tennis, fishing, and her pets. The private guest suite has its own bath, deck, and, of course, the view.

Dogs and cats in residence; no pets or children; full breakfast; TV; deck; soaking tub available in hosts' bathroom; good hiking nearby; off-street parking; some French spoken; airport pickup (Ocean Ridge). 10% discount to seniors.

ROOM	BED	BATH	ENTRANCE	FLOOR	DAILY RATES S - D (EP)
A	2T	Pvt	Main	1	$50-$65

Thomas' White House Inn
P.O. Box 132, Bolinas, CA 94924
(Between Stinson Beach and Point Reyes Natio

The magic and mystery of Bolinas lies in its i
of so many other seaside communities that nur
expense of the natural environment. Bolinas is n
been said that if you want to find it, you will. Its _____ beauty is
nowhere more apparent than at this marvelous bluff-side inn overlooking the Pacific. Just to breathe the fresh air here, to savor the
panorama of blue sea, Stinson Beach, the foothills, and Mount Tamalpais, feels like a privilege. The New England-style home of Jackie
Thomas is a crisp white with red trim. It has two stories and, at the top,
an observation deck. Two large, artfully appointed bedrooms and a
half-bath comprise the second floor. The first floor offers a full bath
with an aviary for zebra finches, a living room with a fireplace accented
by Mediterranean blue tile, a sunporch, and an open country kitchen
with dried flowers hanging from the beams. From bedrooms, common
rooms, and from the beautifully cultivated grounds, the view is omni-
present — just as it should be.

No pets; no smoking on second floor; expanded Continental
breakfast; off-street parking.

ROOM	BED	BATH	ENTRANCE	FLOOR	DAILY RATES S - D	(EP)
A	1Q	Shd*	Main	2	$85	($10)
B	1D	Shd*	Main	2	$75	($10)

each Bed & Breakfast   **(707) 464-9086**
Macken Avenue, Crescent City, CA 95531
cross from state beach)

Experience an out-of-the-way surprise at this lovely home situated near a beautiful stretch of coastline you might not otherwise
discover. Pebble Beach Bed & Breakfast is a quiet and gracious place.
Watch sunsets from your room, relax in the guest lounge area, catch
up on work at the desk and phone, or join Margaret Pappas for
music (from an extensive collection of CDs) and a glass of wine. The
entire second floor is for guests, with two main guest rooms, a
lounge, a bath, and an extra bedroom for an additional person in a
party. It's only steps to that gorgeous beach, and Redwood National
Park is within a few minutes' drive. Whatever brings you to this
northwest corner of California, you'll remember it fondly after a stay
at Pebble Beach Bed & Breakfast.

No pets; children by special arrangement; smoking downstairs
only; full breakfast; lounge with telephone, desk, and refrigerator;
cable TV in each room; off-street parking. Third bedroom is $20 for
extra person in party.

ROOM	BED	BATH	ENTRANCE	FLOOR	DAILY RATES S-D (EP)
A	1K	Shd*	Main	2	$65
B	1Q	Shd*	Main	2	$55

Old Town Bed & Breakfast Inn   **(707) 445-3951**
1521 Third Street, Eureka, CA 95501
(Third near P, north end of Old Town district)

Built in 1871, this historic home is one of the few remaining Greek Revival Victorians in the area. It was the original home of the local lumber baron until he built the Carson Mansion. Then it was moved to its present location, just a block and a half from the Mansion. Hosts Leigh and Diane Benson have kept the spirit of the past alive by furnishing the inn with antiques of the period. They've added their own whimsical touches, such as a teddy bear on each bed and rubber ducks and bubble bath for the clawfoot tubs. The result of their labors is the quintessential bed and breakfast inn. Its history is reflected in some of the room names: William Carson, Sumner's, and Sarah's Rose Parfait. After a stroll around Old Town, relax by the fireplace in the Raspberry Parlor with complimentary beverage and cheese. In the morning, sample one of Diane's country breakfast creations such as Eggs Derelict or Lumber Camp Breakfast Pie and homemade biscuits. Old Town Bed & Breakfast Inn's warm atmosphere and convenient location will make your stay in Eureka a memorable experience.

Two cats in residence; no pets; children over ten welcome by prior arrangement; full breakfast; afternoon refreshments; off-street parking; major credit cards (V, MC, AE). Discounts for longer stays and for business travelers.

ROOM	BED	BATH	ENTRANCE	FLOOR	DAILY RATES S - D (EP)
A	2T or 1K	Pvt	Main	2	$60-$70
B	1Q	Shd	Main	2	$50-$60
C	1Q	Shd	Main	2	$50-$60
D	1D	Pvt	Main	2	$50-$60
E	1Q	Pvt	Main	1	$75-$85

The Iseman Residence   **(707) 884-3584**
P.O. Box 888, Gualala, CA 95445
(West of Highway 1, one mile north of town)

I find Gualala appealing for a number of reasons: it isn't too touristy; there's just enough to see and do on a weekend; it feels more remote than it really is; the people have a keen sense of community; and the coastline is just beginning to get that rugged look of the North Coast. At The Iseman Residence, you'll have a private apartment that's connected to the house by an atrium. It has a living room with a wonderful ocean view, a wet bar, a bedroom, and a bath. Jo Iseman's cultural interests include collecting the work of her favorite artists, many of whom are local, which appears throughout the house. The pleasant environment may tempt you to simply curl up with a good book, but exploring the rocky coast is enticing, too. The natural beauty and salty fresh air could be just the elixir you need.

No pets; complimentary wine and soft drinks; TV; phone; robes provided; sofa bed in living room; shops, galleries, and two fine restaurants, plus golf, tennis, canoeing, hiking, whale-watching, and beachcombing nearby; off-street parking; Italian spoken; airport pickup (Ocean Ridge, Sea Ranch). Inquire about weekly rates.

ROOM	BED	BATH	ENTRANCE	FLOOR	DAILY RATES
					S - D (EP)
A	2T or 1K	Pvt	Sep	1	$75-$85 ($10)

Alder House   (415) 669-7218

P.O. Box 644, Inverness, CA 94937
(Just north of Inverness Village at 105 Vision Road)

In a wide, sunny clearing and sharing the property with Susan Brayton's home is Alder House — a true haven for privacy-seekers with its own driveway and entrance. The architect-designed house is unusually spacious and light inside, consisting of a large living room with a woodstove, a dining area, a kitchen, a bedroom and bath, a sunroom and deck. The fine artwork that graces the interior portrays landscapes of local scenes; colorful rugs are from Afghanistan. Wonderful views of Inverness Ridge and Mount Vision are yours from the living room, deck, and sunroom. The feeling of soothing greenery outside permeates the interior through its many windows and skylights. In the large yard and beyond, riparian bird life thrives; a creek flows nearby. Walk three minutes to Tomales Bay or ask Susan about taking a "paper trail" to the village. The beaches, trails, and wildlife of Point Reyes National Seashore could satisfy nature lovers for days and days. Alder House is large enough for a family vacation, quiet enough to nurture your creative spirit, and private enough for the most romantic of interludes.

Pets welcome (small charge for dogs); children welcome; smoking outside only; expanded Continental breakfast left for guests to prepare at their leisure; off-street parking; handicapped accessible. Inquire about weekly rates, monthly rates, or vacation rentals. Brochure available.

ROOM	BED	BATH	ENTRANCE	FLOOR	DAILY RATES
					S - D (EP)
A	1Q & 2T	Pvt	Sep	1	$95 ($20)

The Ark   **(415) 663-9338**
P.O. Box 273, Inverness, CA 94937
(Inverness Ridge, one mile up from village)

If you're longing for a secluded little paradise where you can be temporarily removed from the rest of the world, The Ark is the place for you. This rustic artist's studio on Inverness Ridge is absolutely private. You'll have decks and sheltered open space for enjoying woods and meadow, an octagonal bath house, and a barbecue/ picnic area — all to yourself! The structure was designed and built of recycled building materials by an architecture class in the early seventies. It was recently refurbished as a guest cottage and displays some artwork by its early inhabitants. It has unique architectural details, high ceilings, and many windows. The light-flooded studio has a wood-burning stove, a full kitchen, and a bath. A drawing room and a loft provide extra sleeping space; six can be comfortably accommodated. The Ark is ideal for a family, a gathering of friends, or a romantic retreat.

Full breakfast provided by hosts, who can be reached by phone from The Ark; double futon in loft; off-street parking; Spanish and French spoken. $20 extra for one-night stay on weekend.

ROOM	BED	BATH	ENTRANCE	FLOOR	DAILY RATES S - D	(EP)
A	1Q & 2T	Pvt	Sep	1	$95	($15)

MacLean House   **(415) 669-7392**
P.O. Box 651, Inverness, CA 94937
(One block above town of Inverness and Tomales Bay)

What could be a more perfect setting than Inverness for the perfect Scottish guest house? Among trees overlooking Tomales Bay is the redwood-shingled home of Jinny and Bob Cuenin. It has been renovated and furnished with great attention to detail, carrying out the Scottish theme through the main quarters and the guest rooms below. The clan MacLean tartan provides the color scheme, looking crisp and clean against the white walls of each spacious room. Lovely antiques and brass accents complete the picture, adding up to the utmost in quality lodgings. Flowers and birds abound in this quiet, often sunny location. Point Reyes National Seashore and some excellent local restaurants have always been good reasons to visit the area; now the Cuenins and MacLean House are also high on *my* list.

No pets or RV parking; smoking in rooms discouraged; private patio; decks; off-street parking.

ROOM	BED	BATH	ENTRANCE	FLOOR	DAILY RATES	
					S - D	(EP)
A	1D & 1T	Pvt	Sep	1	$85	($10)
B	1Q	Pvt	Sep	1	$85	($10)

Rosemary Cottage
(415) 663-9338

75 Balboa Avenue, P.O. Box 619, Inverness, CA 94937
(Just south of village and west of Sir Francis Drake Boulevard)

A wall of windows overlooks a dramatic sylvan scene — a sunlit wooded gulch that is sanctuary to many wild birds of the Point Reyes National Seashore. You lie on the deck at night and marvel at stars that never seemed so bright before. A romantic French-country cottage is your own private hideaway; luxuriate in its seclusion and the beauty surrounding it. Designed and built by owners Suzanne and Michel, Rosemary Cottage is about fifty yards through a forest from their home. It has many handcrafted details, a wood-burning stove, a full kitchen, and space that will comfortably sleep four. Under an old oak tree, the large deck overlooks an herb garden. It is a marvelous setting for alfresco meals. Settle into quiet relaxation or take off to enjoy the beaches, hiking trails, and prolific wildlife of the Seashore. Rosemary Cottage is near it all — in a world of its own.

Families welcome; full breakfast; off-street parking; Spanish and French spoken. $20 extra for one-night stay on weekend.

ROOM	BED	BATH	ENTRANCE	FLOOR	DAILY RATES S - D (EP)
A	1Q & 2T	Pvt	Sep	1	$95 ($15)

Mendocino Farmhouse   **(707) 937-0241**
P.O. Box 247, Mendocino, CA 95460
(One and one-half miles from Mendocino Village)

If you're seeking the quintessential farmhouse in Mendocino for your north coast getaway, look no further. The home of Marge and Bud Kamb provides superb accommodations in the quietest possible setting, so near and yet so far from the busy village scene. Here, there's a permanent warm glow to the interior that feels authentic to the core — not "decorated." Sloped ceilings, pretty fabrics and rugs, and country antiques give the bedrooms an ambient coziness. Two of the rooms are quite spacious; Room A has a wood-burning stove; a slightly smaller one (C), also with a wood-burning stove, is irresistibly romantic. Newer accommodations have been added in the converted barn overlooking the garden. Each room (D and E) has a separate entrance and a charm all its own, as well as such inviting features as stone fireplaces, coffee makers, and small refrigerators. In the morning, savor a sumptuous farmhouse breakfast in the sun room of the main house while taking in the views of redwood forest, beautiful gardens, a pond, and a meadow. The aura of this lovely home makes an indelible impression on those fortunate enough to stay here.

Children or pets by arrangement; smoking outside only; full breakfast; off-street parking.

ROOM	BED	BATH	ENTRANCE	FLOOR	DAILY RATES	
					S - D	(EP)
A	1K	Pvt	Main	2	$60-$70	($12)
B	1Q & 1T	Pvt	Main	2	$70-$80	($12)
C	1Q	Pvt	Main	2	$70-$80	($12)
D	1Q	Pvt	Sep	1	$80-$90	($12)
E	1Q	Pvt	Sep	1	$80-$90	($12)

The Wool Loft   (707) 937-0377
32751 Navarro Ridge Road, Albion, CA 95410
(Ten miles south of Mendocino)

The Wool Loft's setting overlooking the sea reminds me of some B&Bs in Ireland or Scotland. Sheep graze in nearby fields; the family garden and henhouse contribute food to the table. Jan and Sid offer three cheery guest rooms with private baths in the main house to guests who prefer traditional B&B treatment. The Wool Loft itself is a separate accommodation (A). It's a spacious studio apartment with queen-sized bed, fully equipped kitchen, bath, wood-burning stove, and huge windows with stunning river and ocean views. Quiet and cozy seclusion on the famous Mendocino coast is yours if you choose The Wool Loft.

No pets, children, or smoking; gather eggs for breakfast if desired; deck and fireplace in main house; firewood provided in Wool Loft; Room B has river and ocean view; off-street parking. *Open weekends only (Friday-Sunday).* Two-night minimum; three-night minimum on holiday weekends. Special weekly rate for Room A, $490; no breakfast served during week. Brochure available.

ROOM	BED	BATH	ENTRANCE	FLOOR	DAILY RATES S-D (EP)
A	1Q	Pvt	Sep	2	$85
B	1Q	Pvt	Main	1	$75
C	1Q	Pvt	Main	1	$55
D	1Q	Pvt	Main	1	$55

Arbor Cottage   **(415) 663-8020**
P.O. Box 748, Point Reyes Station, CA 94956
(Just south of Inverness Village)

You'll feel at home in an in-
stant when you enter this comfy
guest cottage set amid live
oaks, bay laurels, and redwoods.   The light pine interior is accented by colorful
handmade quilts, dark green
carpeting, and a large rose wing
chair that invites you to kick back
and take it easy. Light a fire in the
woodstove — it's ready for you —
and settle in for a spell. Louvered
doors lead from the spacious bed-
sitting room to a smaller bedroom;
together they can accommodate two
couples or a family. The cottage has
a fully equipped kitchen, a good collection of naturalist literature, and
lots of privacy. Stargazing through
the skylight above the bed is part of
this perfect escape to the country.

Smoking outside only; breakfast
delivered to cottage; coffee and tea
available in kitchen; radio; phone; adjacent to Point Reyes National Seashore and
Tomales Bay State Park; off-street parking. Rates
are $10 extra for one-night stays and $5 less per person without
breakfast; ask about midweek discounts. Brochure available.

ROOM	BED	BATH	ENTRANCE	FLOOR	DAILY RATES	
					S - D	(EP)
A	1Q & 1D	Pvt	Sep	2	$75	($10)

The Country House   **(415) 663-1627**
P.O. Box 98, Point Reyes Station, CA 94956
(On mesa overlooking village of Point Reyes Station)

On an acre at the end of a quiet street where old-time houses share the landscape, The Country House stands surrounded by an apple orchard and English-style flower gardens. You'll get a wonderful view of Inverness Ridge from the property, as well as frequent glimpses of resident wildlife. The house itself exudes a casual, let-your-hair-down version of "Welcome home!" A hearth with a wood-burning Franklin stove is the focal point of the spacious living area that includes the dining area and kitchen. Cook pots hang from the open rafters, and an old Oriental rug covers the floor by the stove — a heartwarming, comfortable scene. Two antique furnished bedroom suites have queen-sized beds and private baths. A third suite has its own sitting room with a fireplace, a queen-sized bed in a loft with a spectacular view, and a private bath. Hosts live in separate quarters, but they're on hand when you need them. In the morning you'll savor a huge country breakfast featuring specialties such as blue cornmeal pancakes and a variety of omelettes. You will be treated as a favored house guest in Ewell McIsaac's relaxing country retreat.

No pets; children over seven welcome; smoking outside only; full breakfast; cable TV; Tomales Bay, villages of Point Reyes Station and Inverness, and the many natural wonders of the Point Reyes National Seashore nearby; off-street parking; wheelchair access. Excellent for families and reunions; inquire about midweek and extended stay rates. Brochure available.

ROOM	BED	BATH	ENTRANCE	FLOOR	DAILY RATES S - D	(EP)
A	1Q	Pvt	Main	1G	$75	($15)
B	1Q	Pvt	Main	1G	$75	($15)
C	1Q	Pvt	Sep	1G	$80	($15)

Horseshoe Farm Cottage (415) 663-5⟍
P.O. Box 332, Point Reyes Station, CA 94956
(Between Point Reyes and Inverness atop Drake's Summit)

A desire to commune with nature in utter solitude could inspire a getaway to Horseshoe Farm Cottage. Surrounded by enormous old live oaks, pines, and Douglas fir, the cottage is hidden from the view of any other dwelling. An unspoiled panorama of mountains can be yours from the lovely, secluded deck. A peaked roof gives the interior a light and spacious feeling, with shoji screen skylights and other Japanese touches. The main room is colorful and casual, featuring a built-in redwood bed, a Vermont Castings woodstove, a dining table with three chairs, a fold-out futon, a settee and reading chair. The bathroom is just down the stairs. There's a kitchen for light housekeeping and a fridge stocked with goodies for an expanded Continental breakfast to be enjoyed at your convenience. Horseshoe Farm Cottage is a beautiful place for some serious relaxation. Go with someone whose company you appreciate — even if it is just your own.

Ocean beaches, mountain forests, miles of hiking trails, whale-watching, year-round birding in adjoining Point Reyes National Seashore; off-street parking. Two-night minimum on weekends; inquire about midweek and extended stay rates. Brochure available.

ROOM	BED	BATH	ENTRANCE	FLOOR	DAILY RATES
					S - D (EP)
A	1Q & 1T	Pvt	Sep	2	$90 ($25)

Jasmine Cottage   **(415) 663-1166**
11561 Coast Route #1, Point Reyes Station, CA 94956
(Two blocks above village of Point Reyes Station)

If you like being on your own in total peace and seclusion, Jasmine Cottage could be the hideaway you've been looking for. It is the guest cottage for the original Point Reyes Schoolhouse, built in 1879. Karen Gray lives in the masterfully renovated schoolhouse. She has done a remarkable job with the cottage, too. It opens onto a pasture with a beautiful view of Inverness Ridge and backs onto an herb and flower garden. There is a private drive for guests. The interior is a perfect blend of modern efficiency, family antiques, and local artwork. I particularly like the queen-sized bed alcove. There is a fully equipped kitchen, bath, living area with wood-burning stove, two patios, garden room, and plenty of windows. A desk holds a collection of naturalists' writings and guides to the Point Reyes area. Jasmine Cottage can be what you want it to be — romantic haven, family vacation spot, nature lover's retreat. It is a place to make some dreams come true.

    Children welcome; crib available; minutes from Point Reyes National Seashore and Tomales Bay State Park; children's playground across road; off-street parking. Inquire about weekly rates.

ROOM	BED	BATH	ENTRANCE	FLOOR	DAILY RATES S - D (EP)
A	1Q & 2T	Pvt	Sep	1G	$95 ($15)

Terri's Homestay   (415) 663-1289
P.O. Box 113, Point Reyes, CA 94956
(83 Sunnyside Drive, Inverness Park)

High atop Inverness Ridge in a remote, "above it all" location adjoining Point Reyes National Seashore is Terri Thornton's comfortable redwood home. Here guests have plenty of space and privacy in quarters that include a large bedroom with a sitting area, a private bath, separate entrance, wood-burning stove, deck access, and an amazing view over ridges of Bishop pine toward the sea. Guatemalan artwork and fabrics add zest to the natural environment. Feel like exploring? Take a forty five-minute hike to the top of Mount Vision for a rewarding panorama; spend some time on secluded, bluff-lined beaches; see how many different species of wildlife you can spot. In the evening, enjoy a soak in the outdoor spa. To round out a thoroughly relaxing holiday, schedule a massage by Terri, who specializes in polarity therapy. This quiet, sunny spot offers an array of pleasures you won't soon forget.

Dogs on premises; children and outdoor dogs welcome; no smoking; no RV parking; expanded Continental breakfast; antique piano, CD player, and futon in room; small charge for use of spa; massage by appointment; ample street parking. Inquire about off-season and extended stay rates.

ROOM	BED	BATH	ENTRANCE	FLOOR	DAILY RATES S - D	(EP)
A	1Q	Pvt	Sep	1	$80-$90	($15)

Thirty-nine Cypress   **(415) 663-1709**
P.O. Box 176, Point Reyes Station, CA 94956
(Near Point Reyes National Seashore)

Julia Bartlett feels a special connection to the Point Reyes area and, in particular, to the spot where she's made her home. One easily understands this after being a guest at Thirty-nine Cypress. The passive solar house is on 3.5 acres of land, set on a bluff overlooking a pastoral scene where cattle graze and all seems right with the world. Inside, there's a strong feeling of *home* — a cozy fireplace, floors covered with aging Oriental rugs, warm quilts to sleep under. The house is natural and rustic, with an ambiance of warmth and comfort. Throughout the house, original works of art catch the eye. There are skylights in two of the rooms, and from your bed at night you may see stars and hear the hooting of owls. There is a state-of-the-art spa halfway down the bluff where you can relax after a day of hiking or beachcombing. Julia can provide a wealth of information for guests about the Point Reyes-Inverness area.

Cat and dog in residence; no pets or young children; TV; patio; spa; off-street parking. Midweek rates, $5 less.

ROOM	BED	BATH	ENTRANCE	FLOOR	DAILY RATES S - D	(EP)
A	1K	Shd	Main	1G	$85-$90	
B	1D	Pvt 1/2	Main	1G	$85-$90	
C	1Q	Pvt 1/2	Main	1G	$85-$90	

Howard Creek Ranch   **(707) 964-6725**
P.O. Box 121, Westport, CA 95488
(Three miles north of Westport on Highway 1)

Sally and Sonny invite you to retreat to the romance of yesteryear at Howard Creek Ranch. Their ranch house was built in 1872 by Alfred Howard, newly arrived from the coast of Maine. At one time a stagecoach stop, it is now a quaint and cozy home filled with collectibles and antiques. The guest suites allow privacy, and the old fireplace inspires conversation and fun. The house is set in a wide, secluded valley at the mouth of Howard Creek. It faces the ocean and a vast, sandy beach where you can walk for miles at low tide. Several uniquely constructed, private guest units on the property offer additional accommodations. At this bed and breakfast resort, you can find your own pace and tune in to the natural beauty all around you.

Dog and two cats in residence; full ranch breakfast; kitchen privileges by arrangement; decks; barbecue; swimming pool; wood-heated hot tub; sauna; massage by appointment; off-street parking; major credit cards (V, MC). All guest units have sinks; A has a balcony; C has a loft; all except B have skylights. Unit D is a boathouse; E and F are cabins; both have woodstoves and electricity. Inquire about off-season and midweek rates. Brochure available.

ROOM	BED	BATH	ENTRANCE	FLOOR	DAILY RATES S - D	(EP)
A	1Q & 1D	Pvt	Main	2	$75	($10)
B	1K & 1T	Shd	Sep	1	$68	($10)
C	1Q & 1T	Shd	Main	2	$58	($10)
D	1D	Pvt	Sep	1	$75	
E	1D	Shd	Sep	1	$48	
F	1Q & 1D	Pvt	Sep	1	$85	($10)

DINING HIGHLIGHTS: NORTH COAST

Please read "About Dining Highlights" on page *ix*.

ALBION

Albion River Inn, 3790 North Highway 1; (707) 937-1919; local seafood and pasta

The Ledford House at Salmon Point, 3000 North Highway 1; (707) 937-0272; new American cuisine

EUREKA

Ramone's Opera Alley Café, 409 Opera Alley; (707) 444-3339; international cuisine

The Sea Grill, 316 E Street, Old Town; (707) 443-7187; fresh local seafood and steaks

Sergio's, Second & "C" Streets; (707) 443-8187; Italian/fresh pasta and seafood

FORT BRAGG

Coast Hotel Café, 101 North Franklin; (707) 964-6443; fresh seafood and Creole cuisine

The Purple Rose Restaurant, 24300 North Highway 1; (707) 964-6507; Mexican

The Restaurant, 418 Main Street; (707) 964-9800; eclectic menu

INVERNESS

Inverness Inn Restaurant, 2 Inverness Way; (415) 669-1109; specialty, fresh oysters

MARSHALL

Tony's Seafood Restaurant, 18863 Highway 1; (415) 663-1107; local seafood

MENDOCINO

955 Ukiah Street Restaurant, 955 Ukiah Street; (707) 937-1955; creative seafood, pasta, meat, and fowl dishes

POINT REYES STATION

Chez Madeleine, 10905 Highway 1; (415) 663-9177; French

The Station House Café, Main at Third Street; (415) 663-1515; local seafood and chicken, steak, and pasta specialties

WESTHAVEN

The Larrupin Café, 1150 South Westhaven Drive; (707) 677-0230; ribs and chicken

Central
Coast

San Francisco
MONTARA
Half Moon Bay
SAN GREGORIO
PESCADERO
DAVENPORT   SCOTTS VALLEY
SANTA CRUZ
WATSONVILLE   152
Monterey
Carmel   Pacific Grove
Big Sur
              1
                        101
San Simeon   SAN MIGUEL
CAMBRIA   PASO ROBLES   42
Morro Bay
LOS OSOS   San Luis Obispo
ARROYO GRANDE

              1

"The Coastside," as the area surrounding Half Moon Bay is known, remains a part of the Pacific's edge where travelers can still make their own discoveries. A favorite country café tucked back in the farmlands, a pebble beach where you can still find jade, a redwood grove that stands as a memorial to the dedicated environmentalists who fought for it (the lumber company slashes still visible on the venerable giants marked for cutting) are some of the little-known treasures of the area. The Año Nuevo State Reserve, the James Fitzgerald Marine Reserve, and the Pescadero Wildlife Refuge provide sanctuary for the abundance of coastal wildlife that is yours for the watching, while several state and county parks offer hideaways in the redwoods. A respite from bustling tourism, this stretch of coast allows time and tide their ebb and flow.

Monterey Bay, with its crescent of sandy beaches from Santa Cruz to Carmel, is the heartland of the Central Coast. Here beach-lovers sun, surf, and even swim in the quieter waters of the bay. On the northern shore of the bay, Santa Cruz enjoys a unique ambiance, a mixture of the spontaneous street fun concocted by musicians, dancers, and impromptu actors along the Pacific Garden Mall, the lazy sea lions snoozing beneath the feet of anglers on the municipal pier, and the staid Victorians that keep an eye on the goings-on.

Monterey, on the southern shore, offers a different mood entirely, one steeped in California history and natural beauty. The adobe buildings on the city's Path of History mark its nineteenth-century prominence, while Cannery Row, no longer Steinbeck's turbulent cauldron of the sardine industry, survives as a complex of shops and restaurants. The diverse sea life of the bay may be studied up close in the Monterey Bay Aquarium, at the end of Cannery Row .

The adjoining town of Pacific Grove has many visitors, some of whom fly in on velvety orange-and-black wings. The Monarch butterflies hang out in select groves of pines from October to March. Carmel-by-the-Sea, a few miles to the south, is still trying to be a quaint little village in the forest, but its bumper crop of shops, galleries, and restaurants gives it an air of sophistication.

For some people, the poetry of the Monterey Peninsula is to be found at Point Lobos State Reserve. The wind-twisted Monterey cypress, the soft sighs of pines, the azure water foaming milky white around dark rocks that host the miniature worlds of the tidepools — all say Monterey.

Farther south, travelers experience an exquisite fragility riding the thin ribbon of Highway 1 through Big Sur country, under the imposing brow of the Santa Lucia Mountains and along the precipitous cliffs overlooking the Pacific. Gradually, the landscape softens into something less wild, more idyllic. Just when you're thinking it's the perfect place for a fairy-tale castle — Shazam! There it is! San Simeon, William Randolph Hearst's fantasy made real. A concourse of gardens, classic pools, and mansions displaying a dazzling collection of art make San Simeon the wonder of the Central Coast. Nearby Cambria, a tiny coastal town in the pines, is a delightful country contrast.

Dune buggies wheel up and down the dramatic sand dunes of Pismo Beach, where those little bubbles may mean you're onto something big. A Pismo clam can be the size of a fist.

San Luis Obispo's history tour is a surprise, covering nearly every period and contributing culture of California history. Architecture ranges from adobe to Frank Lloyd Wright. To the east, rolling countryside provides pastoral scenes to inspire an old-fashioned Sunday drive — even on Mondays.

NOTICE TO CENTRAL COAST TRAVELERS:

Although Scenic Highway 1 between San Simeon and Big Sur is often closed due to slides, Hearst Castle and Cambria are always accessible via U.S. 101 and Highway 46. They are well worth the detour when necessary.

The Guest House (805) 481-9304
120 Hart Lane, Arroyo Grande, CA 93420
(Off U.S. 101, seventeen miles south of San Luis Obispo)

Homesick New Englanders, look no further than The Guest House at Arroyo Grande. It was built in the 1850s by a sea captain from the east and bears an unmistakable resemblance to the homes he left behind. Present owners Mark Miller and James Cunningham have kept the flavor of old New England alive in the house. Stenciled wall designs, American primitives, Oriental rugs, and family heirlooms add to the mellow, inviting atmosphere. A crackling fire in the hearth and comfortable places to sit make the living room a haven for easy conversation. The afternoon social hour often takes place in the bay-windowed sunroom with French doors that lead out to the garden. Breakfast is appropriately hearty fare, served in the sunroom or out in the garden. For traditional Yankee hospitality at the sign of the pineapple, The Guest House is a classic.

Cat in residence; no pets, children, or RV parking; full breakfast; afternoon refreshments; city park in turn-of-the-century village of Arroyo Grande; off-street parking; airport pickup (San Luis Obispo).

ROOM	BED	BATH	ENTRANCE	FLOOR	DAILY RATES	
					S - D	(EP)
A	1Q	Shd*	Main	2	$40-$55	($10)
B	1D	Shd*	Main	2	$40-$55	($10)
C	1D	Shd	Main	1	$40-$55	($10)

Duane & Miriam Benell   **(805) 927-3112**
340 Weymouth, Cambria, CA 93428
(Just east of Highway 1)

The Benells look forward to spending the summers in their lovely Cambria home, and it's no wonder. They are just seven miles south of Hearst Castle, two blocks from Moonstone Beach, and within walking distance of charming Cambria village. The guest room is on the ground level, and the living-dining area is on the upper level with a view of the ocean. Having greatly enjoyed B&Bs abroad, hosts are pleased to extend hospitality to foreign visitors traveling in California. The Benells are in residence June through Labor Day, and often at other times. B&B is available the rest of the year with *advance reservations* by calling (805) 927-3112, (213) 695-5431, or writing 12002 Beverly Drive, Whittier, CA 90601.

No pets or smoking; one or two children OK; full breakfast; small RV parking; TV and fireplace upstairs; off-street parking. Room B used only for people in same party as Room A. Advance reservations *essential* year-round for Hearst Castle tours.

ROOM	BED	BATH	ENTRANCE	FLOOR	DAILY RATES	
					S - D	(EP)
A	2T or 1K	Pvt	Main	1G	$35-$50	
B	1Q		Main	1G	Inquire	

Whispering Pines   **(805) 927-4613**
P.O. Box 326, Cambria, CA 93428
(1605 London Lane, off Ardath)

For many, discovering Cambria is an added bonus to visiting the magical Hearst Castle at San Simeon. The quaint coastal town retains its homespun charm even though it becomes more arty and sophisticated each year. In a lovely, tranquil area just a short drive from the old Cambria village is Jack and Ginny Anderson's multi-level contemporary home with views of rolling hills and pines — Whispering Pines, that is. Guests may retreat to the total privacy of a deluxe, tri-level apartment with its own entrance and a hot tub just outside. Light, immaculate, and tastefully decorated, the unit consists of a living room with TV and VCR, dining area, kitchenette, full bath, and large loft bedroom. A tantalizing choice of breakfast entrees is offered, along with the luxury of delivery to your quarters. Simply put, Whispering Pines is a great little hideaway on the Central Coast.

No pets; smoking outside only; no RV parking; full breakfast; day bed in living room; off-street parking; $25 for extra couple. Hosts also operate Bed & Breakfast Homestay, a reservation service listing $50-$85 rooms and apartments in the area. Brochure available.

ROOM	BED	BATH	ENTRANCE	FLOOR	DAILY RATES
					S - D (EP)
A	2T or 1K	Pvt	Sep	2&3	$70 ($10)

New Davenport Bed & Breakfast   **(408) 425-1818 or 426-4122**
Davenport, CA 95017
(Nine miles north of Santa Cruz)

The New Davenport Bed & Breakfast is located in one of Davenport's original old buildings, just across the Coast Highway from the ocean. Four bright, comfortable rooms, furnished with antique beds and oak dressers, are available to B&B travelers. Delicious breakfasts are served in the sitting room and next door at the New Davenport Cash Store (pictured). Dinner is served on Friday, Saturday, and Sunday nights, as well as the rest of the week in summer. Weekend festivities often include live music and a lively crowd. This landmark also houses a pottery, gift, and craft gallery. The New Davenport is an ideal getaway from the Bay Area. Though the trip is short, there's a wonderfully remote feeling about the place. And when you don't have to spend hours driving, there's much more time for fun.

No pets; no children under twelve; no smoking in rooms; off-street parking; major credit cards (V, MC, AE); bus service from Santa Cruz. Additional rooms available on the second story of the main (Cash Store) building, most with ocean views. Rates range from $80-$105 for two. 20% midweek discount in winter. Brochure available.

ROOM	BED	BATH	ENTRANCE	FLOOR	DAILY RATES S - D	(EP)
A	1D	Pvt	Main	1G	$55	
B	1D	Pvt	Main	1G	$60	
C	1Q	Pvt	Main	1G	$65	
D	1D	Pvt	Main	1G	$60	

Gerarda's Bed & Breakfast   **(805) 528-3973**
1056 Bay Oaks Drive, Los Osos, CA 93402
(Just south of Morro Bay)

The section of the Central Coast between Morro Bay and San Luis Obispo is a very special and largely undiscovered wonderland. The Los Osos/Baywood Park area offers a scenic seven-mile drive blessed with rocky shores, isolated coves, sandy beaches, prolific wildlife, and stunning views. Spectacular Montana de Oro State Park is a joy to explore. On a quiet residential street in Los Osos, the warmest of welcomes awaits you at Gerarda's Bed & Breakfast. Surrounded by burgeoning flower beds (mostly roses), Gerarda's home is a haven of Dutch hospitality. You're meant to enjoy the entire house as your own. The living room and Room A offer a vista of the ocean and Morro Rock; B is a master room with ensuite bath. The art and needlework throughout Gerarda's home, as well as the ample breakfasts, impart a European flavor. Her friendly, accommodating nature makes being her guest a relaxing pleasure.

Cat in residence; smoking outside only; full breakfast; TV in each room; tennis and golf nearby; off-street parking; Dutch and Indonesian spoken; wheelchair access. Rate drops to $35 after first night. Brochure available.

ROOM	BED	BATH	ENTRANCE	FLOOR	DAILY RATES S - D	(EP)
A	2T or 1K	Shd	Main	1G	$25-$39	
B	2T or 1K	Pvt	Main	1G	$25-$39	

The Goose & Turrets Bed & Breakfast (415) 728-5451
P.O. Box 370937, Montara, CA 94037-0937
(One-half mile from coast; twenty-five minutes from San Francisco)

Proximity to the Bay Area, a colorful history, and natural beauty that hasn't been overtaken by development make the coastal hamlet of Montara an ideal country escape. Raymond and Emily Hoche-Mong welcome guests to The Goose & Turrets — built around 1908 in the Northern Italian villa style — with "creature comforts, bonhomie, and solitude." The wonderful old building has been refurbished and decorated to reflect the hosts' myriad interests and world travels. Each of the five guest rooms has been fashioned with taste and imagination to convey a distinct personality. They feature German down comforters, English towel warmers, and bathrobes. Step out back to the old-fashioned gardens and "chat" with the resident mascot geese, hike down to beaches and rocky coves, or lounge about at The Goose & Turrets where you can lose yourself in a good book or practice the art of doing absolutely nothing.

No pets; smoking outside only; full breakfast; afternoon tea; common room with woodstove, piano, game table, stereo, and eclectic book collection; Room A has sitting area with woodstove; off-street parking; major credit cards (V, MC, AE, D); French spoken; airport pickup by host/pilots (Half Moon Bay, San Carlos, Palo Alto) by prior arrangement; also, pickup for sailors at Pillar Point Harbor at Princeton). Brochure available.

ROOM	BED	BATH	ENTRANCE	FLOOR	DAILY RATES	
					S - D	(EP)
A	1Q	Shd*	Main	1	$85	
B	1D	Shd*	Main	1	$70	
C	1D	Pvt	Main	1	$85	
D	1K	Shd*	Main	1	$80	
E	2T	Shd*	Main	1	$75	

Montara Bed & Breakfast   **(415) 728-3946**
P.O. Box 493, Montara, CA 94037
(One-half mile from coast; twenty-five minutes from San Francisco)

Bill and Peggy Bechtell have remodeled their inviting country home to include a private guest suite on two floors. The bedroom, attractively decorated in a seaside motif, opens onto a redwood deck where you might catch a bit of morning sun. Upstairs, a sitting room has a woodstove and a distant view of the ocean through the trees. A full breakfast is served in a solarium overlooking the garden. This rustic, cozy retreat is just moments away from beaches, seaside dining, historic Montara Lighthouse, Fitzgerald Marine Reserve, and miles of hiking trails at the largely undiscovered McNee Ranch State Park. Other Coastside towns to the south offer further pleasures. The Bechtells want you to enjoy your privacy while feeling very much at home during your stay at Montara Bed & Breakfast. No problem.

Dog, ducks, rabbit, and other critters on premises; no children or smoking; full breakfast; ample street parking; major credit cards (V, MC); airport pickup (Half Moon Bay). Two-night minimum on weekends; seventh consecutive night free.

ROOM	BED	BATH	ENTRANCE	FLOOR	DAILY RATES S-D (EP)
A	2T or 1K	Pvt	Sep	1	$55-$65 ($15)

Darken Downs Equestre-Inn   (805) 467-3589
Star Route, Box 4562, San Miguel, CA 93451
(Nine miles northeast of Paso Robles)

    The ranch of Darlene and Ken Ramey offers a unique combination of a blossoming sporthorse facility and a bed and breakfast on their nine-acre parcel. The Spanish-style ranch house reflects the flavor of the southwest and overlooks the pasture, barn area, paddocks, ring, and the arena. Set in the midst of a burgeoning wine country (over twenty-five wineries nearby), Darken Downs is just one of many horse operations in what is recognized also as horse country. If room is available, guests may also bring their own horse(s) for an additional fee. Two bedrooms are available to guests, one with a double antique sleigh bed, the other with twin beds; each has a private bath. Cambria, Hearst Castle, and Morro Bay are an hour's drive away. The County Fair in August is considered one of the best in the country. For a taste of true western hospitality, visit Darken Downs Equestre-Inn. Don't wait too long — the Central Coast has been discovered!

    Small poodle in residence; no pets; smoking outside only; afternoon refreshments; wine-tasting and touring nearby; off-street parking. Inquire about equestrian facilities and services. Evenings best to phone for reservations. Three people using two rooms, $75. Brochure available.

ROOM	BED	BATH	ENTRANCE	FLOOR	DAILY RATES S - D (EP)
A	1D	Pvt	Main	1G	$50-$60
B	2T	Pvt	Main	1G	$50-$60

Bob & Jane Rynders (415) 879-0319
P.O. Box 478, Pescadero, CA 94060
(Adjacent to Butano State Park)

Make your way along a narrow country road as it winds its way into Butano Forest to a small community of sequestered homesites alongside Butano Creek. Steelhead spawn here, and occasionally a blue heron drops in. A profusion of fuchsias, azaleas, and rhododendrons share space with native forest plants. Here, nestled in the ferns and redwoods, the Rynders' guest cabin offers a respite from bustling tourism and the hectic pace of modern life. The *shibui* (quiet, tasteful) decor of the sitting room and bedroom, echoing the Rynders' two-year sojourn in Japan during the sixties, creates an atmosphere conducive to relaxation, meditation, study, or sleep. To this end, books, candles, incense, reading lamps, and extra blankets and pillows are kept on hand. A small kitchenette with a refrigerator is equipped with essentials for preparing a light lunch or dinner. And a full country breakfast is delivered to your doorstep on a tray each morning.

No pets or RV parking; TV, VCR, AM/FM stereo, CD player, and cassette deck; deck; barbecue; heated community swimming pool nearby; off-street parking. $10 extra charge for one-night stays; two-night minimum on holiday weekends; vacation rentals by prior arrangement.

ROOM	BED	BATH	ENTRANCE	FLOOR	DAILY RATES S - D (EP)
A	2Q	Pvt	Sep	1G	$65-$75 ($20)

Rancho San Gregorio   **(415) 747-0810**
P.O. Box 21, San Gregorio, CA 94074
(Five miles east of Highway 1)

When you wend your way from the coast highway through the idyllic valley of San Gregorio, it's easy to feel that you're back in the time of the Spanish land grants. Then you arrive at Bud and Lee Raynor's fifteen-acre rancho, where peace and quiet abound. Every arched window of the Spanish Mission-style house frames a scenic view of hills, gnarled oak trees, and wide open sky. The interior offers a comfortable blend of natural colors and materials, country antiques, and Indian artifacts. Rooms in the guest wing are named for creeks in the area, and historical pictures provide rare glimpses of the valley's past. Numerous Coastside excursions from the rancho are possible, or you may choose to do nothing more than walk, picnic under old apple trees, plop down by a rambling creek, or sun yourself on a patio. The Raynors invite you to an utterly relaxing retreat at Rancho San Gregorio.

No pets; children by special arrangement; smoking outside only; full ranch breakfast on weekends; coffee, tea, other beverages, snacks, and refrigerator in guest wing; extra double bed in Room A; decks, patios, and gazebo; off-street parking. Room D is a suite with woodstove, refrigerator, VCR, and balcony. Inquire about midweek rates. Brochure available.

ROOM	BED	BATH	ENTRANCE	FLOOR	DAILY RATES	
					S - D	(EP)
A	2T or 1K	Pvt	Main	2	$65	($15)
B	1Q	Pvt	Main	2	$65	($15)
C	1Q	Pvt	Main	2	$75	($15)
D	1K & 2T	Pvt	Main	2	$90	($15)

The Victorian Manor   **(805) 467-3306**
P.O. Box 8, San Miguel, CA 93451
(North end of town where U.S. 101 and North Mission converge)

A good midway point between San Francisco and Los Angeles is the historic old mission town of San Miguel. In a beautiful rural setting, The Victorian Manor is an operating Morgan Horse ranch as well as a fine guest house. With over 5,000 square feet of living space, the home is open and airy; its attributes include a full library, formal dining room, game room, and large screened porch. Four bedrooms complete with sinks are available to guests. Two rooms with a shared bath are on each end of the second floor. While you're enjoying the relaxed, easy living at Ed and Catherine Allen's country estate, you may wish to explore the property and surrounding area on foot, view the horses, take a walk to the old mission, or picnic at a local winery. The Allens will make sure your stay is a comfortable one.

No indoor pets; smoking permitted on porch; TV and pool table in game room; off-street parking. Brochure available.

ROOM	BED	BATH	ENTRANCE	FLOOR	DAILY RATES S - D	(EP)
A	1D	Shd*	Main	2	$50	
B	1D	Shd*	Main	2	$50	
C	1D	Shd*	Main	2	$50	
D	1K	Shd*	Main	2	$50	

Bruce & Susan Bangert   **(408) 476-1906**
2501 Paul Minnie Avenue, Santa Cruz, CA 95062
(One quarter-mile from Highway 1, Soquel Avenue Exit)

The Bangerts' inviting old farmhouse seems to welcome you as you draw near, and once inside, the feeling is complete. Restored with loving care over the last few years, the house stands ready to delight any traveler lucky enough to discover it. The decor centers around the many works of art collected by the Bangerts. A dazzling array of ceramic pieces have been selected by Bruce, former head of the Ceramics Department at UC Santa Cruz. Two artists-in-residence work in the studio behind the house, where visitors can examine their wares. The Bangerts have a baby grand piano, a warm patio, and a relaxing deck that they enjoy sharing. Two gable-roofed bedrooms with an adjoining half-bath are available to B&B guests. The truly welcoming atmosphere, along with some nice surprises, have turned many guests into friends.

TV; refrigerator and barbecue available; shared full bath on first floor; off-street parking; bus transportation.

ROOM	BED	BATH	ENTRANCE	FLOOR	DAILY RATES	
					S - D	(EP)
A	1 D	Shd	Main	2	$40	
B	1 D	Shd	Main	2	$40	

Valley View (415) 321-5195 (Reservations)
P.O. Box 66593, Santa Cruz, CA 95066
(Santa Cruz Mountains, off State Highway 17)

Total privacy and seclusion, a fabulous view, all the comforts of home, and only two minutes to Highway 17 and another twelve to the beaches of Santa Cruz? Indeed. Valley View can make your fantasy getaway a reality. The home was designed with many elements of Frank Lloyd Wright's style by his protege, John Taggart. Walls of glass on the back side of the house bring in the beauty of the more than 20,000 acres of redwood forest that the home overlooks. A large deck has the same view, a Jacuzzi, and comfortable places to relax. The sound of trickling water from the circulating pond on the property adds to the feeling of serenity. The interior features a unique kitchen-in-the round, mirrored walls, luxurious carpeting throughout, and a large stone fireplace. Imaginatively shaped rooms offer wide vistas of the valley of redwoods. Unwind in country splendor, take a hike along redwood-lined paths, or head for Santa Cruz and the beach. It's all here to be savored by a fortunate few.

No children or pets; smoking outside only; no RV parking; fully stocked refrigerator, including provisions for a generous Continental breakfast; sofa bed in living room ($20 for fifth or sixth person in same party); barbecue; cable TV; stereo and large selection of tapes; piano; off-street parking; German spoken; major credit cards. House used for only one couple or group at a time; Room A is filled first. Hosts may be present upon request; more often, guests prefer to have exclusive use of the home with complete privacy. Two-night minimum.

ROOM	BED	BATH	ENTRANCE	FLOOR	DAILY RATES	
					S - D	(EP)
A	1K	Pvt	Sep	1G	$95	
B	1Q	Pvt		1G	$65	

Dunmovin   **(408) 728-4154**
1006 Hecker Pass Road, Watsonville, CA 95076
(Between Watsonville and Gilroy)

Located at the top of Hecker Pass, Ruth and Don Wakefield's rambling gray Tudor home is set on twenty-two acres with a giant redwood grove, Christmas trees, and free-roaming wildlife. The view from the many-windowed home is unsurpassed (a delight during breakfast in the family room). Dunmovin is situated partway between Santa Cruz and Monterey at such an elevation that you can see both towns plus the entire Monterey Bay. There is a separate wing for guests. Room A can be closed off and entered by its own door. Room B can be added to the accommodations and share the bath, ideal for couples traveling together. Room C is great for families; it's removed from the main part of the house and is entered separately. It has long, built-in twin beds and a queen-sized sofa bed. If you stay at Dunmovin, you can partake of the U-Pick fruits and vegetables of Watsonville; go wine-tasting at the small, family-run Hecker Pass wineries; and discover the many thrills of the Monterey Bay area.

Dog, cat, and two peacocks on premises; no pets in house; full breakfast; TV; tennis court; hot tub; near Mount Madonna Park with restaurant and golf course; off-street parking; airport pickup (Watsonville). If bath is shared by Rooms A and B, rate is $60 per room. $5 extra for one-night stays; two-night minimum preferred.

ROOM	BED	BATH	ENTRANCE	FLOOR	DAILY RATES	
					S - D	(EP)
A	1Q	Pvt	Sep	1	$65	
B	1D	Shd*	1		$60	
C	1Q & 2T	Pvt	Sep	1	$55	($10)

Please read "About Dining Highlights" on page *ix*

ARROYO GRANDE

Finch's Restaurant & Bar, 110 East Branch; (805) 489-0576; Cajun, Italian, fresh fish, and pasta

BIG SUR

Deetjen's Big Sur Inn, Highway 1; (408) 667-2377; homemade vegetarian, fish, and meat dishes

Nepenthe, Highway 1; (408) 667-2345; American

CAMBRIA

The Hamlet at Moonstone Gardens, Highway 1; (805) 927-3535; American/Continental

The Grey Fox, 4095 Burton Drive; (805) 927-3305; seafood, chops, and steaks

Ian's, 2150 Center Street; (805) 927-3535; prime rib, steaks, and local abalone

The Moonraker, 6500 Moonstone Drive; (805) 927-3859; fish, meat, and Cajun dishes

The Sea Chest, 6216 Moonstone Drive; (805) 927-4514; seafood

The Sow's Ear, 2248 Main Street; (805) 927-4865; ribs, chicken, fish/down-home cooking

CAPITOLA

Balzac Bistro, 112 Capitola Avenue; (408) 476-5035; informal Continental

Masayuki's, 427 Capitola Avenue; (408) 476-7284; sushi, etc.

Shadowbrook Restaurant, 1750 Wharf Road; (408) 475-1511; specializing in prime rib and fresh seafood

CARMEL

Casanova Restaurant, Fifth Street between San Carlos and Mission; (408) 625-0501; country-style French and Italian

Flaherty's Seafood Grill & Oyster Bar, Sixth Street between San Carlos and Dolores; (408) 625-1500; seafood

La Boheme Restaurant, Dolores Street near Seventh; (408) 624-7500; European country cuisine

L'Escargot, Mission Street at Fourth; (408) 624-4914; French

Rio Grill, 101 Crossroads Boulevard; (408) 625-5436; creative American food

DAVENPORT

New Davenport Cash Store Restaurant, Highway 1; (408) 426-4122; fresh home cooking, California style

EL GRANADA

Anchorage, 4210 Cabrillo Highway; (415) 726-2822; seafood and pasta

The Village Green, 89 Avenue Portola; (415) 726-3690; English

HALF MOON BAY

San Benito House, 356 Main Street; (415) 726-3425; French and northern Italian

Pasta Moon, 315 Main Street; (415) 726-5125; homemade pasta and sauces

MONTEREY

The Fishery, 21 Soledad Drive; (408) 373-6200; seafood

MORRO BAY

Abba's Pacific Café, 1150 Embarcadero; (805) 772-2965; varying menu of seafood, chicken, steak, and pasta dishes

PASO ROBLES

Berardi and Sons, 1202 Pine Street; (805) 238-1330; Italian

Joshua's Restaurant, Thirteenth and Vine Streets; (805) 238-7515; steak house

Lolo's, 555 Twelfth Street; (805) 239-1515; Mexican

PESCADERO

Duarte's Tavern, 202 Stage Road; (415) 879-0464; seafood and local specialties

RIO DEL MAR

Café Rio, 131 Esplanade (408) 688-8917; seafood

SAN LUIS OBISPO

Café Roma, 1819 Osos Street; (805) 541-6800; cucina rustica Italiana

SANTA CRUZ

Hollins House, 20 Clubhouse Road; (408) 425-1244; Continental

India Joze, 1001 Center Street; (408) 427-3554; Asian and Middle Eastern

Keffi, 2-1245 East Cliff Drive; (408) 476-5571; vegetarian

O'mei Restaurant, 2361 Mission Street; (408) 425-8458; Chinese

Peachwood's Grill & Bar, 555 Highway 17 at The Inn at Pasatiempo; (408) 426-6333; Continental

Pontiac Grill, 429 Front Street; (408) 427-2290; updated fifties diner food

Sala Thai Restaurant, 1632 Seabright Avenue; (408) 427-2559

Zanzibar, 2332 Mission Street; (408) 423-9999; seafood and vegetarian specialties

SCOTTS VALLEY

Zanotto's Pasta & More, 5600 Scotts Valley Drive; (408) 438-0503; pasta and Italian dishes

SOQUEL

The Salmon Poacher Restaurant, 3035 Main Street; (408) 476-1556; fresh seafood

Theo's, 3101 Main Street; (408) 462-3657; French

Tortilla Flats, 4724 Soquel Drive; (408) 476-1754; Mexican

San Francisco
& the
Bay Area

When you hear the clang of a cable car and the moan of a foghorn, you know where you are. San Francisco is like nowhere else, a city for all senses. Bounded on three sides by water, the feathery touch of sea mist is a pleasant certainty. Views from its famous hills — Telegraph, Russian, Nob, and Twin Peaks — are feasts for the eyes. Delicate, mysterious aromas arising from Chinatown contrast with the sharp sea smells of Fisherman's Wharf. Taste buds are tempted by over 2,600 restaurants with an astounding choice of menus — Basque, Moroccan, Hungarian, Greek, Armenian, Swiss, Jewish, Indian, Chinese, Japanese, Thai, Filipino, Korean, Italian, Scandinavian, Mexican, Spanish. Truly, San Francisco is a city to savor.

The city is really several. One out of every seven San Franciscans is either foreign-born or a first-generation citizen. San Francisco streets belong to the neighborhoods, ethnic communities whose diverse customs and lifestyles make San Francisco more than a sum of its parts. Whether you are a resolute explorer or a dawdling gadabout, the streets of San Francisco are guaranteed to fascinate.

Crossing the Golden Gate Bridge, travelers are often surprised to find themselves in a spot of wilderness, the Marin headlands. Hiking the headlands is exhilarating. The intense blue of the bay, often dotted with sailboats, and hills that can be either spring green or summer gold have a lucid radiance.

Hiking the streets of Sausalito is equally heady, although in quite a different way. This Marin town is a favorite of window-shoppers and trend-spotters. Go with the flow, if only for an afternoon. Only slightly farther north, Mount Tamalpais offers a more challenging hike as well as an unforgettable view. Muir Woods, at its foot, is a refuge of redwood and fern.

The Other Bridge (the Bay) takes you straight to Oakland, where the Oakland Museum answers more questions about California than you ever thought to ask. And Oakland must be one of the few cities in the country with a downtown saltwater lake, Lake Merritt.

Just south of the City is the Peninsula. The cities of Palo Alto and Menlo Park bustle at the base of oak-studded foothills. Many people have found their way to San Jose, one of the nation's fastest-growing cities. But not everyone has found the way to the hidden wine country surrounding it. More than fifty small to medium-sized wineries flourish in Santa Clara County. Tours and tastings are often unhurried and homey. The pastoral atmosphere may seem a world away from cosmopolitan San Francisco, but it's a mere fifty miles or so. In the Bay Area you can enjoy both.

Webster House   (415) 523-9697
1238 Versailles Avenue, Alameda, CA 94501
(East side of island in San Francisco Bay, adjacent to Oakland)

Since Susan and Andrew McCormack rescued this historical treasure, they've been delving into its fascinating past. The 1854 Gothic Revival cottage is the oldest house on Alameda Island and a documented historical landmark. The McCormacks are glad to share their discoveries with interested guests by way of old photos, books, and other documentation. Selected period antiques grace each of three cozy guest rooms and a Library Suite (D). A parlor fire glows in cool weather, while a redwood deck with a waterfall entices on warmer days. Webster House is located in a pleasant residential neighborhood where you can stroll or cycle with ease. Good restaurants, shops, a swimming beach (really!), and other outdoor recreation lure visitors to experience this unique island in the bay.

No pets; smoking on deck only; afternoon tea, champagne or sherry, espresso variations, and warm bedtime drinks available; good public transportation; airport pickup (Oakland International). Room with private bath available when possible.

ROOM	BED	BATH	ENTRANCE	FLOOR	DAILY RATES S - D (EP)
A	1D	Shd*	Main	1	$65
B	1Q	Shd*	Main	1	$65
C	1Q	Shd*	Main	1	$75
D	1D	Shd*	Sep	1	$85

Diablo Vista   **(415) 634-2396**
2191 Empire Avenue, Brentwood, CA 94513
(Just east of Antioch, off Lone Tree Way)

This elegant ranch-style home is set on two acres of fruit and nut trees, with a view of Mount Diablo in the distance. It is an hour from San Francisco and just ten minutes from the Sacramento River Delta. For hikers and cyclists, Black Diamond Regional Park, with its many trails and historic sites, is only four miles away, as is Contra Loma Lake for swimming, windsurfing, and fishing. Brentwood is famous for its many "U-Pick" fruit and vegetable farms. Maps showing the various farms and their offerings are are available from the hosts. The guest room at Diablo Vista is located at the far end, well separated from the rest of the house. The huge space has its own entrance, bath, kitchenette, small library, TV, and stereo system. A harmonious, soothing effect is created by the use of subtle colors, Oriental rugs, custom-made window cushions, and American antiques. You're welcome to swim in the pool, soak in the hot tub, sip a drink in one of the two gazebos, or relax in the lovely garden. Guests often comment on the peaceful surroundings and the brilliance of the nighttime sky. Hosts Dick and Myra Hackett have thoroughly searched out the best restaurants in the area, a boon to those of us who take our dining seriously.

No pets; children over eight (swimmers) welcome; smoking outside only; TV; stereo; swimming pool; hot tub; jogging and biking trails surround property; off-street parking; some Spanish spoken; airport pickup (Antioch).

ROOM	BED	BATH	ENTRANCE	FLOOR	DAILY RATES S - D (EP)
A	1Q	Pvt	Sep	1G	$45-$50

Frank & Virginia Hallman   (415) 376-4318
309 Constance Place, Moraga, CA 94556
(Five miles from Orinda BART station and Freeway 24)

At the Hallmans' Moraga home, you can have the best of both worlds while visiting the Bay Area. You can take off to "do" San Francisco in the ideal (car-less) fashion, then scoot back across the bay to the quiet luxury of this tastefully appointed home. The Hallmans will see that you have all the restorative comforts you need. There's a large pool and redwood hot tub in a private garden setting. Guest rooms are particularly pleasing. Moraga is usually sunny and is centrally located to many places of interest in the Bay Area. Hosts will help you find your way to the City, Berkeley, Napa Valley, Muir Woods, and elsewhere.

No pets or young children; no smoking preferred; full breakfast optional; TV (B); swimming pool; hot tub; living room with fireplace for guests; five miles to JFK University, ten to UC Berkeley, twelve to Mills College; network of hiking trails through Moraga and Lafayette, as well as other East Bay regional parks, nearby; bus and BART service; airport connections from San Francisco and Oakland; street parking. Inquire about weekly and family rates.

ROOM	BED	BATH	ENTRANCE	FLOOR	DAILY RATES S - D (EP)
A	1Q	Shd*	Main	1G	$40-$45 ($10)
B	1Q	Shd*	Main	1G	$40-$45 ($10)

Faye & Robert Abbey (415) 892-5478
55 Grande Vista, Novato, CA 94947
(Twenty-eight miles north of Golden Gate Bridge)

Novato is the northernmost city in Marin County and best known to some as the site of the annual Renaissance Pleasure Faire. Its location in the "Valley of Gentle Seasons" gives it a mild, healthful climate. Faye and Robert Abbey live in an older, well-groomed neighborhood. Their huge back yard is a beautiful landscape of flowers, ferns, and trees, with sitting areas for enjoying the park-like environment. Two bedrooms on the main floor and a suite on the upper floor comprise the B&B accommodations. A front room (A) is cheerfully decorated in red and white; the one across the hall (B) is done in peach with ivory lace and ruffles. The large master suite (C) offers complete privacy and a balcony with a view of the back yard. The Abbeys' home is an appealing place to stay, and its location poises the traveler for a foray into the Sonoma Wine Country, San Francisco, or Marin County's unique towns, parks, and coastline.

TV (in suite and family room); living room with fireplace available to guests; off-street parking.

ROOM	BED	BATH	ENTRANCE	FLOOR	DAILY RATES S - D (EP)
A	2T	Pvt	Main	1	$35-$45
B	1Q	Pvt	Sep	1	$35-$45
C	1K	Pvt	Main	2	$55

OAKLAND

Bruce & Helen Maxfield   **(415) 654-9616**
343 Modoc Avenue, Oakland, CA 94618
(Oakland Hills, off Broadway Terrace)

The Maxfields' home is in a quiet, secure residential area with attractive homes nestled along the hillside. Wonderful views of San Francisco, the Golden Gate Bridge, and Mount Tamalpais abound as you walk or jog through the neighborhood. Bruce and Helen offer B&B guests a bright, open room with a private bath on the lower level of their home. Sparkling white walls are accented by dashes of color and interesting artwork. The ambiance is at once fresh and relaxing. Enjoy the privacy of your room or share the living room fireplace, TV, and VCR. Hosts can suggest city hikes, country hikes, restaurants, museums, and theaters close at hand. The great location and comfortable room, plus the Maxfields' kind hospitality, assure a satisfying stay in the exciting Bay Area.

No pets or smoking; public transportation; ample street parking. Two-night minimum.

ROOM	BED	BATH	ENTRANCE	FLOOR	DAILY RATES S - D (EP)
A	1D	Pvt	Main	LL	$45

Jessie & Pete Taylor   **(415) 531-2345**
59 Chelton Lane, Oakland, CA 94611
(Oakland Hills)

    The Taylors love sharing their home, which is set on a quiet lane in the hills above Oakland and the San Francisco Bay. Here you'll be assured of a gracious welcome and a good night's rest — but that's only the beginning. For these generous-spirited hosts, taking special care of guests is a top priority. Two lovely guest rooms and a bath on the lower level of the house can be closed off for an extra measure of privacy. You may have breakfast on the front deck enclosed by a soothing Japanese garden, or on the rear deck facing the bay. View jewel-like San Francisco by night from your bedroom, the living room, or the deck. Three islands (Yerba Buena, Alcatraz, and Angel) and two bridges (Bay and Golden Gate) are visible by day. Need I say more?

    No RV parking; full breakfast; TV; decks. Two parties traveling together may share the bath or use an additional bath at the top of the stairs; inquire about street parking. Two-night minimum.

ROOM	BED	BATH	ENTRANCE	FLOOR	DAILY RATES S - D (EP)
A	2T	Pvt	Main	LL	$35-$45 ($10)
B	1D	Pvt	Main	LL	$35-$45 ($10)

Ruth Simon & Hy Rosner   (415) 237-1711
2723 Esmond Avenue, Richmond, CA 94804
(Off San Pablo Avenue)

In this quiet Richmond neighborhood, a new contemporary home that fits in agreeably with the older homes around it was recently built. The lot is small, but the house was cleverly designed to seem spacious inside. The owners are Ruth Simon, a writer and seismologist, and Hy Rosner, who's retired. Their home is filled with books, art, and music, making the ambiance one of civility and comfort. The large upstairs guest room is light and airy, with a crewel-embroidered bedspread, a sofa bed, and a private half-bath. While you're in Richmond, explore picturesque Point Richmond Historical District. All the bridges across the Bay are visible from the waterfront, and you'll find some beautifully restored buildings and good restaurants there as well.

No pets or smoking; TV; VCR; crib and single rollaway bed available; shared full bath; garden hot tub; swimming at nearby municipal indoor pool; good public transportation; ample street parking; airport pickup (Buchanan, Oakland, San Francisco).

ROOM	BED	BATH	ENTRANCE	FLOOR	DAILY RATES S - D	(EP)
A	1D	Pvt 1/2	Main	2	$30-$35	($5)

Mario & Suellen Lamorte (415) 456-0528
45 Entrata Drive, San Anselmo, CA 94960
(Walking distance from central San Anselmo)

To stay at the Lamortes' three-story brown-shingled house is to savor the taste of old Marin. It's on a quiet, tree-lined lane that was cut into a hillside long ago; from here, the views of the hilly terrain are a visual feast. The lower floor of the house is a private guest suite that can accommodate up to four people. Natural wood paneling and floors, Oriental rugs, unique paned windows, and a curved redwood sleeping alcove give the interior a warm rustic charm. French doors lead to a private deck where sunlight filters through a canopy of fruit and oak trees. The home is within walking distance of fine restaurants, shops, hiking trails, and lakes. San Anselmo is less than an hour from the wine country and Point Reyes National Seashore, yet only fourteen miles from the Golden Gate Bridge. Whether you plan to do the town or explore the country, the Lamortes' is a good place to start.

Children welcome ($10 extra for one or two); no smoking; full breakfast; kitchen; TV; phone; rollaway bed available; off-street parking; Italian spoken.

ROOM	BED	BATH	ENTRANCE	FLOOR	DAILY RATES S - D (EP)
A	1D & 1T	Pvt	Sep	LL	$70 ($10)

Casa Arguello   **(415) 752-9482**
225 Arguello Boulevard, San Francisco, CA 94118
(Presidio Heights, between California and Lake)

Mrs. Emma Baires makes her B&B guests feel right at home in Casa Arguello, a large, two-floor flat located in a safe residential area; it's within easy walking distance of shops and restaurants on Sacramento Street, Clement Street, and in Laurel Village. Spacious, immaculate rooms feature brass or iron beds with comfortable mattresses. The view from each room is a constant reminder that you couldn't be anywhere *but* San Francisco. Casa Arguello celebrates its twelfth year as a B&B home in 1990, and, not surprisingly, it has more return visitors than ever. People appreciate the cheerful, homelike accommodations that Mrs. Baires so graciously provides.

No pets or smoking; expanded Continental breakfast; TV in each room; large living room for guests; inquire about street parking; Spanish spoken; good public transportation and airport connections. Room D is a two-room master suite. $5 extra charge for one-night stays; two-night minimum preferred.

ROOM	BED	BATH	ENTRANCE	FLOOR	DAILY RATES S - D	(EP)
A	1D	Shd*	Main	3	$45	
B	2T	Shd*	Main	3	$50	
C	1K	Shd*	Main	3	$50	
D	1K & 2T	Pvt	Main	2	$70	($10)
E	1K	Pvt	Main	3	$60	

A Country Cottage (415) 931-3083
P.O. Box 349, San Francicso, CA 94101
(#5 Dolores Terrace)

Discovering A Country Cottage is like finding a surprise tucked away in a pocket you didn't know you had. Dolores Terrace is a hidden little pocket just off Dolores Street and very close to downtown. Susan and Richard Kreibich have restored this small, brown-shingled house to top condition. The exterior has modern lines; the interior is crisp, clean, and loaded with country comfort. The house is larger than it appears. Breakfast is served in the sunny kitchen on the main floor. A cheery guest bedroom with a pineapple theme (D) is also on this floor. Other B&B guests are accommodated downstairs, where there are three bedrooms, a bath, a pretty patio with trees and birds, and a separate entrance. The carpeted rooms have beautiful brass or oak beds and country antiques. Hosts also operate "American Family Inn," a reservation service with private homes all over the City. If you're making late reservations or looking for a particular kind of lodging, chances are they can help. For a taste of quiet country living in the midst of San Francisco, the Cottage is a winner.

No children; full breakfast; complimentary wine; patio; travel information provided; wholesale shopping tours arranged; good public transportation and airport connections; no RV parking; inquire about limited car parking; German spoken; major credit cards (V, MC, AE). Two-night minimum; $5 extra for one-night stays.

ROOM	BED	BATH	ENTRANCE	FLOOR	DAILY RATES	
					S - D	(EP)
A	1Q	Shd*	Sep	LL	$45-$55	
B	1Q	Shd*	Sep	LL	$45-$55	
C	1D	Shd*	Sep	LL	$45-$55	
D	1Q	Shd*	Sep	1	$45-$55	

Dorothy Franzblau   **(415) 564-7686**
2207 Twelfth Avenue, San Francisco, CA 94116
(South of Golden Gate Park and UC Medical Center)

Dorothy Franzblau's home is nestled in Golden Gate Heights, one of San Francisco's many interesting neighborhoods. Some of its assets include exhilarating views, good places for walking and running, and proximity to the lively shops and restaurants near Ninth and Irving. Guests in Dorothy's home are treated with care. Breakfast is a potpourri of her special creations, served in the dining room with a vast Pacific panorama as a backdrop. The guest room, decorated in blue and white, is a calm haven to return to after a busy day. And a peaceful night's sleep is assured in this quiet, safe neighborhood.

No pets; limited smoking; full breakfast; TV; extra bed; good public transportation; inquire about parking.

ROOM	BED	BATH	ENTRANCE	FLOOR	DAILY RATES S - D (EP)
A	2T or 1K	Shd	Main	2	$50-$60 ($10)

The Garden Studio   **(415) 753-3574**
1387 Sixth Avenue, San Francisco, CA 94122
(Two blocks from Golden Gate Park and UC Medical Center)

John and Alice Micklewright are the second owners of this 1910 Edwardian-style home. It is quite handsome in appearance, from the unusual sloped roof to the extensive interior woodwork. The house feels rich, solid, and handcrafted. The Garden Studio was recently completed on the garden level. It has a separate entrance from the street and a fully carpeted interior. The peach and green color scheme accents the fully equipped kitchen with slate floor and marble counters, and is carried throughout the bath and dressing rooms. The queen-sized iron bed has a down comforter and a cover with a Marimeko green and white motif. The light and airy apartment opens onto a compact city garden with lawn, flowering border, and a private, serene feeling. Well-traveled guests appreciate the attention to detail hosts have shown in providing many conveniences to enhance their stay in the City.

No pets or smoking; TV; iron and ironing board; private telephone (with deposit); rollaway bed; information and maps for neighborhood and City attractions provided; good public transportation and airport connections; inquire about parking; French spoken. Brochure available.

ROOM	BED	BATH	ENTRANCE	FLOOR	DAILY RATES S - D (EP)
A	1Q	Pvt	Sep	1G	$60-$65 ($15)

Moffatt House (415) 661-6210
431 Hugo Street, San Francisco, CA 94122
(Between 5th & 6th Avenues, near U.C.S.F.)

This pale blue Edwardian home is in close proximity to the popular neighborhood haunts of Ninth and Irving, Golden Gate Park, and U.C. Medical Center. Ruth Moffatt knows the area well and offers assistance with just about anything her guests might need. The four guest rooms are neat and cheerful, with artistic touches in the decor and, typically San Franciscan, shared split baths. The quiet, safe location of Moffatt House makes walking a pleasure — neighborhood shops, cafes, bakeries, and markets invite browsing. A "Cafe Walk" through the nearby Haight-Ashbury district can be arranged, an experience that's both fun and memorable. The new exercise discount really pays off in a form most everyone can enjoy. Moffatt House pays a quarter a mile for any running or walking guests do in Golden Gate Park. Yes, Ruth puts the cash right in your hand! Moffatt House puts San Francisco at your feet — the possibilities are endless....

Cat in residence; kitchen privileges; crib available; one-night stays and late arrivals OK; Spanish, Italian, and French spoken; good public transportation and airport connections; inquire about parking; major credit cards (V, MC).

ROOM	BED	BATH	ENTRANCE	FLOOR	DAILY RATES S - D	(EP)
A	2T	Shd*	Main	2	$39-$44	
B	1D	Shd*	Main	2	$39	
C	1Q & 1T	Shd*	Main	2	$49-$54	($5)
D	1Q	Shd*	Main	2	$49-$54	

The No Name Bed & Breakfast   **(415) 931-3083**
P.O. Box 349, San Francisco, CA 94101
(North of Market Street, six blocks west of Civic Center area)

Located near historic Alamo Square and the row of Victorians pictured on many post cards of San Francisco, Susan and Richard Kreibich's 1880s Victorian offers a friendly, hospitable stay in a tastefully renovated home. The three individually decorated bedrooms have private baths and fireplaces. There's a deck with a hot tub for guests to enjoy in the evening, perhaps after having dinner at one of the Kreibichs' choice restaurant discoveries. Next morning, Richard will serve your full breakfast in the cheerful kitchen with a view of the garden.

Full breakfast; hot tub; travel information provided; wholesale shopping tours arranged; German spoken; inquire about parking; good public transportation and airport connections; major credit cards (V, MC, AE). Two-night minimum; $5 extra for one-night stays.

ROOM	BED	BATH	ENTRANCE	FLOOR	DAILY RATES S - D	(EP)
A	1Q	Pvt	Main	2	$65-$75	
B	1Q	Pvt	Main	2	$65-$75	
C	1Q	Pvt	Main	2	$65-$75	

Ed & Monica Widburg   **(415) 564-1751**
2007 Fifteenth Avenue, San Francisco, CA 94116
(South of Golden Gate Park and UC Medical Center)

The Widburgs' home has an individual charm of its own, both inside and out. Their wide, quiet street is elevated to allow striking views of the ocean and the Golden Gate. The rose-beige stucco home and landscaped yard have a look of understated elegance. European and Indonesian art objects, antiques, maps, and family heirlooms fit well into an interior graced with exquisite finishing details. At the front of the main floor, a bed/sitting room (A) and adjacent bath are available to guests. Another bed/sitting room (B) is just off the hallway and, when occupied, shares the bath. Hosts sleep downstairs, so there's an extra degree of privacy. Large view windows across the back of the house make the dining and living rooms unusually pleasant. The Widburgs' European background contributes to their unfailing graciousness: they are not only well traveled but accustomed to hosting visitors from other countries. Bed and breakfast is a way of life to them, and sharing their special city by the sea is second nature.

No pets, children, or smoking; TV in Room A; European languages spoken; good public transportation and airport connections; ample street parking.

ROOM	BED	BATH	ENTRANCE	FLOOR	DAILY RATES S - D (EP)		
A	1Q	Shd*	Main	2	$50-$65		
B	1Q	Shd*	Main	2	$45-$55		

The Briar Rose   **(408) 279-5999**
897 East Jackson Street, San Jose, CA 95112
(North downtown San Jose)

The Briar Rose, an 1875 Victorian, once served as the farmhouse for a flourishing walnut orchard. Now it is a fine home in a quiet, intown neighborhood near a lovely city park. Owners Cheryl and James Fuhring have spent years restoring it to its former grandeur in every detail. Carefully chosen period furnishings grace rooms that have been fabulously wallpapered in the authentic Victorian designs of Bradbury & Bradbury, specialists in the field. Even the grounds around The Briar Rose recall an earlier era; some original trees remain, as well as a pond, an arbor, and a quaint little Victorian cotttage. A wide, wrap-around porch, delightful gardens, and a gazebo complete the picture. The Fuhrings invite you to step back in time, if only for a little while, and be pampered in the style befitting their gracious home.

No pets; smoking outside only; full breakfast; TV optional for any room; all antique beds; Murphy bed in Room B; clawfoot tub in Room D; good public transportation and airport connections; ample street parking; garden weddings and receptions; major credit cards (V, MC, AE). Informative brochure available.

ROOM	BED	BATH	ENTRANCE	FLOOR	DAILY RATES S - D	(EP)
A	1 D	Shd*	Main	2	$65	
B	1 D	Shd*	Main	2	$65	($5)
C	1 D	Shd*	Main	2	$55	
D	1 D	Pvt	Main	2	$70	
E	1 D	Pvt	Main	1	$85	

Barbara & George Kievlan   **(408) 559-3828**
14497 New Jersey Avenue, San Jose, CA 95124
(Near Campbell, Los Gatos, and Highway 17)

Although you'd never guess it, this sprawling suburban home occupies part of the old Blossom Valley Ranch, and the historic ranch house still stands in the vicinity. The first thing you notice upon entering the spacious living room is an oversized fireplace that dominates the room, offering its warm glow when the weather's chilly. In warmer weather, the large family room and adjacent patio with pool and spa are the usual gathering places. The Kievlans are very accommodating people. Their home conveys the feeling that you can truly do as you please, whether your urge is to socialize, do some light cooking, or spend some time alone. As a guest here, you'll soon feel like just blending into this comfortable household.

No pets; smoking outside only; TV; extra bed in room, $20; swimming pool; spa; pool table; IBM computer for business use; off-street parking; wheelchair access. Inquire about weekly rates.

ROOM	BED	BATH	ENTRANCE	FLOOR	DAILY RATES	
					S - D	(EP)
A	1K	Pvt	Sep	1G	$38-$48	
B	2T	Pvt	Sep	1G	$38-$48	

The Palm House   **(415) 573-7256**
1216 Palm Avenue, San Mateo, CA 94402
(A block east of El Camino Real, between 12th and 13th Avenues)

Alan and Marian Brooks have enjoyed creating The Palm House, and they're justifiably proud of it. Built in 1907, it's a picture-book, Craftsman-style home in a quiet residential area of San Mateo. The interior has a warm, European ambiance created by multi-paned windows and dark wooden panels and beams. Some of the stunning works of art on the walls were done by Alan, an accomplished and successful painter. B&B guests are treated to gracious breakfast service and sun-dried, 100% cotton sheets and towels. The Palm House is located within walking distance of shops and restaurants; San Francisco International Airport is a short ride away by bus or taxi. You can get to San Francisco, Stanford University, or the Pacific Ocean in less than thirty minutes, and all can be reached by public transportation. Alan and Marian wish to convey the spirit of English bed and breakfast to their guests — and you'll see a surprising bit of evidence to prove it.

Children welcome; ample street parking.

ROOM	BED	BATH	ENTRANCE	FLOOR	DAILY RATES	
					S - D	(EP)
A	1Q & 1T	Pvt	Main	2	$45-$50	($10)
B	1T	Shd	Main	2	$40	

Madison Street Bed & Breakfast   **(408) 249-5541**
1390 Madison Street, Santa Clara, CA 95050
(Near Santa Clara University and San Jose Municipal Airport)

One doesn't necessarily associate the Santa Clara Valley with historic homes and genteel living, but that is exactly what you'll find at Theresa and Ralph Wigginton's completely restored Victorian on Madison Street. The result of their painstaking work is a unique lodging establishment with turn-of-the-century style and personal service. The high-ceilinged rooms are appointed with wallcoverings of authentic Victorian design, Oriental rugs, antique furnishings, brass beds, and one romantic four-poster. Deluxe breakfasts are served in a dining room that overlooks landscaped grounds with a pool, spa, and barbecue area. Hosts will try to accommodate your business or personal needs; they can arrange for such things as private meetings and intimate, home-cooked dinners. A most pleasant atmosphere for work or relaxation is yours at Madison Street Bed & Breakfast.

No smoking; full breakfast; TV and movies available; sink in Rooms C and D; robes provided; telephones in rooms; dry cleaning services; pool and spa; dinners (from a tantalizing menu!) for four to sixteen guests by arrangement; private meetings; Winchester Mystery House and Great America Amusement Park ten minutes away; ample street parking; major credit cards. **KNIGHTTIME PUBLICATIONS SPECIAL RATE: 10% discount with this book.

ROOM	BED	BATH	ENTRANCE	FLOOR	DAILY RATES S - D (EP)
A	1Q	Pvt	Main	1	$85
B	1D	Pvt	Main	1	$75
C	1D	Shd*	Main	1	$60
D	1D	Shd*	Main	1	$60
E	1D	Pvt	Sep	LL	$85

Bed & Breakfast in Tiburon   **(415) 435-0605**
27 Old Landing Road, Tiburon, CA 94920
(Marin County, on San Francisco Bay)

Sandy Paul's ranch-style adobe home is set among trees and faces the bay. Deer roam freely through the yard. The home's interior is the essence of coziness and country charm. There's a small, private beachfront across the street where some guests favor sipping their morning coffee while contemplating the day ahead. A "must" for many visitors is the ferry trip from Tiburon to Angel Island (dock ten minutes away), a good place for hiking, picnicking, and riding bicycles. With the variety of unique shops and restaurants in Tiburon and nearby Sausalito — not to mention the stunning views of San Francisco from both spots — you don't really *need* to venture further to have a perfect holiday.

Cat in residence; no pets; good airport connections from San Francisco International by Marin Airporter; off-street parking.

ROOM	BED	BATH	ENTRANCE	FLOOR	DAILY RATES S - D (EP)
A	1D	Pvt	Main	1G	$45-$50

Christine's Bed & Breakfast   **(415) 947-1845**
530 Dover Drive, Walnut Creek, CA 94598
(Near north entrance to Mount Diablo State Park)

Mount Diablo offers, among other things, outstanding views of the entire Bay Area. Carved right out of the mountain is the popular Concord Pavilion. Whether you're taking in a concert, visiting friends or relatives, or doing business in Contra Costa County, a luxurious stay can be yours at Christine Scott's rambling ranch-style home. A huge, two-sided, old brick fireplace dominates the living and family rooms. A grand piano stands ready to be played. Two attractive bedrooms and a master suite comprise the sleeping quarters. In summer, a California-style breakfast is served in the garden. Nature lovers may wish to explore Briones Regional Park or one of the many wilderness areas nearby. Booming Contra Costa has something for just about everyone. Christine's makes a quiet home base while you're there.

No pets; children over six welcome; full breakfast; exercise equipment available; ample street parking. Two-night minimum.

ROOM	BED	BATH	ENTRANCE	FLOOR	DAILY RATES S - D	(EP)
A	1D	Shd	Main	1	$50	
B	1Q	Shd	Main	1	$55	
C	1K	Pvt	Main	1	$65	

Please read "About Dining Highlights" on page *ix.*

ALAMEDA

Beau Rivage, 1042 Ballena Boulevard; (415) 523-1660; French

BERKELEY

Café at Chez Panisse, 1517 Shattuck Avenue; (415) 548-5525; fresh, inventive California cuisine

Café Fanny, 1603 San Pablo Avenue; (415) 524-5447; fresh and simple breakfasts and lunches

Café Pastoral, 2160 University Avenue; (415) 540-7514; Oriental/French

Caffé Venezia, 1903 University Avenue; (415) 849-4681; Italian

Cha-Am, 1543 Shattuck Avenue; (415) 848-9664; Thai

Fatapple's, 1346 Martin Luther King Junior Way; (415) 526-2260; burgers

Plearn Thai Cuisine, 2050 University Avenue; (415) 841-2148

Ristorante Venezia, 1902 University Avenue; (415) 644-3093; Italian

Sedona Grill & Bar, 2086 Allston Way; (415) 841-3848; American Southwest cuisine

BETHEL ISLAND

Artist's Table, 6277 Bethel Island Road; (415) 684-3414; Continental

CONCORD

Doc's American Diner, 4600-A Clayton Road; (415) 682-7313; updated fifties-style diner food

Sabina India Cuisine, 4607 Clayton Road; (415) 827-9112

T.R.'s Bar & Grill, 2001 Salvio Street; (415) 827-4660; American

CORTE MADERA

Il Fornaio, 233 Corte Madera Town Center; (415) 927-4400; Italian

Savannah Grill, 55 Tamal Vista Boulevard; (415) 924-6774; American

DANVILLE

The Danville Hotel Restaurant & Saloon, 155 South Hartz Avenue; (415) 837-6627; early California cuisine

Saro's, 254 Rose Street; (415) 838-2008; Italian

Tiger Alley Courtyard Restaurant & Bar, 400 South Hartz Avenue; (415) 743-1700; Continental/American

EMERYVILLE

Bucci's, 6121 Hollis Street; (415) 547-4725; Italian

Homemade at Hollis, 5900 Hollis Street; (415) 655-5929; contemporary American

LAFAYETTE

Spruzzo! Ristorante, 210 Lafayette Circle; (415) 284-9709; Italian

LARKSPUR

Dalecio, 286 Magnolia Avenue; (415) 924-4814; Italian

Lark Creek Inn, 234 Magnolia Avenue; (415) 924-7766; American

LOS ALTOS

Beau Sejour Restaurant, 170 State Street; (415) 948-1382; French/nouvelle cuisine; also in Sunnyvale at 704 Town & Country (Mathilda and Washington); (408) 720-0273

LOS GATOS

il pastaio, 15466 Los Gatos Boulevard; (408) 358-1848; fresh, inventive Italian dishes

MILL VALLEY

The Avenue Grill, 44 East Blithedale Avenue; (415) 388-6003; American

MORAGA

Chez Maurice, 360 Park Street; (415) 376-1655; French/Continental

MOUNTAIN VIEW

Chez T.J., 938 Villa Street; (415) 964-7466; French

OAKLAND

Bay Wolf Restaurant, 3853 Piedmont Avenue; (415) 655-6004; California/ Mediterranean

Broadway Terrace Café, 5891 Broadway Terrace; (415) 652-4442; California/seasonal fresh

Creme de la Creme, 5362 College Avenue; (415) 420-8822; California/ country French

Pescatore, 57 Jack London Square; (415) 465-2188; classic and northern Italian

Sabina India Cuisine, 1628 Webster; (415) 268-0170

Thornhill Café, 5761 Thornhill Drive; (415) 339-0646; Thai-influenced French cuisine

PALO ALTO

Fresco, 3398 El Camino Real; (415) 493-3470; fresh California cuisine

ROSS

Alessia, 23 Ross Common; (415) 925-9619; contemporary Italian

SAN ANSELMO

Comforts, 337 San Anselmo Avenue; (415) 454-6790; eclectic menu

SAN FRANCISCO

The Ace Café, 1539 Folsom Street; (415) 621-4752; California cuisine

Buca Giovanni, 800 Greenwich Street; (415) 776-7766; Italian

Café For All Seasons, 350 West Portal Avenue; (415) 665-0900; American

China Moon Café, 639 Post Street; (415) 775-4789; California/Chinese

Clement Street Bar & Grill, 708 Clement Street; (415) 386-2000; American

Courtyard Restaurant, 2436 Clement Street; (415) 387-7616; American

E'Angelo Italian Restaurant, 2234 Chestnut Street; (415) 567-6164

Fog City Diner, 1300 Battery Street; (415) 982-2000; contemporary American

Golden Turtle, 2211 Van Ness Avenue; (415) 441-4419 - and - 308 Fifth Avenue; (415) 221-5285; Vietnamese

Gypsy Café, 687 McAllister Street; (415) 931-1854; French

Gypsy North Beach, 353 Columbus Avenue; (415) 781-6880; Italian

Hayes Street Grill, 320 Hayes Street; (415) 863-5545; seafood

I Fratelli, 1896 Hyde Street; (415) 474-8240; cucina Italiana

Julie's Supper Club, 1123 Folsom Street; (415) 861-0707; American

Kabuto, 5116 Geary Boulevard; (415) 752-5652; sushi

L'Avenue, 3855 Third Avenue; (415) 386-1555; Mediterranean, provencale, and traditional American

Le Central, 453 Bush Street; (415) 391-2233; French bistro/brasserie

Le Trou, 1007 Guererro Street; (415) 550-8169; regional French

Little Italy, 4109 Twenty-fourth Street; (415) 821-1515; neighborhood Italian

Little Thai, 2348 Oak Street; (415) 771-5544

Manora's Thai Restaurant, 1600 Folsom Street; (415) 861-6224

Pacific Heights Bar & Grill, 2001 Fillmore Street; (415) 567-3337; specializing in mesquite grilled fish; oyster bar

Pauline's Pizza Pie, 260 Valencia Street; (415) 552-2050

Ryan's, 4230 Eighteenth Street; (415) 621-6131; hearty California cuisine

Sea Chanteys, 1233 Van Ness Avenue; (415) 673-0558; chef-owned, seafood

690, 690 Van Ness Avenue; (415) 255-6900; California cuisine

South Park Café, 108 South Park (between Second and Third, Brannan and Bryant); (415) 495-7275; French

Stars Café, 555 Golden Gate Avenue; (415) 861-7827; light food and fish & chips

Stoyanof's, 1240 Ninth Avenue; (415) 664-3664; Greek

Ton Kiang, 3148 Geary Boulevard; (415) 752-4440 - and - 5827 Geary Boulevard; (415) 386-8530; northern Chinese

Tre Fratelli, 2101 Sutter Street; (415) 931-0701; neighborhood Italian

Trio Café, 1870 Fillmore Street; (415) 563-2248; casual neighborhood cafe serving breakfast and lunch

Tung Fong, 808 Pacific Avenue; (415) 362-7115; dim sum

Yank Sing, 427 Battery Street; (415) 362-1640; dim sum

Zuni Café, 1658 Market Street; (415) 552-2522; Mediterranean

SAN JOSE

Eulipia Restaurant & Bar, 374 South First Street; (408) 280-6161; California cuisine

SAN MATEO

Eposto's Four Day Café, 1119 South B Street; (415) 345-6443; Italian

SAN RAFAEL

Adriana's Ristorante, 999 Anderson Drive; (415) 454-8000; Italian

Café Monet, 100 Smith Ranch Road; (415) 499-8668; American

Royal Thai Restaurant, 610 Third Street; (415) 485-1074

SAN RAMON

Mudd's, 10 Boardwalk (off Crow Canyon Road); (415) 837-9387; fresh California cuisine

SANTA CLARA

Birk's, 3955 Freedom Circle; (408) 980-6400; classic American grill

4-5-6, 2362 Pruneridge Avenue; (408) 985-8456; Szechuan Chinese

Fresco, 1103 East El Camino Real; (408) 984-7474; fresh California cuisine

SAUSALITO

The Chart House, 201 Bridgeway; (415) 332-0804; seafood

North Sea Village, 300 Turney; (415) 331-3300; Chinese

TIBURON

Guaymas, 5 Main Street; (415) 435-6300; upscale Mexican

Rooney's Café & Grill, 38 Main Street; (415) 435-1911; American and California cuisine

Sam's Anchor Café, 27 Main Street; (415) 435-4527; American/seafood

WALNUT CREEK

The Cantina, 1470 North Broadway; (415) 934-3663; Mexican

Crogan's, 1387 Locust Street; (415) 933-7800; American/seafood

Devil Mountain Brewery, 850 Broadway; (415) 935-2337; American

Mai Thai, 1414 North Main Street; (415) 937-7887

Max's Opera Café, 1676 North California Boulevard; (415) 932-3434; American/New York-style deli

Pasta Mania, 1375 North Broadway; (415) 933-0180; Italian

Prima Café, 1522 North Main Street; (415) 935-7780; California cuisine

Scott's, 1333 North California Boulevard; (415) 934-1300; seafood

Spiedini, 101 Ygnacio Valley Road; (415) 939-2100; Italian

Takao, 1690 Locust Street; (415) 944-0244; Japanese

Also recommended is California Café Bar & Grill *in the following locations:* Almaden, Corte Madera, Los Gatos, Palo Alto, San Francisco, San Ramon, Santa Clara, Sunnyvale, and Walnut Creek.

Wine
Country

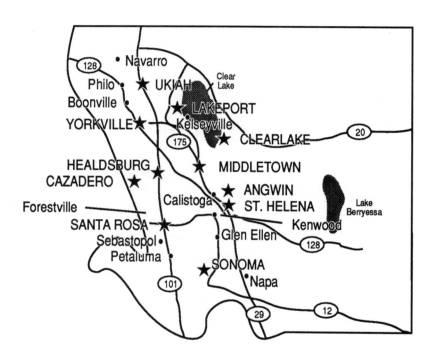

"How simple and frugal a thing is happiness: a glass of wine, a roast chestnut, a little brazier...." Everyone probably has a taste of simple happiness they would add to Nikos Kazantzakis's list, but most of us would keep a glass of wine at the top. The varied character of wine, its surprises and revelations, transform a day in the country into a celebration.

The Wine Country is not a homogeneous plain of back-to-back vineyards, but rather several unique valleys separated by peaks and foothills. Napa and Sonoma are the best known valleys, but wine connoisseurs are eagerly following up new leads in the Alexander, Anderson, Russian River, and Ukiah Valleys as well. Each valley has its own community of wineries, often clustered like grapes on a vine, making traveling from one to another convenient.

A picnic is *de rigeur*. A loaf of bread, a chunk of cheese, deli delights, and the season's fruit provide the makings of a main event. A good place to stock up is the Rouge et Noir Cheese Shop in Petaluma, where they have been making Camembert, Brie, Schloss, and their special breakfast cheese for over a century. Petaluma's Victorians and "Iron Front" buildings, with their factory-made fronts of cast or sheet iron, are well worth a walking tour.

Sonoma Valley has many excellent wineries and some equally excellent sun-dappled settings for picnics. These vary from open valley vistas to shaded crannies near elusive streams. The back roads are famous for pick-your-own fruits and vegetables.

Sonoma itself is a reflection of the past. Somehow the early California ranchos are real again, the Bear Flag Rebellion might erupt at any moment, and wasn't it just yesterday that Kit Carson dropped by the Blue Wing Inn? Jack London's ranch near Glen Ellen looks down on his beloved Valley of the Moon, a name he borrowed from the Suisun Indians.

Napa Valley, with microclimatic conditions ideal for grape growing, has been called an agricultural preserve. Over 20,000 acres are under cultivation here. Highway 29, running through Yountville, Oakville, Rutherford, and St. Helena, is the hotline of the Napa wineries. A parallel road, the Silverado Trail, is a more leisurely route, high enough for panoramic views of the vineyards. The two roads meet at various crossroads, so you can zigzag back and forth to visit the wineries of your choice.

Roving the Napa Valley turns up some interests extracurricular to enology. One of the world's three regularly erupting geysers, California's Old Faithful, shows off every fifty minutes just north of Calistoga. The town itself is famous as a health resort of hot springs and mud baths. Fans of Robert Louis Stevenson can haunt the Silverado Mine near St. Helena to look for ghosts.

The southwestern end of the Russian River, especially near Guerneville, is a river playground. Cruising down the river — in inner tubes, rafts, or canoes — is favorite family fun in the summertime. In fall and winter, it's the scene of serious fishing.

Northwest of Cloverdale, the Navarro River flows to the sea through the Anderson Valley, a fifteen-mile stretch where the wineries are within shouting distance of one another along Highway 128. The Anderson Valley is also known as apple country. One orchard alone produces thirty different varieties. Historical Boonville is a treat, whether or not you harp (speak) Boontling, the imaginative dialect spoken by old-time Boonters who live here.

Many people think of boating, fishing, and water skiing when you mention Clear Lake, but wine lovers will be glad to know that a re-emergence of Lake County wineries is well under way. In the early 1900s, more than thirty Lake County wineries produced wine that won gold medals in American and European competitions. The difficulty of shipping wine over the rugged mountains that surround the county, and then Prohibition, caused most of the wineries to die on the vine. Today these are no longer problems, and a number of important wineries flourish here to tempt travelers. And, of course, there is still the attraction of Clear Lake, the largest natural lake within California's borders (Lake Tahoe is bigger, but it is shared by Nevada). A park along its shores is the perfect place to picnic and dream up some additions to Kazantzakis's list.

Big Yellow Sunflower   **(707) 965-3885**
235 Sky Oaks Drive, Angwin, CA 94508
(Above east side of Napa Valley)

The Big Yellow Sunflower is a private apartment suite and a bedroom adjacent to the home of Betty and Dale Clement. It is situated near Angwin in a lush little valley on top of Howell Mountain, a gorgeous ten-minute drive from the Napa Valley. Decorated in golds and browns, the spacious suite (A) includes a living area with a large fireplace as its focal point, a kitchenette, bath, loft bedroom, and private deck. The bedroom (B), decorated in blue, white, and gold, has its own entrance and private bath. Both offer total comfort and seclusion. Cheese and crackers, fresh fruits, Calistoga water, and Häagen Dazs ice cream are complimentary on arrival (in suite). Each accommodation makes a wonderful hideaway retreat where you may relax and catch up on your reading or find refuge after an exciting day in the Napa Valley. A gracious welcome is yours at the sign of the Big Yellow Sunflower, as well as some of the Napa Valley's most reasonable rates.

No pets or smoking; children welcome; large brunch; homemade vegetable soup in the evening for $1; TV; VCR; AC; kitchenette; ten-speed bikes; up to seven adults can be accommodated; off-street parking; airport pickup (Angwin). $5 extra charge for one-night stays; two-night minimum preferred; midweek rates, $10 less.

ROOM	BED	BATH	ENTRANCE	FLOOR	DAILY RATES	
					S - D	(EP)
A	2Q	Pvt	Sep	1G	$75	($15)
B	1Q	Pvt	Sep	1G	$49	

House of a Thousand Flowers   **(707) 632-5571**
P.O. Box 369, Monte Rio, CA 95462
(Five miles east of Jenner-by-the-Sea)

  When you arrive at the House of a Thousand Flowers, you know right away how it got its name. Greenery, including fuchsias and other blossoming plants, bedeck the house and infuse it with cheer. Host Dave Silva takes pride in the family home that is now a remote country haven for harried city folk in need of escape. The house is set high on a bluff above the Russian River and has two cozy guest rooms on its lower level. Each has its own deck, separate entrance, and access to an enclosed, plant-filled spa. Look toward the sea and you may witness the magical effect created as fingers of fog move through the redwoods. The main floor is also yours to enjoy, with grand piano, extensive library, and dining room where Chef David serves his famous omelettes. Coffee is ready by your room when you wake up, and breakfast is served at your convenience anytime during the morning. Discover a little slice of paradise at the House of a Thousand Flowers.

  Dog and cat in residence; full breakfast; afternoon refreshments; rollaway bed available; spa; river and ocean activities, good restaurants and wineries nearby; off-street parking; major credit cards. Brochure available.

ROOM	BED	BATH	ENTRANCE	FLOOR	DAILY RATES S - D (EP)
A	1Q	Shd*	Sep	LL	$69 ($15)
B	1Q	Shd*	Sep	LL	$69 ($15)

Big Canyon Bed & Breakfast   **(707) 928-5631**
P.O. Box 1311, Lower Lake, CA 95457
(Seigler Springs, at foot of Cobb Mountain)

The remote and woodsy mountain setting makes Big Canyon Bed & Breakfast a perfect place to escape to the quiet, natural world that inspires true relaxation. The Cape Cod-style home has two spacious rooms for guests on its upper floor. One (A) has its own entrance, woodstove, skylight, and kitchenette, while the other (B) has a cozy alcove window seat. The entire floor makes an ideal family or group accommodation. In the immediate surroundings you may enjoy identifying spring wildflowers, gazing at bright stars, and finding Lake County diamonds. Or take a twenty-minute drive to the Lake and get into the swim of things. The casual country atmosphere of Big Canyon is conducive to doing simply whatever you please.

Smoking outside only; AC; (main) kitchen privileges; double sofa bed in Room A (no charge for use); off-street parking. **KNIGHTTIME PUBLICATIONS SPECIAL RATE: Two nights for the price of one Sunday-Thursday with this book. Brochure available.

ROOM	BED	BATH	ENTRANCE	FLOOR	DAILY RATES	
					S - D	(EP)
A	1Q	Pvt	Sep	2	$55	
B	1Q	Pvt	Main	2	$45	

Muktip Manor   **(707) 994-9571**
12540 Lakeshore Drive, Clearlake, CA 95422
(South shore of lake)

The home of Elisabeth St. Davids and Jerry Schiffman (affectionately known as Muktip Manor) has a peculiar, Early California charm of its own. The living quarters are all on the second floor, with doors opening onto a wrap-around veranda. Located opposite the lake, it affords good views and a small, private beach. The guest unit consists of a bedroom, living room, kitchen, and bath. While not luxurious, the decor is delightfully eclectic. Elisabeth is a journalist, and Jerry, a former actor. (Look for him on reruns of *Streets of San Francisco*; Elisabeth says, "He always played a cop or a corpse.") They enjoy sailing their catamaran most every evening. Whatever your particular pleasure might be, there's a host of activities to choose from: boating, windsurfing, swimming, canoeing, fishing, rock-hunting, and wine-tasting at Lake County wineries. The lifestyle at Muktip Manor is casual, unpretentious, and laced with humor — a thoroughly engaging combination.

Dog and cats in residence; no children; pets welcome ($5 extra); full breakfast; TV; kitchen; large deck; launch ramp and public fishing piers nearby; extra meals optional; ample street parking; French, German, and Spanish spoken; airport pickup (Pearce). Animal lovers preferred. $5 discount per day with *current* edition of book.

ROOM	BED	BATH	ENTRANCE	FLOOR	DAILY RATES
					S - D (EP)
A	1D	Pvt	Sep	2	$50

Shelby's Happy House   **(707) 994-2554**
P.O. Box 2079, Clearlake, CA 95422
(Two blocks from Clear Lake on Shelby Lane)

Shelby, a special niece of John and Sharron Lucich, dubbed their home "a happy house," so they honored her when they named their B&B. Inside and out, it inspires a smile. The endearing blue Cape Cod-style home is filled with charm and country comfort. There's a pink confection of a bedroom with a private bath on the main floor. An upstairs bedroom with a canopy bed is decorated in white eyelet and navy blue. The large living room with a fireplace and a restful atmosphere is as inviting as the lovely patio out back. It is an easy walk down to water's edge where you can picnic at delightful Redbud Park. Or spend the day sampling Lake County wines in tasting rooms that operate nearby. Enjoy a contented holiday in this hospitable setting near California's largest natural lake.

No pets; smoking outside only; full breakfast; off-street parking; airport pickup (Pearce Field).

ROOM	BED	BATH	ENTRANCE	FLOOR	DAILY RATES S - D (EP)
A	1Q	Pvt	Main	1	$75
B	1Q	Shd	Main	2	$65

Haydon House   **(707) 433-5228**
321 Haydon Street, Healdsburg, CA 95448
(Five blocks from historic Plaza)

It gladdens the heart to arrive at Haydon House for the first time and realize it's where you'll spend your sojourn. Imagine the appeal of a tree-shaded yard on a quiet little street, roses abloom along a white picket fence, and a house that is clearly someone's work of art. Richard and Joanne Claus restored their 1912 Queen Anne home with painstaking thoroughness, and the interior design shows their meticulous attention to detail. Each of the six guest rooms is an individual creation, featuring handmade Dhurrie rugs, French and American antiques, Laura Ashley prints, dried and silk flowers, and inspired use of color. At Haydon House you are treated like a friend in fine country style, with your every comfort in mind.

Two small dogs in residence; no pets; no children under twelve; no smoking; full breakfast; TV; AC; clawfoot tubs in some rooms; off-street parking; major credit cards (V, MC). Two additional rooms with double whirlpool tubs available in separate two-story Gothic Victorian cottage, $110 each. **KNIGHTTIME PUBLICATIONS SPECIAL RATE: $5 discount on weeknights. Brochure available.

ROOM	BED	BATH	ENTRANCE	FLOOR	DAILY RATES	
					S - D	(EP)
A	1D	Semi-pvt	Main	2	$70	
B	1Q	Semi-pvt	Main	2	$70	
C	1Q	Semi-pvt	Main	2	$70	
D	1Q	Pvt	Main	2	$80	
E	1Q & 1T	Semi-pvt	Main	2	$75	($10)
F	1Q	Pvt	Main	1	$80	

Gee-Gee's   (707) 833-6667
7810 Sonoma Highway, Santa Rosa, CA 95409
(On Highway 12 in the Valley of the Moon)

Gerda Heaton-Weisz has been offering quality lodgings to travelers for many years. In 1981, she moved Gee-Gee's of Quincy from the Feather River country to the wine country. (Numerous wineries are close to Gee-Gee's.) Four pleasant guest rooms are available for bed and breakfast, two in the main house and two in a separate guest cottage. The swimming pool can surely look inviting after an arduous day on the road. Gerda attended the Sorbonne and speaks French fluently. She brings some of her European traditions to the hospitality she provides. What she appreciates most about her present setting is the "view of mountains on three sides, cattle grazing across the road, and seemingly endless stretches of prune and walnut trees bordering my one acre...." I, for one, am glad she decided to share it.

Dog and cat in residence; no pets, children, or smoking; full breakfast; sitting room with fireplace and TV; decks; swimming pool; complimentary bicycles; hiking and jogging trails, horseback riding, and golfing nearby; off-street parking. Clock radios in all rooms; TV in Room B, which has a new sitting room. Rooms A and B share a bath; C and D share a bath. $5 charge for conversion of 2T to 1K in Room D (or vice-versa). 5% discount to AARP members. **KNIGHTTIME PUBLICATIONS SPECIAL RATE: 10% discount with this book.

ROOM	BED	BATH	ENTRANCE	FLOOR	DAILY RATES S - D	(EP)
A	1D	Shd*	Main	1G	$60-$65	
B	1D	Shd*	Main	1G	$75	
C	1Q	Shd*	Sep	1G	$75	
D	2T or 1K	Shd*	Sep	1G	$80	

The Forbestown Bed & Breakfast Inn   (707) 263-7878
825 Forbes Street, Lakeport, CA 95453
(One block from Clear Lake in downtown area)

Buzz and Janet Bruns are pleased to have opened Lakeport's first bed and breakfast inn. The family lived for many years in the 1869 home, which was built when the town was known as Forbestown. Expert restoration has given the beautiful old home all its original charm. Each of the four luxurious guest rooms is a tasteful creation named after a historical figure of the Forbestown era. (A colorful cast of characters, I might add!) American oak antiques and designer fabrics highlight the decor, and gentle strains of music add to the calm elegance within. Outside, a secluded garden beckons one to relax in a lounge chair or to take a dip in the inviting pool or spa. Hosts can help with arrangements for visiting a gold mine, geothermal steam wells, wineries, and fine restaurants; water recreational equipment may be rented nearby. A rare glimpse of Lake County history coupled with splendid hospitality await you at The Forbestown Bed & Breakfast Inn.

No pets; no children under twelve; smoking outside only; full breakfast; afternoon refreshments; AC; ample street parking; major credit cards (V, MC); airport pickup (Lampson Field). Off-season rates for business travelers. Brochure available.

ROOM	BED	BATH	ENTRANCE	FLOOR	DAILY RATES S - D (EP)
A	1Q	Shd*	Main	1	$85
B	1K	Shd*	Main	1	$95
C	1Q	Pvt	Main	2	$85
D	1Q	Shd*	Main	2	$75

Fritz's Place   (707) 9█
P.O. Box 327, Middletown, CA 95461
(Just off Highway 29)

After a scenic trip over Mount St. Helena, Highway 29 straightens out at Middletown. Just beyond the town, it's easy to spot Fritz's Place on a lane to the left paralleling the highway. There's no doubt about it — Fritz *is* the place. He's known as a genial host who makes people comfortable; drop by for a chat and a beer, maybe a picnic, and some of the county's best wines. You can buy your supplies here — bread, cheeses, patés, soft drinks, wines, and imported beers — and savor them at a table under the wisteria arbor. If you want to explore Lake County a bit, consider staying overnight at Fritz's. His European approach is part of the appeal. He offers a couple of simple, affordable (and perfectly adequate) rooms to one party at a time. He prepares an ample breakfast that includes eggs from his own chickens. It's a given at Fritz's Place: Everyone has a *good time*.

Various animals on property; no smoking in bedrooms; full breakfast; TV in living room; deck; tasting room; volleyball and horseshoes; public tennis courts nearby; off-street parking; German and French spoken; major credit cards (V, MC). Accommodations are for one to four people traveling together. Brochure available.

ROOM	BED	BATH	ENTRANCE	FLOOR	DAILY RATES S-D (EP)
A	1Q	Pvt	Main	1	$35-$49
B	1K				$35-$49

...:akfast   **(707) 963-3794**

...in Road, St. Helena, CA 94574

...Highway 29, above the Napa Valley)

As you wind your way along the road up Spring Mountain, glancing back occasionally for views of the valley below, the anticipation begins to build. Once you reach Deer Run, you will be well rewarded. It's a rustic gem of a home on four acres belonging to Tom and Carol Wilson. There are two antique furnished guest units in the main house, each with a private bath and entrance, one with a fireplace (B). A third unit (C), a spacious carriage room in a separate building with private bath, entrance, and deck, offers the advantage of having your breakfast delivered each morning. The swimming pool looks enticing, and the deck is a great place to relax among the trees. You may even see some deer, for the property really *is* a deer run. You can enjoy this private hideaway in its tranquil, secluded setting and still be only minutes from shops, restaurants, spas, and the wineries for which the valley is famous. Spring Mountain itself (Tom's birthplace) boasts a number of wineries that give special consideration to Deer Run's guests. In every respect, the Wilsons aim to provide top-notch hospitality.

Dog and three cats in residence; no pets or children; no smoking preferred; TV and complimentary sherry in each room; swimming pool; off-street parking.

ROOM	BED	BATH	ENTRANCE	FLOOR	DAILY RATES S - D (EP)
A	1Q	Pvt	Sep	1	$71
B	1K	Pvt	Sep	1	$81
C	1Q	Pvt	Sep	2	$91

Judy's Bed & Breakfast   **(707) 963-3081**
2036 Madrona Avenue, St. Helena, CA 94574
(One-half mile west of Main Street, or Highway 29)

You'll get a warm, wine-country welcome at Judy's. Bob and Judy Sculatti have lived on their nine-acre vineyard for many years. They've converted a spacious, private room at one end of their home to a B&B accommodation of great charm and comfort. The large space is furnished with lovely antiques, Oriental rugs, and a romantic brass bed. There is also a wood-burning stove with a glass door. Complimentary beverage and cheese are served upon your arrival. After a day of touring and tasting, or even a hot-air balloon ride, you can come back to Judy's for a refreshing dip in the pool. To round out your perfect day, dine at one of the Napa Valley's superb restaurants.

No pets or RV parking; no smoking preferred; TV; AC; swimming pool; sauna; barbecue; off-street parking; Italian spoken. Midweek rate, $10 less. **KNIGHTTIME PUBLICATIONS SPECIAL RATE: 10% discount with this book. Brochure available.

ROOM	BED	BATH	ENTRANCE	FLOOR	DAILY RATES S - D (EP)
A	1Q	Pvt	Sep	1G	$75

Judy's Ranch House   (707) 963-3081
701 Rossi Road, St. Helena, CA 94574
(Just west of Silverado Trail in Conn Valley)

The Sculatti family operates an additional B&B home on the opposite side of the Napa Valley but just as accessible to it. The spacious, comfortable ranch-style home is built around an interior courtyard. Everywhere you look, there are idyllic views of the Conn Valley countryside. Guests have use of an inviting living room with fireplace, a large country kitchen, and a Jacuzzi spa — a marvelous place to unwind while watching cattle, deer, and quail feed in neighboring pastures and vineyards. Relax on the front patio, which looks out upon century-old oak trees lining a seasonal creek. Each bedroom has a ceiling fan, private bath, and hillside view; one has a woodburning stove. Your hosts can help you with plans for enjoying the Napa Valley's many attractions.

No pets; smoking outside only; Jacuzzi spa; off-street parking. **KNIGHTTIME PUBLICATIONS SPECIAL RATE: 10% discount with this book. Brochure available.

ROOM	BED	BATH	ENTRANCE	FLOOR	DAILY RATES	
					S - D	(EP)
A	2T or 1K	Pvt	Main	1G	$75	
B	1Q	Pvt	Main	1G	$85	

Spanish Villa   **(707) 963-7483**
474 Glass Mountain Road, St. Helena, CA 94574
(Off Silverado Trail)

In a quiet wooded setting just off the scenic and leisurely Silverado Trail, a remarkable Mediterranean villa welcomes visitors to the Napa Valley. It puts the riches of Calistoga and St. Helena at your fingertips, yet retains the exotic, faraway flavor of a retreat to paradise. Neatly manicured grounds with ancient oak trees, palms, and flower gardens surround the villa and provide stunning views from the many arched windows. "La Galleria," a large sitting room where breakfast is served, sets the tone. Here and throughout the guest quarters, crisp white plaster walls are strikingly accented by brightly colored stained glass, tile work, Tiffany-style lamps, and selected paintings. Guest rooms are well-separated; they feature king-sized beds and handpainted sinks. A world of beauty, privacy, and serenity is waiting for you at Spanish Villa.

No pets or smoking; AC; patio; off-street parking; Italian, Spanish, and Portuguese spoken. Two rooms with a sitting area are ideal for two couples. Brochure available.

ROOM	BED	BATH	ENTRANCE	FLOOR	DAILY RATES	
					S - D	(EP)
A	1K	Pvt	Main	2	$85	
B	1K	Pvt	Main	2	$85	
C	1K	Pvt	Main	2	$85	

Hilltop House Bed & Breakfast (707) 944-0880
9550 St. Helena Road, Santa Rosa, CA 95404
(Near Napa/Sonoma County line)

Poised at the very top of the ridge that separates the famous wine regions of Napa and Sonoma is a country retreat with all the comforts of home and a view that you must see to believe. Annette and Bill Gevarter built their contemporary home with this mountain panorama in mind, and the vast deck allows you to enjoy it at your leisure with a glass of wine in the afternoon, with breakfast in the morning, or with a long soak in the hot tub. From this vantage point, sunrises and sunsets are simply amazing. Enter your lovely room through sliding glass doors from the deck and be assured that everything you need to make your stay a pleasure is there. After a restful night's sleep, look to a day of exploring either the Napa Valley (fifteen minutes to the east) or the Sonoma Valley (twenty minutes to the west). At Hilltop House, you'll cherish the natural setting, the caring hospitality, and the prize location.

Dog in residence; no pets or smoking; no children under twelve; queen sofa bed extra in Room C; hot tub; hiking trails nearby; full complement of amenities; off-street parking; major credit cards (V, MC). Midweek rate for Room A, $75; B and C, $90. Brochure available.

ROOM	BED	BATH	ENTRANCE	FLOOR	DAILY RATES	
					S - D	(EP)
A	1Q	Pvt	Main	1G	$85	
B	1Q & 1T	Pvt	Main	1G	$95	($15)
C	1Q	Pvt	Main	1G	$95	($15)

Pygmalion House   **(707) 526-3407**
331 Orange Street, Santa Rosa, CA 95407
(Convenient to downtown and historic Railroad Square)

How fittingly named is Pygmalion House, a rare Santa Rosa survivor of the 1906 earthquake. Once a fading Queen Anne Victorian, it underwent a painstaking transformation to its present beauty. Everything about the home speaks a heartfelt welcome, from the (seasonal) glow of the parlor fire to the presentation of afternoon refreshments to the multi-course breakfast. Most of all, it is Lola Wright who makes her home feel like your home. She is ever ready to help guests in any way and has many who return again and again. Each of five guest rooms, mostly on the ground floor with its own entrance, is an individual creation. Selected antiques and an abundance of handwork — needlepoint, quilting, embroidery, and lace — lend warmth and personality to the decor. Pygmalion House, notable for its history and hospitality, is a treasure.

No pets; smoking outside only; full breakfast; AC; showers and clawfoot tubs available; off-street parking. Brochure available.

ROOM	BED	BATH	ENTRANCE	FLOOR	DAILY RATES S - D (EP)
A	1Q & 2T	Pvt	Sep	1G	$60-$65 ($15)
B	1K	Pvt	Main	1	$60-$65
C	1Q	Pvt	Sep	1G	$50-$55
D	1Q	Pvt	Sep	1G	$50-$55
E	1Q	Pvt	Sep	1G	$50-$55

Sunrise Bed & Breakfast   **(707) 542-5781**
1500 Olivet Road, Santa Rosa, CA 95401
(West of Santa Rosa in the Russian River Valley)

Imagine a home in the Sonoma wine country, surrounded by orchard and vineyard, where you can taste award-winning wines made on the premises, view the vineyard from a hot-air balloon, and be served a different delicious breakfast each morning. Denyse and Bob Linde provide these experiences for their guests to take with them as beautiful memories. Bob is a winemaker, hot-air balloon pilot, and building contractor, among other things — a very talented chap. Denyse is the creator of the gracious, serene atmosphere that makes Sunrise Bed & Breakfast an ideal place to unwind and remember what living is all about. Two lovely bedrooms share a bath off the hallway; the luxurious master suite has an oversized private bath and exquisite decorator touches. You'll find fresh flowers and fruit, American oak antiques, and a place to relax, undisturbed, until you feel like moving again.

No pets, children, or smoking; full breakfast; TV; VCR; bicycles for rent; balloon rides by reservation; many wineries nearby; off-street parking; airport pickup (Sonoma County). Brochure available.

ROOM	BED	BATH	ENTRANCE	FLOOR	DAILY RATES	
					S - D	(EP)
A	1Q	Shd*	Main	1G	$75	
B	1Q	Shd*	Main	1G	$75	
C	1Q	Pvt	Main	1G	$95	

Alene Maches   **(707) 996-7178**
18860 Melvin Avenue, Sonoma, CA 95476
(Off Highway 12 in the Valley of the Moon)

You'll be warmly received in the home of Alene Maches. It's located in a quiet, secure neighborhood on the northern edge of Sonoma. Two of her three tidy bedrooms are used for B&B guests. Breakfast is served in the large, sunny kitchen. Through the window, you can view the well-tended yard where flowers and fruit trees display their seasonal bounty. When staying at Mrs. Maches's home, you'll be only a short distance from the Valley of the Moon, the Plaza in Sonoma, and an interesting mix of historical and enological attractions unique to this part of Sonoma County. If you do a little research in advance, you're sure to make some intriguing discoveries.

Children welcome; TV; VCR; kitchen privileges; patio and garden; barbecue; ample street parking.

ROOM	BED	BATH	ENTRANCE	FLOOR	DAILY RATES S - D	(EP)
A	1D	Shd	Main	1G	$30	
B	1T	Shd	Main	1G	$25	

Oak Knoll Bed & Breakfast   **(707) 468-5646**
P.O. Box 412, Ukiah, CA 95482
(Seven miles south of Ukiah)

Surrounded by classic wine country scenery of rolling hills and vineyards, Oak Knoll is a contemporary home of generous proportions and sweeping views. Shirley Wadley, a former college music teacher, keeps an immaculate house that's both elegant and comfortable. Guests are invited to enjoy the piano in the living room, a fire in the fireplace and perhaps a movie on the 40-inch screen in the family room, and games, reading, or television in the study/sitting room adjacent to the bedrooms. Snacks and breakfast are often served on the spectacular 3,000 square-foot deck. It is beautifully landscaped and features an enormous solar spa that is ever so enticing to the weary traveler. Oak Knoll's location is central to many attractions: the coast, the redwoods, Lake Mendocino, and wineries of Mendocino County. It's an altogether satisfying bed and breakfast stop.

No pets or children; smoking outside only; TV; VCR; AC; study; deck; spa; off-street parking; airport pickup (Ukiah). Brochure available.

ROOM	BED	BATH	ENTRANCE	FLOOR	DAILY RATES S - D (EP)
A	1Q	Shd*	Main	2	$50-$60
B	1Q	Shd*	Main	2	$50-$60

Redwood House   **(707) 895-3526**
21340 Highway 128, Yorkville, CA 95494
(Twenty miles from Cloverdale and U.S. 101)

I call Redwood House a buried treasure. It's tucked into the woods in a part of the wine country which is only just being discovered — a real "find." The Hanelts have a private guest cottage that's all redwood and glass. It has a living room with a woodstove, a kitchenette, a bath, and a spiral staircase leading to a sleeping loft. The views from within are of trees, sky, and a creek you can swim or row in during the summer. There are wooded paths to explore, a small children's beach, and two decks overlooking the creek. The Hanelts take pleasure in sharing this heavenly spot with their guests, whose options include wine-tasting at fine Anderson Valley wineries, side-tripping to the Mendocino coast (thirty-five miles away), or simply settling into the freedom and joy of country living.

Children welcome; smoking outside preferred; sofa bed and crib available; sauna; playhouse; off-street parking. Two-night minimum.

ROOM	BED	BATH	ENTRANCE	FLOOR	DAILY RATES	
					S - D	(EP)
A	1D & 1T	Pvt	Sep	2	$55-$60	($10)

Please read "About Dining Highlights" on page *ix.*

BOONVILLE

The Boonville Hotel, Highway 128; (707) 895-2210; California cuisine

CALISTOGA

Calistoga Inn, 1250 Lincoln Avenue; (707) 942-4101; fresh seafood/ American

Jamee's Restaurant, 1880 Lincoln Street; (707) 942-0979; California/ American

CAZADERO

Cazanoma Lodge, 1000 Kidd Creek Road; (707) 632-5255; German and American

CLEARLAKE

Kathie's Inn, 14677 Lakeshore Drive; (707) 994-9933; steak and seafood/ Continental

FORESTVILLE

Russian River Vineyards Restaurant, 5700 Gravenstein Highway North; (707) 887-1562; Continental/Greek

GLEN ELLEN

The Grist Mill Inn, 14301 Arnold Drive; (707) 996-3077; fresh California cuisine

HEALDSBURG

Jacob Horner, 106 Matheson Street; (707) 433-3939; Sonoma County fresh

Madrona Manor, 1001 Westside Road; (707) 433-4231; California cuisine

Plaza Grill, 109 A Plaza Street; (707) 431-8305; California cuisine

Tre Scalini, 241 Healdsburg Avenue; (707) 433-1772; fine Italian cuisine

KELSEYVILLE

Konocti Klines Oak Barrel, 6445 Soda Bay Road; (707) 279-0101; seafood

Loon's Nest, 5685 Main Street; (707) 279-1812; California cuisine

KENWOOD

Oreste's Golden Bear, 1717 Adobe Canyon Road; (707) 833-2327; northern Italian

LAKEPORT

The Garden Room Café, 1303 South Main Street; (707) 263-3294; Hungarian and more

Park Place Café, 50 Third Street; (707) 263-0444; homemade pasta

PHILO

The Flood Gate Store & Grill, 1810 Highway 128; (707) 895-3000; regional dishes and grilled items

ST. HELENA

Miramonte, 1327 Railroad Avenue; (707) 963-3970; French

Spring Street Restaurant, 1245 Spring Street; (707) 963-5578; American country cuisine

Tra Vigne, 1050 Charter Oak; (707) 963-4444; rustic Italian

SANTA ROSA

John Ash & Co., 4330 Barnes Road at U.S. 101 and River Road; (707) 527-7687; wine country cuisine

La Gare, 208 Wilson Street; (707) 528-4355; Swiss/French

La Province, 525 College Avenue; (707) 526-6233; French Continental

Mixx, 135 Fourth Street; (707) 573-1344; Continental

Restaurant Matisse, 620 Fifth Street; (707) 527-9797; new French/new American

Ristorante Siena, 1229 North Dutton Avenue; (707) 578-4511; innovative Italian

SEBASTOPOL

Chez Peyo, 2295 Gravenstein Highway (116); (707) 823-1262; country French

YOUNTVILLE

California Café Bar & Grill, 6795 Washington Street; (707) 944-2330; California/American cuisine

Mama Nina's, 6772 Washington Street; (707) 944-2112; northern Italian

Mustards Grill, 7399 St. Helena Highway; (707) 944-2424; American grill

The traveler was active; he went strenuously in search of people, of adventure, of experience. The tourist is passive; he expects interesting things to happen to him. He goes "sightseeing."

—Daniel J. Boorstin

Central
Valley
to
Mount
Shasta

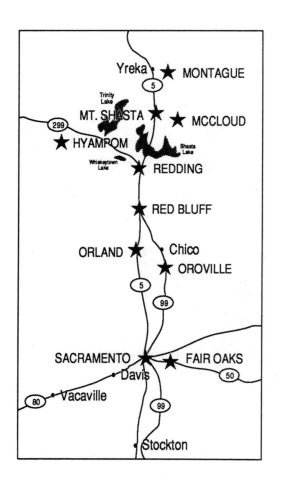

110

California's Central Valley is the richest, most varied agricultural area in the nation. Everything from fruit to nuts, literally, is grown here; well over two hundred different farm products are cultivated within these nineteen counties.

What this means for the traveler is that Interstate 5 need not be boring. Although designed for people on their way to Somewhere Else, I-5 (and parallel Highway 99) has many treats in store for the traveler. Many farms near the highways are open for tours, and farmers' markets and stands do a brisk business. There are good picnic spots, too, cool oases where you can sample those melons you bought in Kings County and that dessert wine from Fresno.

The Central Valley is really two valleys. The southern valley is drained by the San Joaquin River, and the northern one is drained by the Sacramento. The two rivers meet in one of California's nicest surprises, the delightful Delta.

At the northern tip of the Delta is Sacramento. In 1849, Sacramento was the gateway to the gold rush, and a visit to restored "Old Sac" brings back the days of the prospectors, plank sidewalks, and the Pony Express. A bronze rider is a monument to the boys who answered the following ad: *Wanted — Young, skinny, wiry fellows not over eighteen. Must be expert riders, willing to risk death daily. Orphans preferred.*

Sutter's Fort and the State Indian Museum are other historical highlights, as is the Railroad Museum. The restored State Capitol building is a living work of art well worth a visit.

North of Sacramento lies the Feather River country with fern-filled canyons, pine-covered mountains, and chaparral slopes. The river was dubbed by Don Luis Arguello, who happened to be out exploring during the migration of band-tailed pigeons that filled the river with feathers.

Oroville, in the center of the Feather River region, is rich in history. California's largest Chinatown flourished here in the 1870s, and the Chinese Temple still stands. Another landmark is the Lott home, a Gothic Revival-style Victorian, surrounded by Sank Park.

Redding marks the beginning of California's water wonderland. The Big Three — Whiskeytown, Shasta, and Trinity (Clair Engle) Lakes — make up a paradise for boaters, anglers, swimmers, water skiers, sailors, and windsurfers.

Rivers, creeks, and streams abound throughout the area, and there are many smaller lakes as well. One stunner is Lake Siskiyou, a natural mirror for Mount Shasta's majestic profile. Nearby, glacier-polished Castle Crags rear up 6,000 feet.

The Mount Shasta area would be an idyllic destination for a highway, but I-5 does not stop there. It continues on into Oregon and beyond. But that, of course, is Somewhere Else.

Riverview Bed & Breakfast   **(916) 961-1994**
3926 Ridge Street, Fair Oaks, CA 95628
(Overlooking American River)

Just twenty minutes from downtown Sacramento via Highway 50, the village of Fair Oaks is a largely undiscovered vacation spot. It has the charm of another era but functions as a lively community in the present. There's an interesting assortment of antique shops, restaurants, and an amphitheater offering summer Shakespeare as well as other plays and musical performances. Within a short walk is Riverview Bed & Breakfast, a spacious bluffside home overlooking the American River. One guest accommodation is a huge bedroom with a sitting area, a large private bath, a fireplace, and a private deck overlooking the river. Another attractive bedroom has a sloped ceiling, a river view, and country furnishings. If you're eager to be out and about, amble down to the historic bridge and the American River Parkway where walking, jogging, and cycling are popular. Rafting and fishing enthusiasts find the lure of the river irresistible. Educator Karen Blake invites you to make her home your own while discovering the pleasures of Fair Oaks for yourself.

Dog in residence; no pets; smoking outside only; full breakfast; TV in Room A; TV available for Room B; AC; cable TV and good book collection in library; off-street parking.

ROOM	BED	BATH	ENTRANCE	FLOOR	DAILY RATES S - D (EP)
A	1Q	Pvt	Main	2	$55-$60
B	1D	Shd	Main	2	$40-$45

The Areys　　　　　　　　　　　　　　　　**(916) 628-5953**
P.O. Box 1, Hyampom, CA 96046
(Shasta-Trinity Wilderness Area, between Redding and Eureka)

Hyampom is, to date, the most remote location is this book. Imagine how pleased I was, after two hours on winding mountain roads, to find a bucolic little valley where life goes on largely untouched by the outside world. It was a rare experience, and I reveled in it. Honey and Joe Arey are long-time residents of Hyampom and thoroughly delightful people. They have a guest apartment, separate from the main house, that is very comfortable and blessed with a view I could stare at for hours: an apple orchard, a green pasture with grazing sheep, a prolific vegetable garden, and a backdrop of beautiful mountains. For anyone seeking to escape the distractions of the modern world for a while, The Areys is a perfect destination. The only problem is, you may not want to leave.

Outdoor animals on property; no pets; smoking outside only; choice of full or Continental breakfast; kitchen; double sofa bed in living room; fishing, swimming, hiking, cookouts, and birdwatching in area; off-street parking; airport pickup (Hyampom).

ROOM	BED	BATH	ENTRANCE	FLOOR	DAILY RATES	
					S - D	(EP)
A	1Q	Pvt	Sep	1	$35-$45	($10)

Hogin House   **(916) 964-2882**
P.O. Box 550, McCloud, CA 96057
(Nine miles east of Mount Shasta)

To visit McCloud is to experience a fascinating slice of timber industry heritage at the foot of Mount Shasta. A small, turn-of-the-century mill town, McCloud appears to have changed very little over the intervening decades. Forested in cedar, fir, pine, and sequoia, it is a beautiful town with a pleasantly remote quality and interesting early architecture. Angie and Rich Toreson have deep roots in McCloud. They now own what was once "the doctor's house," right across the street from the former hospital where Rich was born. They have fully restored it, blending its inherent charm with antiques, collectibles, colorful rugs, fine quilts and linens, wallpaper and wainscoting. The whole house is brimming with nostalgia, each room bearing a distinct personality. As a delightful bed and breakfast experience and a great value, Hogin House is an unqualified standout.

No pets (indoors); no smoking upstairs; Rooms A and B connect to a sunroom with a trundle bed; living room with woodstove, TV, VCR; wide front porch; excellent hiking and fishing nearby; winter sports at nearby Mount Shasta Ski Park; off-street parking; some German spoken; airport pickup (Mott); major credit cards (V, MC). Brochure available.

ROOM	BED	BATH	ENTRANCE	FLOOR	DAILY RATES S - D	(EP)
A	2D	Shd*	Main	2	$40	($10)
B	1Q	Shd*	Main	2	$40	($10)
C	1D	Shd*	Main	2	$40	
D	1Q	Shd*	Main	2	$40	

Julian Beaudroit House, 1903   **(916) 459-5449**
P.O. Box 746, Montague, CA 96064
(Seven miles east of Yreka at I-5)

   Chet and Dora Shelden have put down roots in the picturesque Shasta Valley where Chet recently retired from his teaching post in a one-room country schoolhouse. He and Dora bought a historic Victorian home in the tiny town of Montague in 1983 and have worked hard to restore it to the restrained elegance of its heyday. The home has stained-glass windows, a clawfoot bathtub, and much of its original charm. A pretty bedroom with a bay window and garden view is the main guest room, with an additional room upstairs. For your pleasure, there is a sunroom with TV and library, and a deck by the beautiful rose garden. A stop at the Julian Beaudroit House takes you off the hurried corridor of I-5 and beckons you to just slow down. You'll find back roads to explore, stunning views of Mount Shasta, and fine mountain and lake recreation nearby. The Ashland Shakespeare Festival is forty-five minutes away and the Klamath River, about thirty. An all-day excursion to Lava Beds National Monument is a one-of-a-kind thrill.

   No pets; smoking outside only; older children by arrangement; ample street parking; some Spanish spoken; airport pickup (Montague).

ROOM	BED	BATH	ENTRANCE	FLOOR	DAILY RATES	
					S - D	(EP)
A	1D	Shd	Main	1	$35-$40	($10)
B	2T	Shd	Main	2	$35-$40	

Ward's "Big Foot" Ranch B & B   **(916) 926-5170**
P.O. Box 585, Mount Shasta, CA 96067
(1530 Hill Road; two miles northwest of downtown Mount Shasta)

After their careers as educators in Saratoga, Barbara and Phil Ward returned to Phil's native Mount Shasta. Now they can bask in the glory of the splendid mammoth mountain every day; their rural ranch-style home is situated for maximum views. A huge wrap-around deck is the scene of summer breakfasts. The beautifully maintained ranch has the feeling of a luxury resort with homelike warmth. There are two lovely guest rooms in the main house and a separate guest cottage (C) that sleeps up to six; it has a wood-burning stove, a deck overlooking a stream, and many other attractive features. The Wards are fond of entertaining and cooking for guests. (Phil's delicious *aebleskivers* have become a tradition.) On starry nights, gazing through a telescope from the deck is a sparkling experience. A restful atmosphere, generous hosts, and unprecedented views of Mount Shasta are yours at Ward's "Big Foot" Ranch.

Outdoor pets include dogs, cats, llamas, and a burro; no pets (indoors); full breakfast; refreshments; TV; living room for guests; queen sofa bed extra in cottage (C); hot tub; barbecue; trout stream; hiking trails; horseshoes; Ping-Pong and croquet in summer; Alpine and Nordic ski areas nearby; off-street parking; bus, train, or airport pickup (Dunsmuir, Weed). **KNIGHTTIME PUBLICATIONS SPECIAL RATE: 10% discount with this book. Informative brochure available.

ROOM	BED	BATH	ENTRANCE	FLOOR	DAILY RATES	
					S - D	(EP)
A	1K	Shd*	Main	1	$55-$60	
B	1Q	Shd*	Main	1	$45-$50	
C	1Q & 2T	Pvt	Sep	1	$85	($20)

The Inn at Shallow Creek Farm   **(916) 865-4093**
Route 3, Box 3176, Orland, CA 95963
(North end of Sacramento River Valley; three miles west of I-5)

Who'd ever guess that just three miles away — and worlds apart — from I-5 you'd find a haven like The Inn at Shallow Creek Farm? The ivy-covered turn-of-the-century farmhouse is the centerpiece of this 3.5-acre citrus orchard where chickens, ducks, geese, and guinea fowl roam freely. It was revived in the early eighties by Kurt and Mary Glaeseman. The house and the hospitality have a genuine old-fashioned quality. Common rooms solely for guests' use include a large living room with a fireplace, a sitting room overlooking the orchard, and a cheery dining room. A large, airy suite on the first floor offers space and privacy; two nostalgic rooms on the second floor are perfect for two couples. A separate four-room cottage offers extra privacy. It has a wood-burning stove, a sunporch, and a full kitchen. In every season, The Inn at Shallow Creek Farm delights city-weary folks who relish its quiet rural atmosphere.

No pets; smoking outside only; full breakfast featuring farm fresh eggs and produce; excellent area for walking, cycling, exploring, birdwatching, stargazing, and photography; poultry, produce, and homemade jams and jellies available for purchase; off-street parking; French, German, and Spanish spoken; airport pickup (Orland). Brochure available.

ROOM	BED	BATH	ENTRANCE	FLOOR	DAILY RATES S - D	(EP)
A	1Q	Pvt	Main	1	$55	
B	1Q	Shd*	Main	2	$45	
C	2T	Shd*	Main	2	$45	($15)
D	1Q	Pvt	Sep	1	$75	($15)

Jean's Riverside Bed & Breakfast (916) 533-1413
P.O. Box 2334, Oroville, CA 95965
(1124 Middlehoff Lane)

Jean Pratt's cedar home is set on the west bank of the Feather River. Sliding glass doors open to a deck and a lawn that slopes gently to the waterfront. Lucky visitors are treated to idyllic views of the river and peaceful countryside, as well as easy access to swimming, boating, fishing, and panning for gold. Jean's acreage is so spacious and still that it's a haven for friendly wildlife. Your host, a seasoned traveler herself, knows an amazing variety of places in the area to explore. She recommends Feather Falls, Table Mountain, the Chinese Temple, the Pioneer Museum, historic cemeteries, and the Oroville Dam and Fish Hatchery (with up-to-date facilities, especially interesting during salmon run; personal tours arranged with advance notice). Oroville and the surrounding area are rich in culture, history, recreation, and scenery.

No pets (indoors); children OK if well supervised; TVs and canoes available; off-street parking; major credit cards (V, MC); airport pickup (Oroville); host suggests day trips from Oroville to Sacramento, Grass Valley, Lake Tahoe, Mount Lassen, and Mount Shasta. Private suite available with 1Q at $65 for two. 10% discount for three nights or longer.

ROOM	BED	BATH	ENTRANCE	FLOOR	DAILY RATES S - D	(EP)
A	1D	Pvt	Sep	1G	$49	
B	1Q	Pvt	Sep	1G	$49	
C	1Q	Pvt	Sep	1G	$49	
D	2T	Pvt	Sep	1G	$49	
E	1K	Pvt	Sep	1G	$49	

The Faulkner House   **(916) 529-0520**
1029 Jefferson Street, Red Bluff, CA 96080
(North downtown area)

Its setting beside the Sacramento River and the diverse styles of Victorian architecture to be found here make Red Bluff a unique community. It's also the home of the William Ide Adobe, where California's first and only president lived. And let's not forget dining — Blondie's Diner alone is worth a special stop. Now, where to stay? It must be The Faulkner House, a gracious Queen Anne home on a quiet, shady street where you'll find four inviting guest rooms and a hospitable welcome from Mary and Harvey Klingler. The decor for each room is exactly fitting and the look uncontrived, like an elegant lady aging ever so gracefully. A satisfying and relaxing stop is certain to be yours at The Faulkner House.

No pets or children; smoking outside only; AC; fireplace; ample street parking; airport pickup (Red Bluff, Redding). Brochure available.

ROOM	BED	BATH	ENTRANCE	FLOOR	DAILY RATES S - D (EP)
A	1D	Shd*	Main	2	$43-$45
B	1Q	Shd*	Main	2	$48-$50
C	1Q	Shd*	Main	2	$48-$50
D	1Q	Pvt	Main	2	$58-$60

Palisades Paradise   (916) 223-5305
1200 Palisades Avenue, Redding, CA 96003
(Central Redding, at edge of Sacramento River)

The name Palisades Paradise isn't an exaggeration. What else would you call a beautiful contemporary home of exceptional comfort with a panoramic view of city lights and river bluff? From the Sunset Suite (B), glass doors open onto a patio with a garden spa where you can watch day turn to evening and soak your cares away. Both the suite and the Cozy Retreat (A) are restful indeed, with soft, muted colors and comfortable beds. The work of some local artists adds to the pleasant decor. Gail Goetz welcomes business and pleasure travelers, making them feel totally at home in the relaxed atmosphere of her Palisades Paradise.

Small dog in residence; children welcome when reseving both rooms; no smoking in bedrooms; living room with fireplace, widescreen TV, VCR; AC; spa; off-street parking; major credit cards (V, MC). Brochure available.

ROOM	BED	BATH	ENTRANCE	FLOOR	DAILY RATES S - D (EP)
A	2T	Shd*	Main	1G	$50
B	1D	Shd*	Main	1G	$60

Aunt Abigail's　　　　　　　　　　　　　　　　　**(916) 441-5007**
2120 "G" Street, Sacramento, CA 95816
(Central downtown location)

Besides being at the pulse of California politics and government, Sacramento is quite a pleasant city in which to live, to vacation, or to do business. Manageable in size and layout, it is also rich in history, culture, and dining opportunities. On one of the city's tree-lined streets graced with fine old mansions, Aunt Abigail's opens its doors to those seeking a refined, homelike atmosphere in a most convenient location. Guests are welcomed into the large living room of the 1912 Colonial Revival mansion. A fireplace, comfortable places to sit, and a spirit of friendliness help one to relax and feel at home. A particular charm distinguishes each lovely guest room: Solarium, Uncle Albert, Aunt Rose, Queen Anne, and Margaret. Delicious breakfasts featuring a different entree every morning are served in the sunny dining room. The neighborhood is great for walking; it's a snap to find your way to the state Capitol and other important attractions. Innkeepers Susanne and Ken Ventura offer an oasis of hospitality in the midst of the bustling city.

Two cats in residence; no pets; older children by prior arrangement; smoking outside only; full breakfast; no RV parking; AC; sitting room with games and piano; patio; garden; hot tub; public transportation and airport connections; off-street parking; major credit cards (V, MC, AE, DC, D). Brochure available.

ROOM	BED	BATH	ENTRANCE	FLOOR	DAILY RATES	
					S - D	(EP)
A	1Q	Pvt	Main	2	$65	
B	1Q	Pvt	Main	2	$75	
C	1Q	Pvt	Main	2	$75	
D	1K	Pvt	Main	2	$85	($10)
E	1K	Pvt	Main	2	$90	($10)

DINING HIGHLIGHTS: CENTRAL VALLEY TO MT. SHASTA

Please see "About Dining Highlights" on page *ix.*

HANFORD
Imperial Dynasty, 2 China Alley; (209) 582-0087; Continental/Chinoise
MC CLOUD
McCloud Guest House, 606 West Colombero Drive; (916) 964-3160; Continental
MOUNT SHASTA
Bellissimo, 204-A West Lake Street; (916) 926-4461; vegetarian dishes, seafood, pasta, burgers, etc.
OROVILLE
The Depot, Oliver and High Streets; (916) 534-9101; steaks, fresh seafood, prime rib
RED BLUFF
Blondie's Diner, 604 Main Street; (916) 529-1668; French influenced California cuisine
REDDING
Nello's Place, 3055 Bechelli Lane; (916) 223-1636; Italian

River City Bar & Grill, 2151 Market Street; (916) 243-9003; Cajun, Creole, Continental, and American
SACRAMENTO
Americo's, 2000 Capitol Avenue; (916) 442-8119; Italian bistro

Biba, 2801 Capitol Avenue; (916) 455-2422; northern Italian/Bolognese

The Firehouse, 1112 Second Street; (916) 442-4772; Continental

Pava's, 2330 K Street; (916) 443-2397; Continental/California cuisine
VISALIA
The Vintage Press Restaurante, 216 North Willis Street; (209) 733-3033; California cuisine

Gold
Country
&
the
Sierra

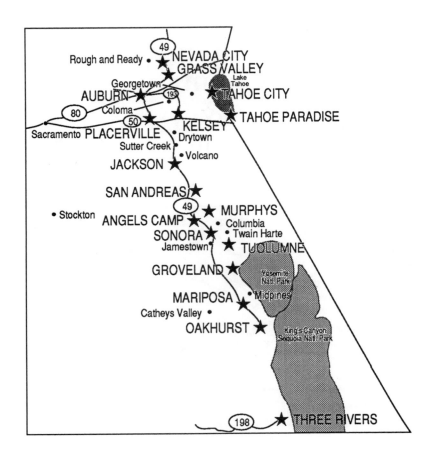

Gold dust still seems to shimmer in the air of the Gold Country, as folded foothills and mahogany manzanita bask in the sun. Imagine: the whoops and hollers of a crowd gathered around the assayer's office as a nugget weighs in at 195 pounds. Imagine: banditos cresting one of these basking hills to descend on a passing stagecoach, their own version of the gold rush. Imagine: Mark Twain writing in a one-room cabin about a major sporting event he's just witnessed — a frog-jumping contest.

The northern gold mines centered around Nevada City and Grass Valley. Walking tours of these and nearby towns unearth some interesting stories about such characters as Lola Montez and Snowshoe Thompson and the secession of Rough and Ready from the Union in the 1850s. It joined up again in 1948, so you won't need a visa. In Grass Valley, the North Star Powerhouse Mine Museum has been called the best mining museum in the Gold Country.

At the eastern end of Nevada County, Truckee marks the gateway to Lake Tahoe. Writing postcards from here is a challenge. What more can be said of this pine-fringed blue eye of the high Sierra?

The seventy-one-mile drive around Lake Tahoe includes coves and casinos, mountains and marinas. Travelers can take their pick. Most people, however, would pick Emerald Bay. Scooped out by a massive glacier, it glitters brightly in its granite setting. At its southern tip is a replica of a Viking castle — Vikingsholm — authentic from its stone foundation to its sod roof. In winter, Lake Tahoe bundles up in snow and plays ski resort. Downhillers take to the steep slopes, while Nordic skiers make their way along the silent snow of the cross-country trails.

History buffs will strike it rich along the Gold Mine Trail, with towns like Sutter Creek, Jackson, Volcano, Amador City, and Drytown. (Drytown had twenty-six saloons in its heyday.) In Jackson, some travelers recommend a stop at St. Sava's Serbian Church and cemetery. The modest clapboard church is the mother church of North America. What it lacks in size it makes up in dignity. An equally eloquent spirit resides at Indian Grinding Rock State Park, where descendants of California's original residents hold annual powwows in the fall.

Visitors to this area have a pleasant surprise in store for them if they have not heard of the rapidly growing wine industry here. The more than twenty wineries are often small, family-run establishments, making tastings a friendly, congenial experience.

The gold rush may be over, but Sonora, former hub of the southern mining district, has never taken a breather. Its hustling heritage blends well with its current role as county seat and trading center.

In Columbia, however, history marches in place. In this completely restored mining town, even the people in sunglasses feel at home riding the stagecoach, drinking sarsaparilla, and eating Cornish pasties. Not too far away, Calavaras Big Trees State Park offers groves of giant sequoias and one of the loveliest rivers in California, the Stanislaus.

Daffodil Hill is a springtime (can we say it?) thrill. Over 200,000 of them trumpet spring. The competition is stiff, though. Poppies, brodiaeas, lupines, larkspur, Mariposa lilies, mullein, and wild roses give their cultivated neighbors a run for their money.

To the southeast is California's gold mine of beauty, Yosemite National Park. Sheer walls of the glacier gorge rise almost vertically to 4,000 feet above the peaceful meadows of the valley floor. In spring, plunging waterfalls veil chasms in perpetual mist. You walk tall in the high country, with its regal peaks and gem-like lakes, and feel small beneath the giant sequoias of the Mariposa Grove. One of the most spectacular spots for beauty in the country, Yosemite is a place for all seasons. The same could certainly be said for the Gold Country in general.

Cooper House
(209) 736-2145

P.O. Box 1388, Angels Camp, CA 95222
(1184 Church Street, one block off South Main Street)

Nearly hidden by trees on a back street well away from the Highway 49 corridor is Cooper House, an entirely restored Craftsman-style bungalow that was once home and office to Dr. George P. Cooper. The interior is graced by elegant woodwork and carefully selected furnishings, some of which belonged to the Stevenot family, one of Calaveras County's oldest. The spacious living room has a characteristic wood-outlined ceiling and a most distinctive fireplace of local greenstone and quartz. A clean, uncluttered look and a calming ambiance prevail at Cooper House. You'll find plenty of room in each elegant suite to settle in and fully unwind. The suites were named for locally grown wine grape varieties: Zinfandel, Cabernet, and Chardonnay. There's a subtle but unmistakable luxury in the choice of linens, accent pieces, carpeting, wallcoverings, and window treatments. Retreat to your private quarters, read or visit in the living room, or get out and explore this fascinating part of the Mother Lode. A memorable visit is certain to be yours at Cooper House.

No pets; smoking outside only; full breakfast; AC; sofa bed in separate room of Cabernet Suite; private deck on Chardonnay Suite; wineries, caves and caverns, state parks, lakes, country back roads, and skiing in vicinity; local swimming pool and tennis courts; off-street and street parking; major credit cards (V, MC). Rates $10 less Sunday-Thursday. Brochure available.

ROOM	BED	BATH	ENTRANCE	FLOOR	DAILY RATES S - D (EP)
A	1Q	Pvt	Main	1	$75 ($10)
B	2T or 1K	Pvt	Main	1	$75
C	1D	Pvt	Sep	2	$75

Dry Creek Bed & Breakfast
(916) 878-0885
13740 Dry Creek Road, Auburn, CA 95603
(Two miles west of I-80 and east of Highway 49)

Dry Creek B&B, nestled in the countryside just outside Auburn, is for active sportslovers as well as those seeking rest and relaxation. It offers free tennis, racquetball, and swimming at the Auburn Racquet Club, five minutes away, and affords nine holes of golf at the beautiful new golf course that adjoins the B&B's acreage. The rustic redwood home is situated on four wooded acres alongside a wild stream. The sounds of rushing water and birdsong will lull you in this setting of natural beauty. Accommodations include the French Country Garden Room (A), a bedroom/sitting room with a unique octagonal bathroom; the Tower Suite (B), three luxurious rooms with views of trees and stream; and the Friendship Room (C). All guests have use of a lovely deck and a large common room with a fireplace. Superb breakfasts are cooked to order and served at the convenience of guests. Although this home isn't far from major highways, other gold rush towns, and all sorts of outdoor recreation, it might as well be hours from civilization.

Small dog in residence; children by arrangement; full breakfast; TV in Room A; AC; large library; refrigerator and laundry privileges; scenic hikes nearby; off-street parking; some French spoken; airport pickup (Auburn). Room C available only for stays of three days or longer; discounts given for stays of two days or longer. *Closed December 20-January 5*. Brochure available.

ROOM	BED	BATH	ENTRANCE	FLOOR	DAILY RATES S-D (EP)
A	1K	Pvt	Sep	1	$65-$70
B	1Q	Pvt	Sep	1	$65-$70
C	2T	Pvt	Main	1	$45-$50

Domike's Bed & Breakfast   **(916) 273-9010**
220 Colfax Avenue, Grass Valley, CA 95945
(In town, just off Highway 49 on Route 174)

Don and Joyce Domike undertook quite a job when they set out to restore one of Grass Valley's largest and most impressive Victorians. The house is set back from the street in an elevated position in keeping with its status. Huge old trees and a lovely lawn are enclosed by a traditional white picket fence. Inside, the Domikes keep the atmosphere pretty casual and are prone to conversation of travel and good books. The upstairs accommodations are appointed with down comforters, clawfoot tubs, air conditioning, and Casablanca fans. Rooms B, C, and D have beds with canopies. You certainly can't go hungry at Domike's. They offer late afternoon beverages and nibbles, plus a hearty breakfast in the morning. Hosts try in every way to make sure your stay in Grass Valley is a satisfying one.

No pets; families welcome; full breakfast served at guests' convenience; TV in Room E; rollaway bed; public transportation; off-street parking; major credit cards; airport pickup (Grass Valley). *Advance reservations recommended.* Inquire about discounts for readers of this book; midweek and off-season rates.

ROOM	BED	BATH	ENTRANCE	FLOOR	DAILY RATES	
					S - D	(EP)
A	1Q	Pvt	Main	2	$58	($10)
B	1K	Pvt	Main	2	$75	($10)
C	1Q	Pvt	Main	2	$68	($10)
D	1K	Pvt	Main	2	$75	($10)
E	1Q & 1T	Pvt	Main	1	$75	($10)

GROVELAND

Jim & Eugenia Colucci   (209) 962-7019
P.O. Box 516, Groveland, CA 95321
(Off Highway 120 enroute to north entrance of Yosemite)

Groveland is a great off-the-beaten-track location on the way to Yosemite. The Coluccis' home is an ideal stopover, but it is also utterly relaxing and could keep one entertained for days. The chalet-style house is set in the pines above a private community lake offering all kinds of water recreation. It has a 180-degree, fifty-mile view toward the mountains of Yosemite. No street lights and very little traffic ensure a good night's rest in one of the comfortable guest rooms. A large loft bedroom with a private bath overlooks the living area; a good-sized room on the main floor has a TV, a sitting area, and a shared bath that is uniquely appointed. The open, airy feeling of the interior is perfectly suited to the alpine surroundings. An old clawfoot bathtub in the living area has been cleverly adapted into a wonderful place to settle in with a good book. While breakfasting under the gazebo on the deck, guests may observe deer feeding close by. Eugenia's Mexican breakfast is a popular specialty, and Jim's French toast is another favorite. These generous, easygoing hosts have a definite knack for making people feel at home.

Pets and children welcome; full breakfast; sofa bed extra in Room A; AC; tennis courts, pool, and lake within walking distance; inquire about parking; Spanish spoken; airport pickup (Pine Mountain Lake).

ROOM	BED	BATH	ENTRANCE	FLOOR	DAILY RATES
					S - D (EP)
A	1K	Pvt	Main	2	$35-$50 ($20)
B	1K	Shd	Main	1	$35-$50 ($20)

The Wedgewood Inn   **(209) 296-4300 or 1-800-WEDGEWD**
11941 Narcissus Road, Jackson, CA 95642
(Six and one-half miles out of Jackson, off Highway 88)

Just ten minutes away from bustling Jackson but hidden in a tranquil, forested setting, The Wedgewood Inn comes as a heady discovery. The stunning Victorian replica is endowed with treasures collected over a lifetime by Vic and Jeannine Beltz. They have lovingly arranged each antique, collectible, family heirloom, objet d'art, handmade Victorian lampshade, and work of stained glass in its perfect place to create a rich haven of turn-of-the-century charm. Each of the five romantic guest rooms has a distinctly memorable character expressed by a special combination of colors, fabrics, furnishings, and nostalgia pieces. Three rooms have clawfoot tubs, balconies, and wood-burning stoves. A parlor grand piano carved in Austria of pecan wood graces the living room, while a collection of tapestries from several countries enhances the formal dining room. Jeannine varies the table settings just as she does the elaborate breakfast specialties that guests are invited to savor at nine every morning. Vic and Jeannine offer a gracious welcome and a most comfortable stay in their dream-come-true, The Wedgewood Inn.

Cocker spaniel (Lacey) in residence; no children; smoking outside only; full breakfast; AC; porch swing; quiet walks; off-street parking; major credit cards (V, MC, D). Additional lodging in Carriage House, $105. Brochure available.

ROOM	BED	BATH	ENTRANCE	FLOOR	DAILY RATES S - D (EP)
A	1D	Pvt	Main	2	$65-$75
B	1Q	Pvt	Main	2	$70-$80
C	1Q	Pvt	Main	3	$75-$85
D	1Q	Pvt	Main	2	$80-$90
E	1Q	Pvt	Main	2	$85-$95

Windrose Inn   **(209) 223-3650**
1407 Jackson Gate Road, Jackson, CA 95642
(Just north of downtown area)

When you cross the footbridge over the creek that runs in front of this turn-of-the-century Victorian farmhouse, it is indeed like stepping into another era. Everything about the Windrose Inn is conducive to a leisurely pace and attitude. Old-fashioned gardens and fruit trees abound on the lovely grounds, and places to take it easy include a wide porch, a gazebo, a hammock by a fish pond, and a patio under an arbor. Each of the inn's three lovely rooms is an individual creation. The Deco Room has a stylishly modern look and an oversized bathroom; The Wicker Room is a vision of seafoam green and peach with white wicker furnishings; The Brass Room, done in tones of rose, has a romantic brass bed. You can experience a bit of gold rush history without even leaving the inn (which you'll be reluctant to do anyway): From the solarium adjoining the kitchen, observe the century-old, hand-dug Chinese well that once served the nearby Kennedy Gold Mine and the schoolhouse across the road. Other historic sites, foothill wineries, and fine restaurants within strolling distance can be suggested by genial hosts Marv and Sharon Hampton; they want your holiday to be special in every way.

No pets; no children under twelve; smoking outside only; full country breakfast; parlor with pot-bellied stove; off-street parking; major credit cards (V, MC); airport pickup (Westover). Unique old Miner's Cottage on property available at $100 ($15EP). Inquire about midweek rates. Brochure available.

ROOM	BED	BATH	ENTRANCE	FLOOR	DAILY RATES S - D	(EP)
A	1D	Pvt	Main	1	$85	
B	1Q	Pvt	Main	1	$85	
C	1Q	Pvt	Main	1	$90	

Mountainside Bed & Breakfast   **(916) 626-0983**
P.O. Box 165, Kelsey, CA 95643
(Eight miles north of Placerville, off Highway 193)

At the top of the Georgetown Divide between the South and Middle Forks of the American River is the rustic family home of Mary Ellen and Paul Mello. These former educators take pleasure in sharing their comfortable abode on eighty acres of wooded paradise with guests who always leave as friends. There are decks galore and many windows that take in a 180-degree view of the foothills and valley. The Mellos have deep roots in the area and are most knowledgeable about its wealth of outdoor recreation and mining history. Three pleasant guest rooms on the main floor have private baths. A large, pine-paneled attic space with its own bath and deck can sleep up to eight people. Weddings, receptions, and group functions work well at Mountainside Bed & Breakfast, as do romantic holidays and family vacations. Outstanding hospitality and country living at its best await you at this wonderful mountain retreat.

Two dogs in residence; no pets or young children; smoking outside only; full breakfast; TV, fireplace, and piano in large parlor; hot tub; off-street parking. Brochure available.

ROOM	BED	BATH	ENTRANCE	FLOOR	DAILY RATES	
					S - D	(EP)
A	1Q	Pvt	Main	1	$55-$60	
B	1Q	Pvt	Main	1	$55-$60	
C	1Q	Pvt	Sep	1	$60-$65	
D	1K, 1Q, 4T	Pvt	Main	2	$55-$60	($10)

Dick & Shirl's Bed & Breakfast   (209) 966-2514
4870 Triangle Road, Mariposa, CA 95338
(Five miles from Mariposa enroute to Yosemite)

Hosts Dick and Shirl Fiester are quite contented living on their fifteen forested acres. It's a quiet, secluded setting where you can slow down, unwind, and tune in to nature — most people leave completely refreshed. The home itself is rustic, commodious, and very relaxing. On the main floor, there's an open living area with a large, stone fireplace and cathedral ceilings of warm, polished redwood. An open kitchen is adjacent, and just off the dining area is a guest suite (A) that can be closed off for complete privacy. A cabin (B) on the property provides additional accommodations. Large breakfasts and friendly conversation are part of the gracious hospitality to be found here. For country lodging on the way to Yosemite (forty miles away), Dick and Shirl's is a fine choice.

Dog and cat in residence; no pets; TV; barbecue; off-street parking; major credit cards (V, MC).

ROOM	BED	BATH	ENTRANCE	FLOOR	DAILY RATES	
					S - D	(EP)
A	1Q	Pvt	Sep	1G	$50	
B	1Q & 1T	Pvt	Sep	1	$50	($10)

The Homestead Guest Ranch   **(209) 966-2820**
P.O. Box 13, Midpines, CA 95345
(Eight miles from Mariposa enroute to Yosemite)

The Homestead isn't the place for a quick stopover. You need some time just to take in the good fortune of having found it, and I promise that you won't want to leave when the time comes. This is a B&B with unusual character and privacy. It's a restored rustic ranch where you'll have an entire house to yourself. Downstairs there's a living room with a big stone fireplace, antiques, a well stocked kitchen, and a large master bedroom and bath. Two smaller bedrooms and a half-bath are upstairs. Enjoy all this *plus* the superlative hospitality of hosts Blair and Helen Fowler, whose home is across a wide meadow from The Homestead. One could easily spend several blissful days in the woodland setting and utter peacefulness of this getaway abode.

Pets and children accepted conditionally; ducks in barnyard; horses graze nearby; barbecue; trails; off-street parking; some German and French spoken; airport pickup (Mariposa). Two-night minimum.

ROOM	BED	BATH	ENTRANCE	FLOOR	DAILY RATES	
					S - D	(EP)
A	1Q	Pvt	Sep	1	$75	($25)
B	3T	Pvt 1/2		2		

Meadow Creek Ranch Bed & Breakfast Inn   **(209) 966-3843**
2669 Triangle Road, Mariposa, CA 95338
(Twelve miles south of Mariposa at Highway 49 S and Triangle Road)

"A pleasant haven of rest" reads the description of this 1858 home in a book on the history of Mariposa. It was once a stop on the Mariposa-Oakhurst stagecoach run that provided overnight lodging for weary travelers. Though many improvements have been made for the sake of comfort, guests today feel the same welcoming spirit of the early days. Hosts Bob and Carol Shockley want you to feel completely at home here, whether you're relaxing in the cozy living room or strolling about the lovely grounds. Guests have a choice of three charming bedrooms, each decorated with a mixture of country and European flavors. After a hard day of traveling, or of exploring the wonder that is Yosemite, you'll be glad to return to this pleasant haven of rest.

No pets; children twelve and older welcome; full breakfast; seasonal refreshments served on arrival; ample street parking; major credit cards (V, MC, AE). Also available at $85 is a "Country Cottage" with private bath, sitting area, queen bed with canopy, and fireplace.

ROOM	BED	BATH	ENTRANCE	FLOOR	DAILY RATES	
					S - D	(EP)
A	1Q	Shd*	Main	2	$60	
B	1Q	Shd*	Main	2	$60	
C	2T	Shd*	Main	2	$60	

Oak Meadows, too   **(209) 742-6161**
P.O. Box 619, Mariposa, CA 95338
(5263 Highway 140 North)

When Don and Francie Starchman built this B&B on the main route to Yosemite, they wanted it to have the same kind of warmth and charm their own home, Oak Meadows, has — hence, the name: Oak Meadows, too. Live-in hosts tend the guest accommodations with care, and the Starchmans are often on hand as well. The B&B features such comforts as air conditioning, private baths, and a fireplace, while the decor is highlighted by brass headboards, hand-made quilts, handpainted china, and country print wallpaper. You'll be served a generous Continental breakfast in the morning. For a party of three, the Rose Room Suite (B), with a sitting room and queen sofa bed, might be a good choice.

No pets; smoking outside only (front porch); children by prior arrangement; AC; off-street parking; major credit cards (V, MC); airport pickup (Mariposa). An additional guest house with three rooms is next door, making visits by larger groups feasible. Brochure available.

ROOM	BED	BATH	ENTRANCE	FLOOR	DAILY RATES	
					S - D	(EP)
A	1K	Pvt	Main	2	$59	
B	1Q	Pvt	Main	2	$59	($10)
C	2T	Pvt	Main	2	$44-$49	

The Pelennor   **(209) 966-2832 or 966-5353**
3871 Highway 49 S, Mariposa, CA 95338
(Five miles south of Mariposa at Bootjack)

Dick and Gwen Foster follow the Scottish tradition of offering simple, low-cost accommodations, which are now in a new building adjacent to their home. They can provide tips on enjoying the area, a bit of hospitality, and even some bagpipe tunes on request. Hosts are pipers in the Clan Campbell Pipe Band; Dick and Gwen occasionally get out the telescope for some stargazing. No other B&B that I know of specializes in "Stars and Pipes," but guests who have sampled this unique combination are not likely to forget it. Each morning the Fosters serve what they term "a solid breakfast." For informal lodgings just off the main route of the Mother Lode and a short hour's drive from Yosemite, The Pelennor makes a welcome stop for the passing traveler.

Hosts have dogs, cat, and cockatiels; other animals roam the property; smoking outside only; lap pool; spa; kitchen in guest building available on a "you use, you clean" basis; off-street parking. At most, two rooms share one bath. Two extra bedrooms in main house available as needed. Available for outdoor weddings. Brochure available.

ROOM	BED	BATH	ENTRANCE	FLOOR	DAILY RATES	
					S - D	(EP)
A	1Q	Shd*	Sep	2	$30-$35	($7)
B	1Q	Shd*	Sep	2	$30-$35	($7)
C	1D	Shd*	Sep	2	$30-$35	($7)
D	2T	Shd*	Sep	2	$30-$35	($7)

Pilgrim's Inn   **(209) 742-6034**
P.O. Box 1969, Mariposa, CA 95338
(Two miles from Highway 140, off Highway 49 N)

Set high on a hill with awesome views of Sierra mountain ridges, this contemporary ranch-style home is ideal for two couples or a small family. The garden entrance takes you into an inviting and comfortable living area. The artistic decor ranges from antique to Oriental, creating an original and appealing environment. Guests sometimes spend leisurely evenings by the fire in the sitting room/library while taking in a movie on the VCR, popcorn and all. Just off this room and well separated from the rest of the house are the guest quarters — two bedrooms and a shared bath. Magnificent vistas are yours from one guest room, from the living area, and from the deck. Mimi Stevenson offers the warmth of a true welcome to people visiting the many historical spots and recreational areas in Mariposa County.

Small dog in residence; small, well-behaved pets welcome; children welcome; extended Continental breakfast; port-a-crib, $15; off-street parking. Two-night minimum on holiday weekends. Brochure available.

ROOM	BED	BATH	ENTRANCE	FLOOR	DAILY RATES S - D (EP)
A	2T	Shd*	Main	1	$30-$45
B	1Q	Shd*	Main	1	$30-$45

Winsor Farms Bed & Breakfast (209) 966-5592
5636 Whitlock Road, Mariposa, CA 95338
(Three miles off Highway 140; seven miles from Mariposa)

Staying near Mariposa offers not only the advantage of good proximity to Yosemite National Park; it also enables one to explore many facets of gold rush history unique to this particular area. Hosts Donald and Janice Haag are well-versed on local attractions and provide all manner of information to enhance one's stay. Both Park employees, their insights can be most valuable to those exploring the myriad wonders of Yosemite. At Winsor Farms, their quiet and comfortable ranch-style home is set on a hilltop surrounded by pine and oak trees. Savor country views from the patio while enjoying an afternoon glass of lemonade or a tasty Continental breakfast in the morning. The large living room, with a huge brick hearth and wood-burning stove, is a relaxing place in which to read or visit. Two guest rooms and a bath can be closed off from the rest of the house for extra privacy. The homey accommodations at Winsor Farms satisfy many year-round visitors to the intriguing Mariposa-Yosemite area.

Dog and cat in residence; smoking outside only; AC; rollaway bed; TV; VCR; off-street parking; wheelchair access. Brochure available.

ROOM	BED	BATH	ENTRANCE	FLOOR	DAILY RATES	
					S - D	(EP)
A	1Q	Shd*	Main	1	$35-$40	($10)
B	1D	Shd*	Main	1	$35-$40	($10)

Dunbar House, 1880   **(209) 728-2897**
P.O. Box 1375, Murphys, CA 95247
(One block off Main Street at 271 Jones Street)

The authentic feeling is the thing I like best about Dunbar House, 1880. From inside you can hear the clip-clop of a horse-drawn buggy taking visitors around, and you are only a few steps from the main street of history-steeped Murphys, "Queen of the Sierra." It's a jewel of a gold rush town, one that's unusually well preserved and lots of fun to explore. Barbara and Bob Costa were drawn to Murphys as well as to the home they purchased in April 1987. The lovely Italianate structure with century-old gardens and wide porches echos another era, and the Costas are keen on preserving the essence of that era at Dunbar House, 1880. As their guest, you can feel a part of it, too.

Dog in residence; no pets; smoking outside only; full breakfast in dining room, in the gardens, or delivered to your room; afternoon refreshments; sitting room with piano, games, books, menus; off-street parking; major credit cards; transfer from airport (San Andreas, Columbia) can be arranged. Brochure available.

ROOM	BED	BATH	ENTRANCE	FLOOR	DAILY RATES S - D (EP)
A	1Q	Pvt	Main	1	$75-$80
B	1Q	Pvt	Main	1	$75-$80
C	1Q	Pvt	Main	2	$75-$80
D	1Q	Pvt	Main	2	$75-$80

Palley Place   **(916) 265-5427**
12766 Nevada City Highway, Nevada City, CA 95959
(Between Grass Valley and Nevada City)

If you're taking in the sights along the Highway 49 detour from I-80 between Lake Tahoe and Sacramento, you'll want to explore both Grass Valley and Nevada City — and you'll find Palley Place a pleasant home base while you're at it. Weaver and fiber artist Meg Palley offers clean, comfortable rooms accented by her own work and that of other local artists. See her loom and spinning wheel in action on most any day. A healthful buffet breakfast is set out in the dining room, where the windows frame beautiful mountain tops in the distance. Meg has a keen interest in the environment, peace, and justice, and she particularly enjoys guests with similar inclinations.

No pets; smoking outside only (patio); FM radio in Room A; TV in Room B; fireplace in living room and on patio; host offers vast knowledge of extensive trails in surrounding areas; off-street parking; airport pickup (Grass Valley). Child on cot, $15 extra. Brochure available.

ROOM	BED	BATH	ENTRANCE	FLOOR	DAILY RATES S - D	(EP)
A	2T	Shd*	Main	1	$30-$60	
B	1Q	Shd*	Main	1	$30-$60	

Ople's Guest House   **(209) 683-4317**
41118 Highway 41, Oakhurst, CA 93644
(Fourteen miles from south entrance to Yosemite)

Ople Smith, long-time resident of Oakhurst, has been taking Yosemite-bound guests into her home for several years. Many make Ople's a regular stop because of the easygoing atmosphere, the clean and pleasant accommodations, and the affordable rates. Set on a hill and half-hidden by trees is the rambling, 1950s-style house where families are welcome and guests may enjoy the whole house as their own. A fireplace and a TV in the living room are shared by all. Ople offers a friendly welcome and any help one needs, but independent travelers appreciate the fact that they are not restricted by rules or schedules in this convenient guest house.

Rollaway bed and cots available; off-street parking; wheelchair access.

ROOM	BED	BATH	ENTRANCE	FLOOR	DAILY RATES S - D	(EP)
A	2T	Shd*	Main	1	$40	($5)
B	1D	Shd*	Main	1	$40	($5)
C	1D	Shd*	Main	1	$40	($5)

River Rock Inn   **(916) 622-7640**
1756 Georgetown Road, Placerville, CA 95667
(Three miles from Placerville via Route 193)

Located directly on the South Fork of the American River, the home of Dorothy Irvin is very quiet and peaceful. From three of the lovely, antique-furnished guest rooms, you can be at eye level with the river flowing by as you lie in bed. An expansive deck stretches by each room, with patio doors opening onto it. Deluxe breakfasts are served here in summer, and there are plenty of lounge chairs for sunbathing. River rafting, fishing, and panning for gold are popular warm-weather activities. In winter there's still lots to do, such as exploring gold rush towns, wine-tasting in foothill wineries, and skiing in Sierra resorts. It's nice, too, having a fireside breakfast in the living room. Dorothy goes out of her way to make sure that her guests are pleased and comfortable.

Dog and cat in residence; no pets; children by arrangement; full breakfast; AC; TV; laundry privileges; hot tub; rafting trips arranged; extra meals possible; off-street parking; airport pickup (Placerville). Rooms A, B, and D face the river. A and B each have a private half-bath; they also share a full bath.

ROOM	BED	BATH	ENTRANCE	FLOOR	DAILY RATES S - D (EP)
A	1D	Pvt 1/2	Main	1	$65
B	1D	Pvt 1/2	Main	1	$65
C	1D	Pvt	Main	1	$65
D	1Q	Pvt	Main	1	$75

The Courtyard   **(209) 754-1518**
Star Route 3, San Andreas, CA 95249
(334 West Charles Street; north end of downtown area)

This small, pleasant-looking house holds many surprises for the first-time visitor. Once inside, you discover its depth, spaciousness, and serene beauty. To the right side of the house is a brick courtyard with a three-century-old oak tree in the center. To the left rear is The Blue Room, decorated in French blue with white wicker and oak furniture and delicate touches of ribbon and lace. In back of the courtyard is The Master Suite, a luxurious space of nearly 600 square feet boasting an antique baby grand piano and a free-standing fireplace. French doors open onto a series of three decks cascading down toward a creek. A hot tub, an outdoor dining area, and an interesting collection of bird-houses delight guests. Lucy Thein makes sure your hot beverage is waiting at your door in the morning and then serves a marvelous breakfast either indoors or out. Partake of afternoon refreshments while pondering which direction to go exploring from this central gold country location — if you can tear yourself away.

No pets; smoking outside only; full breakfast; skiing, boating, wine tasting, visiting museums, browsing quaint shops, touring gold rush towns or caverns and caves in vicinity; available for small weddings, garden parties, luncheons, and showers; off-street parking. Brochure available.

ROOM	BED	BATH	ENTRANCE	FLOOR	DAILY RATES S - D	(EP)
A	1D	Pvt	Main	1	$50	
B	1Q	Pvt	Main	1	$75	

La Casa Inglesa (209) 532-5822
18047 Lime Kiln Road, Sonora, CA 95370
(Two and one-half miles from downtown)

Wooded hills and splendid flower gardens surround the fine English Tudor home of Mary and John Monser, set in the countryside where the Kincaid gold mine once flourished. The baronial elegance of La Casa Inglesa is apparent in its architecture and in the many finishing details throughout the interior. Handsome oak panels, mouldings, and cabinetry create a regal setting in the formal dining room where breakfasts fit for nobility may be served; guests are also drawn to the marvelous country kitchen done in blue and white with lots of brick and copper. Quiet places to relax include a delightful patio and a spacious living room with a fireplace. The entire upper floor is reserved for guests, and the accent is on romance. At one end is a huge suite with a bath featuring beautiful tile work, a whirlpool tub, and a separate shower. All four rooms are exquisitely decorated, with special attention to lightness and privacy (no two rooms adjoin). Wall and bed coverings, original paintings, and lovely iron beds are just a few of the special touches. A large deck with a hot tub and plenty of sun is made to order for basking in the glorious peacefulness of the country.

No pets, children, or smoking; full breakfast; TV in suite; AC; off-street parking; Spanish spoken. Two-night minimum on holiday weekends. Brochure available.

ROOM	BED	BATH	ENTRANCE	FLOOR	DAILY RATES
					S - D (EP)
A	1Q	Pvt	Main	2	$70
B	1Q	Pvt	Main	2	$70
C	1Q	Pvt	Main	2	$70
D	1Q	Pvt	Main	2	$70
E	1Q	Pvt	Main	2	$95

Via Serena Ranch (209) 532-5307
18007 Via Serena, Sonora, CA 95370
(Between Sonora and Jamestown)

Set on beautiful rolling acreage that only *seems* miles from anywhere, Via Serena Ranch is ideally located for sampling the old west flavor of the historic mining towns of Jamestown and Columbia. Sonora, a hub of activity, is just moments away. While you're exploring this rich and varied area, Beverly Ballash will make you feel truly welcome in her elegant ranch-style home. Here you'll find comfortable, immaculate accommodations and a breakfast to remember. Each guest room is a work of art. It's difficult choosing among them, but I found the one with an English hunting theme particularly striking. A large living room and a deck are yours for reading, socializing, or just relaxing. In every way possible, the climate is always perfect at Via Serena Ranch.

No pets, children, or smoking; TV; AC; robes provided; off-street parking; airport pickup (Columbia). Brochure available.

ROOM	BED	BATH	ENTRANCE	FLOOR	DAILY RATES S - D (EP)
A	2T	Shd*	Main	1G	$60
B	1Q	Shd*	Main	1G	$60
C	1Q	Shd*	Main	1G	$60

Cedar Tree   **(916) 583-5421**
P.O. Box 7106, Tahoe City, CA 95730
(Between Highway 89 and Lake Tahoe)

Walt and Doris Genest make it easy for their guests to enjoy Lake Tahoe in a variety of ways. Cedar Tree, an aptly named mountain retreat, is just a short distance from a private beach and pier on the lake. You can try your luck at fishing, or at other games of chance in the North Shore casinos. Golfing, boating, cycling on trails, hiking, rafting, skiing, and fine dining are all possible in the vicinity of Cedar Tree. The second floor loft, with cable TV and extra beds, is popular with the younger set. Doris takes pride in serving nourishing homemade treats for breakfast. If you're looking for a vacation spot with the comforts of home *and* lots of things to do close by, Cedar Tree hits the jackpot.

Bird in residence; smoking outside only; children, kitchen privileges, and fishing by special advance arrangement; sinks in Rooms A and B; barbecue; deck; hot tub; bicycles available; off-street parking. Two-night minimum on weekends.

ROOM	BED	BATH	ENTRANCE	FLOOR	DAILY RATES S - D (EP)
A	1Q	Shd*	Main	2	$45
B	2T	Shd*	Main	2	$45
C	1Q	Pvt	Main	1	$45

Chaney House   **(916) 525-7333**
P.O. Box 7852, Tahoe City, CA 95730
(Overlooking west shore of Lake Tahoe)

Few homes around Lake Tahoe possess the unique sense of history that Chaney House has. Some of the Italian stonemasons who built Vikingsholm at nearby Emerald Bay in the twenties also worked on this impressive home. Eighteen-inch-thick stone walls, elaborately carved woodwork, Gothic arches, and a massive stone fireplace reaching to the top of the cathedral ceiling give the interior an old-world European flavor. Stone arches and walls outline the paths around the three patios; on one of these, superb breakfasts are served on mild days. Across the road, enjoy the private pier that juts out into the crystal clear water or take a bike ride on the path alongside the lake; in winter, choose from the many ski areas close at hand. Hosts Gary and Lori Chaney love the territory around them and they are well-versed on its wealth of outdoor and indoor activities for year-round pleasure. Let the warmth of their hospitality enhance your next visit to spectacular Lake Tahoe.

Dog and cat in residence; no pets; children over twelve welcome; smoking outside only; full breakfast; sofa bed for extra person in Room C; TV, VCR, and barbecue available; ski boat available by advance arrangement; off-street parking. Additional lodging in quaint, European-style honeymoon hideaway on property at $100 ($10EP); weekly rate, $500. Two-night minimum on weekends.

ROOM	BED	BATH	ENTRANCE	FLOOR	DAILY RATES	
					S - D	(EP)
A	1D	Pvt	Main	1	$75	
B	1Q	Shd*	Main	2	$75	
C	1K	Shd*	Main	2	$85	($10)

Chalet A-Capella   **(916) 577-6841**
P.O. Box 11334, Tahoe Paradise, CA 95708
(Near intersection of Highways 89 and 50)

    Richard and Suzanne Capella's chalet-style home blends well with the alpine scenery that surrounds it. You can go cross-country skiing from the doorstep, drive to a number of ski touring trails or downhill slopes in about thirty minutes, or fish right across the street in the Upper Truckee River. South Shore casinos are a short distance away. The interior woodwork and sloped ceilings of the upstairs guest quarters create a snug, rustic feeling. A bedroom and a private bath are just right for a couple. Summer or winter, Chalet A-Capella is a picture-perfect vacation spot.

    No pets; no smoking preferred; TV; deck; off-street parking; Italian spoken. $5 extra for one-night stays; two-night minimum preferred.

ROOM	BED	BATH	ENTRANCE	FLOOR	DAILY RATES S - D	(EP)
A	1Q	Pvt	Sep	2	$45	

Cort Cottage   **(209) 561-4671 or 561-4036**
P.O. Box 245, Three Rivers, CA 93271
(East of Visalia, near entrance to Sequoia National Park)

The setting for this B&B is breathtaking. The private cottage with a panoramic view of mountain and sky was built by architect/owner Gary Cort to fit snugly into a hillside near the Corts' home. At sunrise and sunset, colors play off the rocks in a constantly changing show. Spring wildflowers bloom in profusion along the path you'll probably want to take down to Salt Creek, and you're likely to see a few critters while you're at it. A private outdoor hot tub is located, as Cathy Cort says, "directly under the Milky Way." The cottage is a splendid home base for exploring Sequoia, where you can witness trees that are the largest living things on earth. You'll feel dwarfed by their size and awed by their beauty — and you'll love every minute of it. Those with an interest in art will want to visit the hosts' Cort Gallery in Three Rivers; it is "dedicated to the ideal that art is a part of every moment."

No pets; smoking outside only (deck); no RV parking; sunken bathtub; kitchen; sofa bed in living room; hot tub; off-street parking.

ROOM	BED	BATH	ENTRANCE	FLOOR	DAILY RATES	
					S - D	(EP)
A	1D	Pvt	Sep	1	$55-$60	($5)

Oak Hill Ranch (209) 928-4717
P.O. Box 307, Tuolumne, CA 95379
(Ten miles southeast of Sonora, off Highway 108))

Even though I knew this Victorian ranch home was built in 1980, I had to keep reminding myself that it wasn't here at the turn of the century. Sanford and Jane Grover conceived of the home some twenty-five years ago and began collecting authentic Victorian building materials. Two years of restoring the pieces preceded construction of the home, which was the Grovers' son's senior architectural project in college. Today it stands on fifty-six of the most beautiful acres imaginable. The silence is broken only by the sounds of local fauna, and each room of the home exudes a quietly elegant personality. Oak Hill Ranch is tailored "for a perfect sojourn into the past," to quote an early guest. The superb hospitality offered by the Grovers takes many forms (including a breakfast fit for a gourmet) — I suggest you relax and enjoy the total experience.

No pets; young people over fourteen welcome; smoking outside only; full breakfast; fireplaces; porches, balcony, and gazebo; bicycles available; hiking trails on and off property; tennis courts and swimming pool nearby; one and one-half hours to Yosemite; off-street parking; airport pickup (Columbia). Victorian honeymoon cottage with fireplace, $85. EP rate with rollaway bed, $18. Brochure available.

ROOM	BED	BATH	ENTRANCE	FLOOR	DAILY RATES S - D	(EP)
A	1D	Shd*	Main	2	$65	
B	1D	Shd*	Main	2	$60	
C	1Q	Pvt	Main	2	$70	
D	1Q	Pvt	Main	1	$75	

Please read "About Dining Highlights" on page *ix*.

AMADOR CITY
Au Relais French Restaurant, 14220 Highway 49; (209) 267-5636
ANGELS CAMP
Utica Mansion Inn, 1090 Utica Lane; (209) 736-4209; eclectic menu changes weekly
AUBURN
Headquarter House, 14500 Musso Road; (916) 878-1906; Continental/American
CATHEYS VALLEY
The Chibchas, 2747 Highway 140; (209) 966-2940; Colombian/American
COLUMBIA
City Hotel Restaurant, Main Street; (209) 532-1479; French
COULTERVILLE
Jeffery Hotel & Restaurant, 1 Main Street; (209) 878-3471; American
FISH CAMP
The Narrow Gauge Inn, Highway 41; (209) 683-6446; Continental
GEORGETOWN
Buckeye Restaurant, 7460 Wentworth Springs Road; (916) 333-2200; Greek-influenced Continental cuisine
GRASS VALLEY
The Empire House Restaurant, 535 Mill Street; (916) 273-8272; Continental/Swiss

Main Street Café, 213 West Main Street; (916) 477-6000; fish, game, Cajun, and pasta specialties

The Old California Restaurant, 341 East Main Street; (916) 273-7341; Continental
GROVELAND
Charlotte Hotel & Restaurant, Highway 120; (209) 962-7872; American

Pine Mountain Lake Country Club Restaurant, Mueller Drive; (209) 962-7866; Continental
JACKSON
Amador Inn, 200 South Highway 49; (209) 223-2791; Continental

The Balcony, 164 Main Street; (209) 223-2856; Continental

Teresa's, 1235 Jackson Gate Road; (209) 223-1786; Italian/American
JAMESTOWN
Café Smoke, 18228 Main Street; (209) 984-3733; Mexican

Jamestown Hotel, 18153 Main Street; (209) 984-3902; Continental
MARIPOSA
Bon Ton Café, 7307 Highway 49 North; (209) 377-8229; Guatemalan and American

DINING HIGHLIGHTS: GOLD COUNTRY & THE SIERRA

Charles Street Dinner House, Highway 140 and Seventh Street; (209) 966-2366; Continental

Old Sawmill Restaurant, 5111 Coakley Drive; (209) 742-6101; down-home cooking

MURPHYS

Murphys Hotel, Main Street; (209) 728-3444; Continental

NEVADA CITY

The Apple Fare, 307 Broad Street; (916) 265-5458; American breakfasts and lunches

Country Rose, 300 Commercial Street; (916) 265-6252; country French

Selaya's, 320 Broad Street; (916) 265-5697; California cuisine

York Street Blues Dinner Theatre, 203 York Street; (916) 265-6363; California cuisine

OAKHURST

Erna's Elderberry House, Victoria Lane off Highway 41; (209) 683-6800; European

SONORA

Hemingway's Café Restaurant, 362 South Stewart Street; (209) 532-4900; California Continental cuisine

SUGAR PINE

Kelly's Kitchen, Highway 108; (209) 586-3283; American

SUTTER CREEK

Pelargonium, #1 Hanford Street (Highway 49 N); (209) 267-5008; California cuisine

Sutter Creek Palace, 76 Main Street; (209) 267-9852; American

TAHOE CITY

Bacchi's Inn, 2905 Lake Forest Glen; (916) 583-3324; Italian

Pheifer House, 760 River Road (Highway 89); (916) 583-3102; German/ European

Sunnyside Resort, 1850 West Lake Boulevard; (916) 583-7200; American

Tahoe House, 625 West Lake Boulevard; (916) 583-1377; Swiss and California cuisines

THREE RIVERS

Staff of Life, 41651 Sierra Drive; (209) 561-4937; lunches featuring homemade soups, salads, and sandwiches with vegetarian accent

TWAIN HARTE

Eproson's Restaurant, Twain Harte Drive; (209) 586-5600; Continental

Villa D'Oro, Joaquin Gully and Fuller Roads; (209) 586-2182; Italian

Southern California

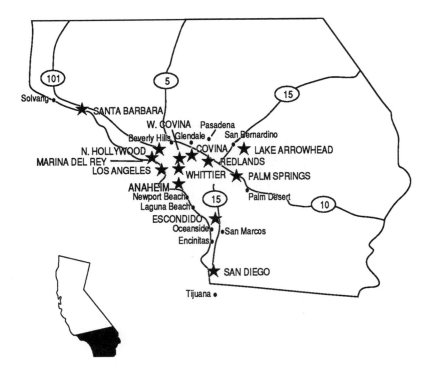

California is a little like Shangri-La, a paradise that is sometimes hard to find. But visitors to Santa Barbara will feel that they have found it. Palm trees, sunny beaches, technicolor sails on blue water, red rooftops and white stucco against a gray-green backdrop of mountains — it's all here, the California of the travel posters. No wonder this was the place chosen as Shangri-La for the original movie version of *Lost Horizons*.

Santa Barbara is a city at home with itself, as a ramble along the terrazzo walks will convince you. A side trip through the County Courthouse buildings will make you feel as if you are in a Moorish castle. Turrets, arched doorways, and curving staircases have a regal air, a mood matched by the exquisitely manicured gardens. From the clocktower, a panorama of city and sea lies below. Another must-see is the "Queen of Missions," one of California's most beautiful, situated alongside a reflecting pool where mission Indians once bathed. Santa Barbara's peaceful pace makes it a good place to relax or gather your energies before heading south for L.A.

L.A. may be the only city in the country known by its initials. Somehow that fits. It expresses the adolescent charm of the unpredictable and offbeat that you find here. It makes this sprawling city of over 460 square miles and more than three million people seem both down-home casual and fast-lane exciting.

Many people are not sure just where L.A. is — exactly. Is it downtown near the Civic Center and the Music Center's cultural constellation of theaters and auditoriums? Or is it more toward the soundstages of the satellite TV and movie studios? Maybe it's over near Chinatown, Little Tokyo, or Olvera Street, that delightful, brick-paved pedestrian street with its colorful wares of serapes and ollas, its taste-tempters of biznaga (candied cactus) or green corn tamales. Wait, isn't it somewhere over on Hollywood Boulevard near Mann's Chinese Theater, where the stars leave footprints? It can't be far from Griffith Park, 3,000 acres supporting a zoo, a planetarium, an outdoor theater, stables, playgrounds, and a mountain wilderness. Or is L.A., as some wags suggest, the La Brea Tar Pits where life-sized models of prehistoric animals (the real skeletons are in the Museum of Natural History) rise from the black murk, as Mercedes Benzes and Porsches whiz by on Wilshire Boulevard? But what about the beaches? Don't all L.A.'s streets lead to the beach?

After you visit L.A., you will undoubtedly have your own opinion about its location. No one leaves L.A. without an opinion.

South of L.A., from Huntington Beach to San Clemente, is the Gold Coast of California. Whether this coastline is named for the golden tans acquired here or the high price of real estate is in dispute.

Either way, the Gold Coast offers a variety of beach topography. Wide, sandy stretches, cliff-clutched coves, tidepools, and balmy breezes delight the senses; swimming, boating, fishing, surfing, scuba diving, snorkeling, and windsurfing strain them to the limit. For your more artistic sensibilities, be sure to stop at the famous artists' colony in Laguna Beach.

For all its glory, the Gold Coast is actually the lesser-known side of Orange County, thanks to the magic wand of Walt Disney. In addition to Disneyland, which needs no description, there are three major amusement parks and seven specialty museums. The area roughly flanking Interstate 5 is a never-ending world's fair. From Knott's Berry Farm (it was an actual farm once) north of Santa Ana down to Lion Country Safari, visitors will be amused, entertained, and informed. Aircraft, crocodiles, roller coasters, wild west shows, chimps, antique cars — it's up to you to cry "Uncle."

Continuing oceanside to the south, you come — of course — to Oceanside. Watch the blue Pacific's lacy hem rise and fall, a slave not to fashion but to time. From here you may wish to explore San Diego's back country, a peaceful landscape including rambling hills, rocky peaks, and desert. Mission San Luis Rey, crowned "King of the Missions" as California's largest, dominates a hill overlooking a tranquil valley.

La Jolla, Jewel of the Pacific, has seven miles of coves, caves, and cliffs that are unsurpassed in the southland. On its northern boundary lies Torrey Pines State Park, where this Ice Age tree can be seen in abundance. Modern Icaruses in brightly colored wings hang-glide off the cliffs here.

La Jolla is the quieter edge of San Diego. In San Diego, the park came first; the city built up around it. Century-old Balboa Park is one of the country's greatest. Nine museums, the Old Globe Theater, and the renowned San Diego Zoo all lie within a public garden of fragrant eucalyptus trees and lush greenery. San Diego's other park, the Mission Bay Aquatic Park, is a water playground near downtown. Water sports and Sea World, a park within a park, are big attractions here. A stroll through Old Town is a stroll through San Diego's past. Nearby San Diego Mission was California's first.

With the diversity of natural and manmade attractions in Southern California, few generalizations apply. Only one seems certain: You will never run out of things to do.

Anaheim Bed & Breakfast   **(714) 533-1884**
1327 South Hickory, Anaheim, CA 92805
(Off Santa Ana Freeway)

Anaheim is the obvious headquarters for anyone planning to visit Disneyland or the convention center, both less than a mile away, or Knott's Berry Farm. Many people also find the location ideal for visiting beaches, L.A., as well as points to the south and east. Disneyland's nightly fireworks can be viewed in summer from the back yard of this suburban home. Margot Palmgren's home exudes a friendly welcome that puts visitors at ease right away. She speaks German fluently and loves meeting people from all over the world. You'll be in good hands with Margot; she knows the area intimately and can give you a real insider's view of things...for example, she remembers when the Knott family ran a little fruit stand nearby — and the day Disneyland opened!

No pets or smoking; TV in each room; AC in Room A; ceiling fan in B and C; AC and fireplace in den; full breakfast; ample street parking; good public transportation and airport connections.

ROOM	BED	BATH	ENTRANCE	FLOOR	DAILY RATES S - D	(EP)
A	1D	Shd*	Main	1G	$30-$40	
B	2T	Shd*	Main	1G	$30-$40	
C	1D	Shd	Main	1G	$30-$40	

Dorothy's Hacienda   (818) 967-4656
1110 East Walnut Creek Road, Covina, CA 91724
(Near I-10 and Grand Avenue; forty minutes east of downtown L.A.)

The Covina Hills area still has a quiet rural beauty that seems rare so near a major city. Find refuge from the madding crowds at Dorothy's Hacienda, a lovely Spanish-style home with an enclosed patio and a large master suite for guests. If you're so inclined, play some tunes on the piano, make yourself comfortable by the fireplace, or soak up a little sun on the patio. Good freeway access makes it a snap to get to shopping centers, dining establishments, and attractions such as Disneyland and Knott's Berry Farm. Desert and mountain resorts are about an hour away. The serenity of Dorothy's Hacienda will ease the strain that can accompany a visit to this fast-paced area.

No pets; no children under ten; TV in master suite (A); AC; gas barbecue; street and off-street parking; three minutes to "restaurant row," which includes six restaurants representing diverse cuisines.

ROOM	BED	BATH	ENTRANCE	FLOOR	DAILY RATES	
					S - D	(EP)
A	1K	Pvt	Main	1G	$40	($10)
B	1T	Shd	Main	1G	$25	

Halbig's Hacienda (619) 745-1296
432 South Citrus Avenue, Escondido, CA 92027
(East of town, off Valley Parkway)

The Halbigs came to Escondido in the fifties and the town literally grew up around them. The home that they built by hand sits on a knoll, removed from the hustle bustle, with wonderful views of the surrounding mountains. Fruit trees dot the property. Long verandas, adobe brick construction, and hand-hewn wooden doors recall the days of the early California ranchos. Two rooms are available for bed and breakfast guests. Escondido makes a good base for exploring San Diego's back country, fishing in nearby lakes, dropping by the Wild Animal Park, or paying a visit to Lawrence Welk's village and dinner theater. Beaches are only twenty minutes away, and San Diego thirty-five. Enjoy a quiet, country-like atmosphere on the edge of town when you visit Halbig's Hacienda.

Children and pets welcome; TV; off-street parking; some Spanish spoken; airport pickup (Palomar).

ROOM	BED	BATH	ENTRANCE	FLOOR	DAILY RATES S - D (EP)
A	1Q	Shd*	Main	1G	$40
B	1D	Shd*	Main	1G	$35

Eagle's Landing   **(714) 336-2642**
Box 1510, Blue Jay, CA 92317
(In San Bernardino Mountains on west shore of lake)

This ingeniously designed home offers all the comfort and charm of a European mountain retreat, with many extra special touches. Finely crafted woodwork, plenty of view windows, and elements of Victorian styling bring to mind a luxury tree house in a romantic alpine setting. Each guest room is unique; all are private, quiet, and tastefully appointed with antiques, art, and handcrafted furnishings. Refreshments are served on a spacious deck or in the Hunt Room by a roaring fire, both with fantastic views of the lake. Breakfast at Eagle's Landing is a memorable event in the "Top of the Tower." Hosts Dorothy and Jack Stone provide unparalleled hospitality and attention to detail. In every respect, Eagle's Landing is a masterpiece.

No pets, children, or smoking; TV in Hunt Room; Room A has private deck; boutique shopping, ice skating, fine dining, and quaint towns of Blue Jay and Arrowhead Village nearby; off-street parking. Also available is a 900-square-foot suite with fireplace, queen bed, TV, stereo, king sofa bed, and expansive lake view at $125. Brochure available.

ROOM	BED	BATH	ENTRANCE	FLOOR	DAILY RATES S - D	(EP)
A	1Q	Pvt	Sep	3	$95	
B	1K	Pvt	Main	3	$75	
C	1K	Pvt	Main	2	$85	

Salisbury House   **(213) 737-7817**
2273 West 20th Street, Los Angeles, CA 90018
(Near Santa Monica Freeway and Western Avenue)

Experience a cozy kind of luxury at Salisbury House, located in the historic West Adams district of Los Angeles. Here you'll find all the amenities of a manor house in the country, yet you'll be only minutes from downtown and major freeways. This turn-of-the-century California Craftsman home is large and sturdy. An expert restoration job has left its original integrity intact. Graciously proportioned rooms are exquisitely furnished with antiques and collectibles. Colors, fabrics, and nostalgia pieces are imaginatively combined to give each room a distinct personality. The total effect is enchanting. The generous breakfasts served here are superb, the hospitality boundless. Hosts Sue and Jay invite you to treat yourself to the many charms of Salisbury House. I can't imagine a more relaxing or romantic intown spot.

No pets; children over ten welcome; no smoking; full breakfast; Room A has a sink; D is the 600-square-foot Attic Suite; E is the Sun Room Suite; ample street parking; major credit cards (V, MC). Inquire about weekly and monthly rates. Brochure available.

ROOM	BED	BATH	ENTRANCE	FLOOR	DAILY RATES S - D	(EP)
A	1Q	Pvt	Main	2	$75	
B	1Q	Shd*	Main	2	$65	
C	1Q	Shd*	Main	2	$65	
D	1K & 1T	Pvt	Main	3	$85	($10)
E	1D & 2T	Pvt	Main	2	$80	($10)

Marilyn & Steve Kalson   **(213) 578-2000**
P.O. Box 10667, Marina del Rey, CA 90295-8823
(Five miles from LAX)

The Kalsons' home is in a residential complex with so many advantages, I hardly know where to start. Chief among them is its location in Marina del Rey, a sparklingly beautiful beach community with enticements at every turn: boating, cycling, skating, fine dining, year-round sunbathing, shopping, and more. The smog and congestion of the city seem worlds away from this beauty spot that claims a nearly perfect climate. The Kalsons, inspired by European bed and breakfast travel, offer guests a quiet, comfortable room with a private bath. Also available for extra people in the same party are one sleeper sofa in a closed-off den and one in the living room. Guests have access to the complex's many options: swimming pools, sauna, health club, tennis courts. You can walk to the ocean or almost anywhere in the neighborhood from the Kalsons', or use the excellent bus service to go where you wish in the L.A. area. When you plan your next trip to Southern California, be good to yourself and include a few days just to relax in gorgeous Marina del Rey.

No pets or smoking; expanded Continental breakfast; kosher kitchen; laundry privileges; inquire about off-street parking and EP rates.

ROOM	BED	BATH	ENTRANCE	FLOOR	DAILY RATES S - D (EP)
A	1K	Pvt	Main	2	$50

Anna's Bed & Breakfast   **(818) 980-6191**
10926 Hamlin Street, North Hollywood, CA 91606
(Two miles north of Hollywood Freeway)

Anyone desiring a quiet little spot convenient to some of L.A.'s main arteries (Ventura, Golden State, and Hollywood Freeways) will be pleased to discover Anna's Bed & Breakfast. It's a neat, Spanish-style bungalow offering one guest room attractively done in shades of blue. Anna's European background and love of travel are apparent in the decor. She enjoys serving breakfast in her delightful backyard garden on pretty days. From Anna's, it's a thirty-minute drive to downtown L.A. and just seven minutes to popular Universal Studios. Nearby Burbank offers a choice of new and noteworthy restaurants. For convenience, value, and homey accommodations, this B&B is a find.

Dog in residence; no children under twelve; no smoking; extra charge for full breakfast; fireplace, TV, VCR in living room; street or off-street parking; German spoken. Inquire about weekly rates.

ROOM	BED	BATH	ENTRANCE	FLOOR	DAILY RATES S - D	(EP)
A	1D	Shd	Main	1	$32-$38	

Sakura, Japanese Bed & Breakfast   (619) 327-0705
P.O. Box 9403, Palm Springs, CA 92263
(Central Palm Springs, a short walk from Palm Canyon Drive)

If you're not able to make it to Japan, do the next best thing. Visit Fumiko and George Cebra's inn in Palm Springs and experience the serene graciousness of the Japanese lifestyle. Here you'll find a Japanese garden for guests, four bedrooms that open onto a beautiful patio with pool and spa, and a striking mountain background. Featured in the rooms are kimonos, futons, bedcovers and draperies designed and made by Fumiko. Refresh yourself in a hot Japanese bath, then don your kimono and slippers and relax as you listen to the delicate music that wafts through the inn. Enjoy a tour movie of Japan or a shiatsu massage and, if you choose, try an authentic Japanese breakfast. If you long for total immersion, join Fumiko (who was born in Hiroshima) and George (a professional musician) on an escorted bed and breakfast tour of Japan. Contact them for details about these moderately priced tours.

No pets or smoking; full Japanese or American breakfast; TV; VCR; AC; futon beds in each room; four rooms share two baths; additional Japanese-style bathing room; swimming pool; spa; shiatsu massage by appointment; off-street parking; airport pickup (Palm Springs). Brochure available.

ROOM	BED	BATH	ENTRANCE	FLOOR	DAILY RATES	
					S - D	(EP)
A	1D	Shd*	Main	1G	$55-$65	
B	1Q & 1D	Shd*	Main	1G	$65-$75	($10)
C	1D	Shd*	Main	1G	$55-$65	
D	2T & 1D	Shd*	Main	1G	$65-$75	($10)

Magnolia House   **(714) 798-6631**
222 South Buena Vista Street, Redlands, CA 92373
(Walking distance to downtown and Redlands Bowl)

Doris and Jim Gentry, formerly of The Lamplighters B&B in Downey, find Redlands much to their liking. Its history, friendliness, cultural orientation, and concentration of genteel Victorian homes give it special appeal. Magnolia House is a three-story Victorian, circa 1902, that looks like a house pictured on a Christmas card. It's in an older residential area on a quiet, magnolia-lined street. Traditional furnishings, selected antiques, and family heirlooms contribute to the nostalgic turn-of-the-century charm. A front bedroom (A) has a Victorian fireplace and a floral motif, while the back bedroom (B) has a bay window seat and a colonial atmosphere. Both are graced with lacy curtains, fresh flowers and fruit, and a decanter of sherry. A generous Continental breakfast (including eggs or meat) is served with a gourmet's touch in the large Victorian dining room. Experience the graciousness of southern hospitality as a guest at Magnolia House.

Dog in residence; no pets; young people over sixteen welcome; smoking outside only; late afternoon refreshments; TV in bedrooms; AC; fireplace in parlor; player piano; off-street parking. Located near Redlands University, Loma Linda University and Hospital, and mountain and desert resorts. Room B shares tub and shower only; Room C is used only for fifth and sixth persons in one party.

ROOM	BED	BATH	ENTRANCE	FLOOR	DAILY RATES S - D (EP)
A	2T	Shd*	Main	2	$40-$45
B	1D	Pvt 1/2	Main	2	$40-$45
C	1D	Pvt	Sep	1	$20-$30

The Cottage   **(619) 299-1564**
P.O. Box 3292, San Diego, CA 92103
(Hillcrest area, near Balboa Park)

   The Hillcrest area is characterized by old homes and canyons, offering an unhurried, isolated atmosphere. Conveniently located on a quiet cul-de-sac, this private cottage (A) recreates the feeling of a Victorian country home. It is furnished with beautiful antiques, including such pieces as an oak pump organ and an old-time coffee grinder that still works. The accommodation includes a living room with a wood-burning stove, a bedroom, a bath, and a fully equipped kitchen; each is uncommonly charming. The Garden Room (B) is a bedroom in the main house with its own entrance and bath. Your hosts, Bob and Carol Emerick, have thought of everything a traveler might need while in residence, and their vast collection of information about the area is yours to peruse (history, architecture, menus, maps, directions, etc.). If ever a place could inspire affection, The Cottage does just that. You may find yourself returning sooner than you think.

   TV; public transportation; inquire about parking; major credit cards. Brochure available.

ROOM	BED	BATH	ENTRANCE	FLOOR	DAILY RATES	
					S - D	(EP)
A	1K & 1T	Pvt	Sep	1	$60	($10)
B	1K	Pvt	Sep	1	$45	

Beverly McGahey   **(619) 279-5435**
6943 Beagle Street, San Diego, CA 92111
(Near Genessee & Balboa in Clairemont district)

Beverly McGahey, an editor and musician, has been known to play chamber music for guests on request. Her piano is an integral part of the house, as is her collection of recorded music. The contemporary home has a fireplace in the living room and glass doors that look out onto a patio and swimming pool. Room A may be used by one party or combined with B to accommodate up to four people with a private bath. Room C is a self-contained unit offering extra privacy and space. Beverly takes a flexible, friendly approach in helping people make arrangements for a visit to San Diego that strikes all the right notes.

No pets or smoking; TV; running trails, golf courses, and free tennis courts nearby; ample street parking. Room C has a kitchenette, a single sofa bed in addition to the double bed, a crib (if needed), and a TV. Two-night minimum. ****KNIGHTTIME PUBLICATIONS SPECIAL RATE: 10% discount with this book.**

ROOM	BED	BATH	ENTRANCE	FLOOR	DAILY RATES	
					S - D	(EP)
A	1D	Pvt	Main	1G	$40-$45	
B	1D	Main	1G		$25	
C	1D	Pvt	Sep	1G	$55	

Bed & Breakfast in Mission Valley   **(619) 283-5146**
Box 100, 4102 - 30th Street, San Diego, CA 92104
(Above Hotel Circle)

You couldn't ask for a more central location than this Mission Valley home; the main attractions of San Diego are only minutes away. Lee Grace could write a book on the fine points of gracious hospitality. Her guests always come away with high praise for the cuisine, amenities, and comfortable lodgings at her B&B. The lower level of the house (a bedroom, bath, and sitting room) can accommodate up to four people and offers extra privacy. Add to all this an outstanding view of Mission Bay from the main floor, and you have an unbeatable combination.

No pets or RV parking; children over eight welcome; afternoon refreshments; TV; laundry privileges; sitting room has queen-sized sofa bed; charge is $55 if both beds are used; $60 for four people; inquire about parking.

ROOM	BED	BATH	ENTRANCE	FLOOR	DAILY RATES S - D (EP)
A	1Q	Pvt	Main	LL	$35-$45 ($10)

Ocean View House   **(805) 966-6659**
P.O. Box 20065, Santa Barbara, CA 93102
(Three blocks from the ocean)

Bill and Carolyn Canfield offer guests an attractive private suite in their home. It has a bedroom, a bath, and an adjoining paneled den with a sofa bed. Interesting books and collections may be perused at your leisure. A generous Continental breakfast featuring fruit from backyard trees is served on the patio, a good vantage point for viewing sailboats and the Channel Islands with a background of vivid blue. Close by are beaches and lovely Shoreline Drive, a popular place for joggers, skaters, cyclists, and sightseers. The harbor and downtown Santa Barbara are within three miles. The playhouse in the back yard is a big favorite with children. If you need a relaxing spot that the whole family can appreciate, Ocean View House has all the necessary ingredients.

Dog and cat in residence; smoking on patio preferred; two TVs; refrigerator; ample street parking. Two-night minimum.

ROOM	BED	BATH	ENTRANCE	FLOOR	DAILY RATES
					S - D (EP)
A	1Q	Pvt	Sep	1G	$45-$50 ($10)

Valli's View (805) 969-1272
340 North Sierra Vista, Montecito, CA 93108
(Foothills of Montecito)

Valerie Stevens has fashioned the house of her dreams in a gorgeous spot. She has reason to be proud: Valli's View is a beauty inside and out. Its ambiance of tranquility and comfort will soothe even the most frazzled nerves. There's a variety of places to relax outdoors — a spacious patio with lounge chairs, a porch swing, or a deck with a view of the mountains. In the evening, it's a pleasure to sit in the living room around the grand piano and fireplace. Guest quarters are at the far end of the house, affording added privacy. Soft-colored fabrics and rich carpeting enhance the charming decor. Valerie offers a choice of tempting breakfasts (using seasonal fruits and vegetables from the garden) which she'll serve to you in bed, on the patio, or by the fireplace. As guest at Valli's View, you'll feel that your every need has been anticipated — a satisfying experience indeed.

No indoor pets or smoking; full breakfast; TV; off-street parking; train or airport pickup (Santa Barbara). Seventh consecutive night free.

ROOM	BED	BATH	ENTRANCE	FLOOR	DAILY RATES S - D	(EP)
A	1D	Pvt	Main	1G	$50	($10)
B	1Q	Pvt	Main	1G	$60	($10)

Mary & George Hendrick   **(818) 919-2125**
2124 East Merced Avenue, West Covina, CA 91791
(Between Freeways 60 and 10, Azusa Exit)

The Hendricks' home in West Covina will give you a real taste of the California lifestyle. The large, rambling house was once photographed inside and out by *Life* magazine. It has a gorgeous deck area with a swimming pool, a separate Jacuzzi, and good outdoor furniture. The master suite (D), a guest room with rainbow motif (B), and one of the living rooms face the deck. There's plenty of space to relax here, and the Hendricks' laid-back style will put you at ease. Genial conversationalists and inveterate travelers, Mary and George can provide all manner of help to people unfamiliar with the area. They'll direct you to special undiscovered spots or to the more popular attractions. Their home is centrally located for visiting Disneyland, L.A., mountains, and desert. If you don't catch some of the California spirit at the Hendricks', consider yourself immune.

No pets; school-age children welcome; refreshments; TV; AC; two living rooms with fireplaces; swimming pool; Jacuzzi; extra meals optional (rave reviews from guests!); good airport connections; off-street parking. Suite (D) only available for stays of three days or longer. A beach home at Ensenada and a cottage on Prudence Island, Rhode Island available for rental or B&B; inquiries welcome.

ROOM	BED	BATH	ENTRANCE	FLOOR	DAILY RATES S - D (EP)
A	2T	Shd*	Main	1G	$40
B	1D	Shd*	Main	1G	$35
C	1T	Shd*	Main	1G	$30
D	1K	Pvt	Main	1G	$50

Coleen's California Casa (213) 699-8427
P.O. Box 9302, Whittier, CA 90608
(Thirty minutes east of downtown L.A.)

Staying at Coleen Davis's contemporary hillside home is one pleasant surprise after another. Park in front, then make your way through the lush foliage to the back where you'll find a delightful patio/garden and the entrance to the private guest quarters. After settling into your comfortable suite, join Coleen on the patio for wine and hors d'oeuvres. After dark you can view the lights of Whittier, and maybe the fireworks of Disneyland, from the large front deck (pictured) where ample breakfast specialties are served. If you're inclined to watch TV, write, or read in bed, the adjustable king-sized bed in Room A will please you. The Casa is a quiet retreat where families can share a private space and get all the help they need to plan a day's adventure in the booming L.A. area. You may even wind up with a little memento from Coleen to remind you of your wonderful visit; she's great with surprises.

No pets; families welcome; full breakfast; TV and robes in each room; refrigerator and microwave available; off-street parking; wheelchair access. If Rooms A and B are used as a suite, rate is $75. Room C is a room off the front deck with king-sized bed and adjoining sitting room with sofa bed; if used as a suite, rate is $75. Host also operates a B&B reservation service called CO-Host, America's Bed & Breakfast; she can help you with reservations throughout California.

ROOM	BED	BATH	ENTRANCE	FLOOR	DAILY RATES	
					S - D	(EP)
A	1K	Pvt	Sep	1G	$55	($15)
B	2T	Pvt	Sep	1G	$55	
C	1K	Pvt	Sep	1G	$55	

Please read "About Dining Highlights" on page *ix.*

ANAHEIM

Gustav's, 2525 East Ball Road; (714) 520-9500; German

The White House Restaurant, 887 South Anaheim Boulevard; (714) 772-1381; Italian with touch of French

BEVERLY HILLS

California Pizza Kitchen, 207 South Beverly Drive; (213) 272-7878; barbecued chicken, calzone, pizza

Chez Helene, 267 South Beverly Drive; (213) 276-1558; country French

The Grill, 9560 Dayton Way; (213) 276-0615; American

BLUE JAY

The Royal Oak, 7187 Highway 189; (714) 337-6018; Continental

CEDAR GLEN

Lilly's by the Lake, Hook Creek Road; (714) 336-3619; Continental

ENCINITAS

Piret M Bistro Gallery, The Lumberyard, 897 First Street; (619) 942-5146; French

ESCONDIDO

Bamboo House, 320 North Midway Drive; (619) 480-9550; Chinese

LA JOLLA

George's at the Cove, 1250 Prospect Place; (619) 454-4244; creative regional cuisine, specializing in fish

Piret's, La Jolla Village Square, 8697 La Jolla Village Drive; (619) 455-7955; French

LOS ANGELES

Anna Maria Ristorante Italiano, 1356 South La Brea Avenue; (213) 935-2089 or 659-6497; neighborhood Italian

California Pizza Kitchen, 330 South Oak, Wells Fargo Center; (213) 626-2616; barbecued chicken, calzone, pizza

Delmonico's, 9320 West Pico Boulevard; (213) 550-7737; seafood

El Cholo, 1121 South Western Avenue; (213) 734-2773; Mexican

Edward's Steak House, 733 South Alvarado Street; (213) 385-0051

Engine Company Number 28, 644 South Figueroa Street; (213) 624-6996; American

Gill's Cuisine of India, Stillwell Hotel, 838 South Grand Avenue; (213) 623-1050

The Grill, 9560 Dayton Way; (213) 276-0615; American

Ho Ban Restaurant, 1040 South Western Avenue; (213) 737-9051; Korean

House of Chandara, 310 North Larchmont; (213) 467-1052; Thai

Katsu, 1972 North Hillhurst Avenue; (213) 665-1891; Japanese

La Bella Cucina, 949 South Figueroa Street; (213) 623-0014; Italian

L.A. Nicola, 4326 Sunset Boulevard; (213) 660-7217; American regional

Le Chardonnay, 8284 Melrose Avenue; (213) 655-8880; French

Mon Kee, 679 North Spring Street; (213) 628-6717; Chinese seafood

Salisbury Manor, 1190 West Adams Boulevard; (213) 749-0573; California influenced old-fashioned home cooking

Trattoria Angeli, 11651 Santa Monica Boulevard; (213) 478-1191; Italian

PALM DESERT

Cedar Creek Inn, 73-445 El Paseo; (619) 340-1236; American

Midori Japanese Restaurant, 73-759 Highway 111 at San Luis Rey; (619) 340-1466

Tanpopo Japanese Country Inn, 72-221 Highway 111; (619) 340-1901

PALM SPRINGS

Bono, 1700 North Indian Avenue; (619) 322-6200; southern Italian

Frying Fish, 123 North Palm Canyon Drive, Suite 433, Desert Fashion Plaza; (619) 322-2356; Japanese seafood and sushi bar

Las Casuelas Terraza, 222 South Palm Canyon Drive; (619) 325-2794; Mexican

REDLANDS

Vesuvio Ristorante, 1687 West Redlands Boulevard; (714) 792-9399; northern Italian

SAN DIEGO

Busalacchi's Ristorante, 3683 Fifth Avenue; (619) 298-0119; traditional Sicilian cooking

California Café Bar & Grill, Horton Plaza; (619) 238-5440; California/American cuisine

Calliope's Greek Café, 3958 Fifth Avenue (619) 291-5588

Celadon, a Thai Restaurant, 3628 Fifth Avenue; (619) 295-8800

Cilantros, 3702 Via de la Valle; (619) 259-8777; Mexican/southwest

City Delicatessen, 535 University Avenue; (619) 295-2747; Jewish/American

The French Side of the West, 2202 Fourth Avenue; (619) 234-5540; French

La Gran Tapa, 611 "B" Street; (619) 234-8272; Spanish

SANTA BARBARA

Cold Spring Tavern, 5995 Stagecoach Road; (805) 967-0066; American

The Epicurean Restaurant, 125 East Carrillo; (805) 966-4789; Continental

La Super-Rica, 622 North Milpas Street; (805) 963-4940; tacos

Mousse Odile, 18 East Cota; (805) 962-5393; French

Presidio Café, 812 Anacapa Street; (805) 966-2428; Continental

WHITTIER

El Patio Mexican Restaurant, 6511 South Greenleaf Avenue; (213) 945-1204

Los Portales Mexican Restaurant, 13033 Philadelphia; (213) 698-2236

Seafood Bay, 13421 Whittier Boulevard; (213) 698-5116

Oregon

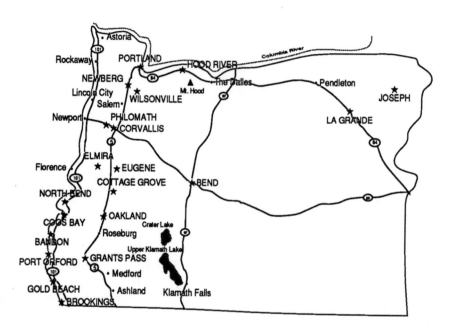

From silken beaches to icy peaks to high desert plateaus to crumbled lava fields, Oregon is a state rich in contrasts. To travel Oregon is to experience both the delicate beauty and the astonishing power of nature.

Brookings, at the southern end of the Coastal Highway, offers the delicate side, with year-round flowers and an unusually mild climate. The thirty-two mile drive north on Highway 101 to Gold Beach will introduce you to the dramatic confrontation of ocean, beach, and forest reaching eastward to the looming Coast Range mountains, which rose gradually in a series of thunderous, continuous volcanic eruptions some forty million years ago.

Oregon's coastline is by law "forever free," which means noncommercial and open to the public. There is a state park every five miles or so. In addition to spectacular scenery, fishing is the main attraction. Try fishing from the rocks, or rent a crab pot at one of the small seaside towns for some luscious Dungeness crab.

Gold Beach, at the mouth of the renowned Rogue River, is a favorite spot for the spring and fall runs of Chinook salmon and steelhead trout. Adventurous souls may wish to take a jet boat excursion through the Rogue's whitewater rapids.

After passing through Port Orford, with its natural deepwater port, and perhaps attending the mid-July Music Festival in Coos Bay, you will be greeted by some of the world's most spectacular coastal dunes. The sand hills of the Oregon Dunes Recreation Area, drifting and sometimes rising hundreds of feet above the water, reach north to the rhododendron city of Florence. At Reedsport, the waters of the Umpqua and Smith Rivers enter Winchester Bay and flow to the ocean, causing the only obvious break in the forty-five mile stretch of dunes.

North of Florence, Highway 101 returns to hugging the shoreline, through Newport to Lincoln City, at times riding the tan shoulders of mountains that tower above the ocean and then down to glorious beaches — some are as long as ten miles, with jagged rocks dotting the surf, spindrift blowing up from the restless waves, and cypress trees clutching at the wind with their tentacle-like branches.

At Cloverdale, you may want to turn west toward one of the state's best surfing beaches, Pacific City. Before entering the surf, ponder: You are standing at the edge of the longest unimpeded expanse of ocean on earth. Neither islands nor reefs stand between Oregon and the beaches of Japan, more than 5,000 miles away.

Roughly paralleling the coast, from its midpoint north, is Oregon's lush heartland, the Willamette Valley. The Eugene-Springfield area occupies its southerly pocket, only sixty miles from the coast.

Eugene, cradled in natural beauty, has all the advantages of a city — museums, shops, cultural and entertainment opportunities, and a major university — yet is also the gateway to unlimited outdoor recreation. Just a few miles to the west, near Elmira, the Fern River Reservoir invites boating, fishing, and swimming. To the east is the McKenzie River, famous for its scenery and watersports like kayaking.

The Willamatte River flows right through the center of Portland, where it joins the mighty Columbia, creating a waterfront setting for the city's skyline of modern glass, complemented by historic brick buildings, many parks, and majestic mountain vistas.

Sixty-two miles east of Portland is the famous Columbia Gorge and towering Mount Hood, the only peak in America to offer year-round downhill skiing. With its gentle southern slope, Mount Hood is the most climbed peak in the nation.

After skiing the slopes of Mount Hood, one can drop to its base and learn the art of skimming the waters of the Columbia near Hood River on a sailboard. Or, for the pro, participate in the annual sailboarding meet, fast becoming an international event. For the less adventurous, stand in awe of some of the Gorge's sparkling waterfalls plunging over huge cliffs formed by the Columbia as it cuts its path through the Cascade Mountain Range, the stony and spectacular backbone of the state.

Further east on Interstate 84, you may wish to experience one of the west's most famous rodeos, the Pendleton Round-Up, held in September each year. Or, in contrast, visit charming LaGrande, named in honor of the beauty surrounding it — the Grande Ronde Valley and the Blue Mountains.

Joseph, a secluded town not far from the Idaho border, is tucked near Wallowa Lake and is the gateway to Hells Canyon National Recreation Area and day-long horse pack trips into the High Wallowas.

The town of Bend, on Highway 97 in central Oregon, is surrounded by recreation areas. One of the loveliest is Drake Park, situated along the Deschutes River and known for its abundant waterfowl.

Some 100 miles south of Bend is Crater Lake National Park, a major volcanic attraction, high in the southern Cascades. The lake is the deepest in the United States; it was formed when Mount Mazama blew its top over 6,000 years ago and collapsed into its own crater, forming a caldern six miles across. The exceptionally clear and brilliant water, looking like melted sapphires, is the result of accumulated snowmelt.

Rushing rivers, rugged peaks, cold blue lakes, stark and lovely deserts, unspoiled beaches...and the peace and quiet in which to enjoy it — some people say Oregon has it all.

Lighthouse Bed & Breakfast   (503) 347-9316
P.O. Box 24, Bandon, OR 97411
(650 Jetty Road)

The contemporary wood home of Linda and Bruce Sisson overlooks Bandon's historic lighthouse and the point where the Coquille River meets the Pacific Ocean. Plant-bedecked rooms are spacious, bright, and comfortable. One (A) offers spectacular sunset views; another (B) has a unique greenhouse bath with a whirlpool tub for two. Park your car for a while and explore the Old Town shopping area on foot. Walk to the beach and join the folks out fishing, crabbing, or clamming; take an easy stroll to one of the fine seafood restaurants close by. The Sissons will be happy to enjoy your company, offer suggestions for making the most of your time in Bandon, or provide you with all the relaxing privacy you need. Your contentment is their aspiration.

Toy poodle in residence; no pets; children over ten welcome; smoking outside only (deck); full breakfast; off-street parking; major credit cards (V, MC); airport pickup (Bandon). Apartment with one or two bedrooms and kitchen available November-February by advance reservation; call for rates. Brochure available.

ROOM	BED	BATH	ENTRANCE	FLOOR	DAILY RATES		
					S - D		(EP)
A	1Q	Pvt	Main	2	$60-$70		($15)
B	1K	Pvt	Main	2	$65-$75		($15)
C	1Q	Pvt	Main	2	$60-$70		($15)
D	1Q	Pvt	Main	2	$55-$65		($15)

Lara House Bed & Breakfast   **(503) 388-4064**
640 NW Congress, Bend, OR 97701
(Downtown Bend, overlooking Drake Park)

Crisp, clean air, sunny skies, and the dramatic beauty of the high desert plateau converging with the eastern slope of the Cascades lure many an adventurous soul to Bend. Hiking in Deschutes National Forest, fishing in mountain streams and lakes, rafting down the Deschutes River, and skiing Mount Bachelor are popular here. So is historic Lara House, located in Bend's most beautiful older intown neighborhood. On a corner wooded lot overlooking spectacular Drake Park, Lara House is large and sturdy, with a wide front porch and a stone foundation. The decor in each of its four spacious guest rooms tastefully conveys some aspect of the local area. On the main floor, a formal dining room and a living room with a big brick fireplace have coffered ceilings and lots of impressive woodwork. An inviting solarium overlooks yard and park, and on the floor below, a sauna and hot tub offer solace after an active day in Bend.

No pets; smoking outside only; full breakfast; TV in living room; rollaway bed available; good restaurants within walking distance; on main route to Mount Bachelor; whitewater rafting trips arranged, discounted for guests; off-street parking; major credit cards (V, MC). Brochure available.

ROOM	BED	BATH	ENTRANCE	FLOOR	DAILY RATES	
					S - D	(EP)
A	1Q	Pvt	Main	2	$50-$60	($10)
B	1Q	Pvt	Main	2	$50 $60	($10)
C	1Q	Pvt	Main	2	$50-$60	($10)
D	1Q	Pvt	Main	2	$50-$60	($10)

Mirror Pond House   (503) 389-1680
1054 NW Harmon Boulevard, Bend, OR 97701
(Overlooking Mirror Pond and Drake Park)

Inside and out, Beryl Kellum's Cape Cod-style home is impressive enough in its own right. It's been thoroughly refurbished in every detail to create the ultimate in refined comfort. Yet no aspect of the decor, however fine, takes precedence over the scene that greets you as you enter through the front door: Giant picture windows across the back of the house reveal an expanse of unparalleled natural beauty. The house is twenty feet from the edge of Mirror Pond, a wildlife preserve inhabited by a variety of waterfowl, including two trumpeter swans. Other creatures such as otter or mink drop by occasionally. Enjoy the pond in your own way: feed the ducks, paddle the house canoe, or sit on the deck and let the magical scene transport you. Inside, two deluxe guest suites offer all you could want in the way of comfort and appeal; the larger one on the second floor overlooks the pond. Guests at Mirror Pond House are treated with the gracious care befitting such a marvelous setting.

No pets; children twelve and over welcome; smoking restricted as required by guests; hors d'oeuvres and wine in late afternoon; full breakfast; fireplace and TV in living room; beds in Suite A extra long; queen bed in Suite B is sofa bed in sitting room; extensive mountain and river recreation in area; off-street parking. Brochure available.

ROOM	BED	BATH	ENTRANCE	FLOOR	DAILY RATES S - D	(EP)
A	2T or 1Q	Pvt	Main	1	$60	
B	1K & 1Q	Pvt	Main	2	$80	($15)

The Chetco River Inn   (503) 469-2114, **Radio phone Ext. 4628**
21202 High Prairie Road, Brookings, OR 97415   (Be persistent!)
(Sixteen miles up North Bank Road)

Here's a destination spot that's as out-of-the-ordinary as it is out-of-the-way. Worldly concerns seem to melt away as you drive through pristine countryside following the Chetco River — sparklingly clear and powerfully inviting. In a remote setting on the river bank, Clay, Sandra, and Dan Brugger welcome guests to their new, lodge-type inn. It has modern lines, a spacious interior, and a rustic, old-world flavor. Shiny marble floors, Oriental rugs, and fine traditional furnishings grace the large, open living area. On one end, a wood-burning stove is backed by a wall of native stone; on the other end, there's an open kitchen and dining area where country breakfasts and memorable five-course dinners are served. Two of the guest bedrooms have enchanting river views, crisp white walls, elegant brass beds, and delightful memorabilia in the form of old decoys and photography equipment. Whether you're contemplating the river from a secluded park bench, taking a hike or a swim, angling for steelhead, or just curling up with a good book, an uncommonly relaxing escape awaits you at The Chetco River Inn.

Dog and cat in residence; no pets; older children welcome; smoking outside only (porch); full breakfast; robes provided; dinner with advance notice; picnic lunches available; satellite TV and movies; library; games; fishing and hunting packages available; off-street parking; major credit cards (V, MC). Reservations also through Pelican Bay Travel: 1-800-327-2688. Brochure available.

ROOM	BED	BATH	ENTRANCE	FLOOR	DAILY RATES	
					S - D	(EP)
A	2T	Shd*	Main	2	$50-$60	
B	1Q	Shd*	Main	2	$50-$60	
C	1Q	Pvt	Main	2	$75	

Holmes Sea Cove Bed & Breakfast   (503) 469-3025
7350 Holmes Drive, Brookings, OR 97415
(North side of Brookings overlooking Pacific)

Many a guest has been reluctant to leave Holmes Sea Cove Bed & Breakfast. Who would willingly give up the comfort of a private paradise with a heavenly view of the rugged Oregon coast? Each of three guest accommodations has its own entrance, bath, refrigerator, and color TV. One is a large room with a sitting area, another a large suite, and the third a separate cottage. All have excellent views, but the one from the cottage is panoramic. Hosts Jack and Lorene Holmes know how to make you feel welcome and then leave you alone to savor a total escape. They deliver breakfast to your doorstep in the morning and invite you to make full use of the gazebo overlooking the ocean, the benches and picnic tables, and the pathway leading to the beach. Landscaped grounds and gardens round out a truly perfect setting for making memories with that special someone.

No pets; children limited; smoking outside only; no RV parking; sofa bed in each room; off-street parking; airport pickup (Sierra Pacific); major credit cards (V, MC). Brochure available.

ROOM	BED	BATH	ENTRANCE	FLOOR	DAILY RATES	
					S - D	(EP)
A	1Q	Pvt	Sep	LL	$75	($10)
B	1Q	Pvt	Sep	LL	$80	($10)
C	1Q	Pvt	Sep	1	$85	($10)

Sea Dreamer Bed & Breakfast   **(503) 469-6629**
P.O. Box 1840, Brookings, OR 97415
(Three miles north of California border, just off U.S. 101)

Judy and Bob Blair named the Sea Dreamer after their sailboat, a thirty-foot Bahama Islander docked at the Port of Brookings. Not surprisingly, there's a nautical theme to their home and, best of all, a gorgeous view past lily fields down to the wide open sea. Built in 1912 of redwood, the two-story, blue home is set on spacious grounds of lawn, trees, and flowers. There are four tastefully appointed guest rooms, three with ocean views. Refreshments are served in the living room around sunset time, and a fire is lit in the hearth whenever a chill sets in. As the Blairs can tell you, there is no shortage of things to do along this stretch of coastline. Let the Sea Dreamer add a touch of romance to your seaside vacation.

No pets, children, or smoking; full breakfast; off-street parking. Brochure available.

ROOM	BED	BATH	ENTRANCE	FLOOR	DAILY RATES S - D	(EP)
A	1D	Pvt	Main	1	$50-$55	
B	1Q	Pvt	Main	2	$55-$60	
C	1Q	Shd*	Main	2	$45-$50	
D	2T	Shd*	Main	2	$45-$50	

This Olde House   **(503) 267-5224**
202 Alder Street, Coos Bay, OR 97420
(Just off U.S. 101 at North Second Street)

This stately house on the hill is every inch a lady. She is pale blue trimmed in white, with all her grandeur still intact. Ed and Jean Mosieur moved from Monterey to Coos Bay, trading one coastal location for another. Things are calmer in Coos Bay, slower paced. Renovations and furnishings have made the Mosieurs' new old home a gracious, inviting place for guests to enjoy a special brand of hospitality. There are four generously proportioned guest rooms, three with a bay view and one with a canopied bed. A short drive takes you to one of my favorite parts of the Oregon coast, the fishing village of Charleston (great for buying fresh and smoked fish) and three adjacent state parks that are worth a special trip: Sunset Bay, Shore Acres, and Cape Arago. Ed, Jean, and Brice are sure to make your stop in Coos Bay a memorable one.

No pets or smoking; no children under forty-three (a bit of Jean's humor); ample street parking.

ROOM	BED	BATH	ENTRANCE	FLOOR	DAILY RATES	
					S - D	(EP)
A	1K	Pvt	Main	2	$60	($10)
B	1K	Shd*	Main	2	$50	($10)
C	1D	Shd*	Main	2	$50	($10)
D	1Q	Shd*	Main	2	$50	($10)

Hillcrest Dairy Bed & Breakfast   (503) 942-0205
79385 Sears Road, Cottage Grove, OR 97424
(Northeast Cottage Grove, Saginaw Exit from I-5)

Here's an opportunity to experience Dutch hospitality on a working dairy farm. Mike and Grace Eisenga bring a bit of the old country to their style of bed and breakfast. Accommodations are immaculate, the breakfasts large and nourishing. The comfortable ranch-style home has common rooms where guests may feel free to play games, read, or use the pool table. There are large and small bicycles available for exploring the beautiful area surrounding the farm. They're great for viewing wildlife such as deer, elk, and birds. If the workings of a dairy farm interest you, witness them firsthand as Mike goes about his daily routine. A visit to Hillcrest Dairy will add a pleasant change of pace to your trip.

No pets; infants and children over six welcome; smoking outside only; full breakfast; single cot extra in Room C; off-street parking; bicycles available.

ROOM	BED	BATH	ENTRANCE	FLOOR	DAILY RATES	
					S - D	(EP)
A	1Q	Shd*	Main	1	$30-$40	($10)
B	1D	Shd*	Main	1	$30-$35	
C	2T	Shd*	Main	1	$30-$35	($10)

McGillivrays' Log Home Bed & Breakfast   **(503) 935-3564**
88680 Evers Road, Elmira, OR 97437
(Off Highway 126, fourteen miles west of Eugene enroute to the coast)

The McGillivrays' unique, built-from-scratch log home is well-suited to its environment: five acres mostly covered with pine and fir trees. Much care and hard work went into the construction of the home, which combines the best of the past with the comforts of today. Throughout the interior, there is handcrafted woodwork displaying a variety of different woods. One guest room (A) with private bath is on the ground floor. An impressive stairway of half-logs leads to a balcony which overlooks the living and dining areas. Doors lead from the balcony to a spacious bedroom (B) with a bath and a small deck. Old-fashioned breakfasts are usually prepared on the antique, wood-burning cookstove in the dining room, a good place to linger over coffee and plan your day. Many people are understandably quite taken with the McGillivrays' log home, but I think a child guest summed it up best when he asked them, "You mean you get to live here *all* the time?"

No pets; families welcome; smoking on covered porches only; TV; AC; extra beds; crib; winery touring and tasting nearby (Forgeron Vineyards); outdoor recreation at Fern Ridge Reservoir; off-street parking; wheelchair access; major credit cards (V, MC); airport pickup (Mahlon Sweet).

ROOM	BED	BATH	ENTRANCE	FLOOR	DAILY RATES	
					S - D	(EP)
A	1K	Pvt	Main	1G	$40-$50	
B	1K	Pvt	Main	2	$50-$60	

The House in the Woods   **(503) 343-3234**
814 Lorane Highway, Eugene, OR 97405
(SW Eugene, South Hills area)

The Lorane Highway is a thoroughfare for joggers and cyclists and a convenient route to downtown Eugene, three miles away. The House in the Woods is set back from the road, with a periphery of fir and oak trees, an abundance of azaleas and rhododendrons, and some formally landscaped open areas. Friendly wildlife still abounds on the two acres. Long-time residents Eunice and George Kjaer have restored their 1910 home to its original quiet elegance. There are hardwood floors with Oriental carpets, high ceilings, lots of windows, and three covered porches (one with a swing). A large, comfortable parlor is most pleasant for visiting, listening to music, or reading by the fireplace. Guest rooms are spacious and tastefully decorated. Parks, cultural events, outdoor recreation, and good restaurants can be pointed out by your versatile hosts, but the house and grounds are so peaceful and relaxing that you may be compelled to stay put.

No pets; children over twelve welcome; smoking on outside covered areas; full breakfast (Continental style for late risers); TV; piano; music library; off-street parking; airport pickup (Mahlon Sweet). Additional bedroom with twin bed and shared bath at $38 is available as an alternate choice; winter rates. Brochure available.

ROOM	BED	BATH	ENTRANCE	FLOOR	DAILY RATES S - D (EP)
A	1Q	Pvt	Main	1	$38-$55
B	1D	Shd	Main	2	$35-$50

Wheeler's Bed & Breakfast   **(503) 344-1366**
P.O. Box 8201, Coburg, OR 97401
(Off I-5, seven miles north of Eugene)

    The beautiful Cascades surround this fertile valley where the McKenzie and the Willamette Rivers meet. Whether you're just passing through or staying long enough to explore a bit, Joe and Isabel Wheeler will be happy to share their comfortable home with you. Joe built the house himself, and B&B guests are sure to find it as liveable as he and Isabel do. They offer two spacious, carpeted bedrooms upstairs which are separate enough from the rest of the house to assure complete privacy. Coburg is a unique little farming community; its antique stores and century-old homes are just a short walk from the Wheelers' home. Picturesque surroundings, a taste of history, and a gracious welcome await you at Wheeler's B&B.

    Full breakfast; TV; living room for guests; off-street parking; major credit cards; airport pickup (Mahlon Sweet). Brochure available.

ROOM	BED	BATH	ENTRANCE	FLOOR	DAILY RATES	
					S - D	(EP)
A	2T	Shd*	Main	2	$34-$39	
B	1Q	Shd*	Main	2	$34-$39	

Endicott Gardens   **(503) 247-6513**
95768 Jerrys Flat Road, Gold Beach, OR 97444
(Four miles east of U.S. 101)

Endicott Gardens is the setting for a small nursery and the home of Stewart and Mary Endicott, who have been joined in hosting by their children, Patrick and Beverly. Bed and breakfast accommodations were constructed in a separate wing of the house, consisting of four bedrooms with private baths. Rooms C and D open onto a deck that is blessed with a view of the forest and mountains. As one might imagine, the grounds are spectacular with flowers and shrubs. Breakfast on the deck is a delight, but in cool weather Mary presents hearty morning fare in the dining room while the nearby fireplace crackles and warms. Guests are provided with some thoughtful amenities, and the cordial climate set by your hosts is spiced with humor. Endicott Gardens offers the traveler all this, plus a chance to unwind in a quiet, natural environment.

No pets; full breakfast; TV available; Rogue River, ocean, and forest recreation nearby; off-street parking; airport pickup (Gold Beach). Brochure available.

ROOM	BED	BATH	ENTRANCE	FLOOR	DAILY RATES S - D (EP)	
A	1Q & 1T	Pvt	Sep	1G	$35-$45	($10)
B	1Q	Pvt	Sep	1G	$35-$45	($10)
C	1Q	Pvt	Sep	1G	$35-$45	($10)
D	1Q	Pvt	Sep	1G	$35-$45	($10)

The Handmaidens' Inn   **(503) 476-2932**
230 Red Spur Drive, Grants Pass, OR 97527
(Five miles south of Grants Pass)

This magnificent home is ideally matched to its magnificent setting among shady oaks overlooking the scenic Rogue River Valley. The ten-room cedar house offers incredible views from all windows and decks, while the interior is beautifully appointed with country furnishings and handcrafted accessories. Bette and Jody Hammer do everything first class, and their guests reap the benefits of their homemaking skills. The expertly prepared breakfasts are something to write home about, as are the multiple amenities that make staying here an extraordinary treat. One of the three lovely guest rooms (A) is quite large and features a king-sized bed, vaulted cedar ceiling, private balcony, and bath. At The Handmaidens' Inn, there's one thing you can count on — excellence, in every respect.

Cat in residence; no pets; no children under twelve; smoking outside only; full breakfast; afternoon snacks; TV; VCR and fireplace in family room; AC; deck with hot tub; off-street parking; major credit cards (V, MC, AE); airport pickup (Jackson County).
**KNIGHTTIME PUBLICATIONS SPECIAL RATE: 10% discount with this book. Brochure available.

ROOM	BED	BATH	ENTRANCE	FLOOR	DAILY RATES	
					S - D	(EP)
A	1K	Pvt	Main	2	$65	
B	1K	Shd	Main	2	$50	
C	2T	Shd	Main	2	$45	

Lawnridge House　　　　　　　　　　　　　　(503) 479-5186
1304 NW Lawnridge, Grants Pass, OR 97526
(One-half mile from I-5, Exit 58)

Lawnridge is a tranquil, tree-lined street in a neighborhood of lovely older homes. Set on a shaded corner lot, Lawnridge House looks friendly and inviting. It has been recently restored with exquisite care. The tasteful interior is enhanced by coffered ceilings, lustrous woodwork and floors, and comfortable antique furnishings. Guest rooms are especially attractive. Room A has its own sitting room and balcony. Room B is ideal for honeymooners or other romantics; it has a handcrafted wooden tester bed with a candlewicking comforter and curtains. There are shady, secluded porches and a small orchard in back. The overall effect is gracious and serene. Host Barbara Head features fresh salmon steaks with breakfast, an example of the impeccable quality you'll find at Lawnridge House.

No pets or RV parking; smoking outside only; full breakfast; TV; VCR; AC; porches; bath for Room A is usually private, but is occasionally shared during summer season; host suggests day trips to Crater Lake, the Oregon coast, Ashland, Jacksonville, Wolf Creek Tavern, Rogue River activities, Oregon Caves, wineries, ghost towns, and the Britt Music and Dance Festivals; Spanish, French, and German spoken; off-street parking; airport pickup (Josephine County, Medford). Off-season rates mid-October to mid-May. Brochure available.

ROOM	BED	BATH	ENTRANCE	FLOOR	DAILY RATES
					S - D　(EP)
A	1Q	Pvt	Main	2	$50
B	1K	Pvt	Main	2	$65

Riverbanks Inn (503) 479-1118
8401 Riverbanks Road, Grants Pass, OR 97527
(Northwest of town on bank of Rogue River)

Riverbanks Inn, situated on twelve acres along the scenic Rogue, is as multifaceted as its owner, Myrtle Franklin. The secluded retreat is a rich tapestry woven from the strands of her life — careers, talents, and travels. She lives in an artist's studio on the premises. The completely refurbished main house is generously endowed with view windows and natural materials, and comfortable seating abounds. Two rooms on the lower level evoke two distinct moods: The Jean Harlow (A), a sort of Floridian art deco glamour; The Casablanca (B), exotic romance. Other accommodations include two rooms in an early Oregon river house (C & D) where co-host Faye Hill resides, and a self-contained log cabin (E), both with fireplaces and country comfort. Riverbanks Inn offers a range of options few places can match. Come share in its wealth.

No pets; children by arrangement; smoking outside only; full country breakfast; evening snacks; TV; VCR; fireplace, refrigerator in B and E; robes provided; all beds extra long; outdoor hot tub; indoor Jacuzzi; steam and exercise rooms; massage by appointment; Zen meditation house; swimming and fishing pond; children's playhouse; River Lodge on property for families or fishing groups; seminars, group retreats welcome; river fishing and rafting; bird walks; off-street parking; major credit cards (V, MC). Brochure available.

ROOM	BED	BATH	ENTRANCE	FLOOR	DAILY RATES S - D	(EP)
A	1K or 2T	Pvt	Sep	LL	$75-$85	
B	1Q	Pvt	Sep	LL	$85-$95	
C	1D	Shd*	Main	1	$45-$55	
D	1D	Shd*	Main	1	$45-$55	
E	1D & 1T	Pvt	Sep	1	$75-$85	($30)

Hackett House   (503) 386-1014
922 State Street, Hood River, OR 97031
(One block above Oak Street at Tenth)

 The Columbia River Gorge area around Hood River has become a mecca for windsurfers, hikers, and skiers alike. Spring blossoms bring festivals in one community after another. Visitors enjoying the many outdoor attractions could do no better than making Hackett House their comfortable home base. The handsome 1903 blue Dutch colonial stands at the corner of State and Tenth Streets, near enough to walk to the choice restaurants that hosts Sam Dunlap and Alice Rosebrook can recommend. Both veterans of the U.S. Forest Service, they've achieved a casual, informal atmosphere in which guests tend to relax almost at once. The commodious living room, done in soothing green tones, has a fireplace, large bay windows, and a piano. Sam prepares his famous "buckaroo breakfasts" in the big country kitchen. Four upstairs guest rooms, full of the charm of yesteryear, range from a deluxe room with a sitting area to a room with twin beds and a river view. Friendly hospitality in the midst of scenic beauty — you can count on it at Hackett House.

 No pets; smoking outside only (veranda); no alcoholic beverages; full breakfast; off-street and street parking; AmEx cards; airport pickup (Hood River County). Brochure available.

ROOM	BED	BATH	ENTRANCE	FLOOR	DAILY RATES S - D (EP)
A	2T	Shd*	Main	2	$35-$55
B	2T	Shd*	Main	2	$35-$55
C	1Q	Shd*	Main	2	$35-$55
D	1D	Shd*	Main	2	$35-$55

Chandlers' Bed, Bread, & Trail Inn　　　　　**(503) 432-9765**
P.O. Box 639, Joseph, OR 97846
(700 South Main Street)

My first question was, "Where is Joseph?" I later discovered it amid the enchanting beauty of Wallowa County, which occupies the northeast corner of Oregon; comparisons to Switzerland had not been exaggerated. Wilderness adventurers find a profusion of outdoor activities here, and visiting artists from around the world come to work in Joseph's bronze foundry. Many have found their way to Chandlers' Bed, Bread, & Trail Inn. They appreciate the rustic lodge ambiance, spectacular vistas of mountain peaks, the choice of areas for conversation or contemplation, the fine breakfast cuisine, and the good company of hosts Ethel and Jim Chandler. Open-beamed ceilings and rough-hewn log walls provide a fitting milieu for tasteful country furnishings, collectibles, and family memorabilia. A visit to this wondrous area can only be enriched by making the Chandlers' your snug home base.

No pets; children over twelve welcome; smoking outside in designated areas; full breakfast; robes provided; common guest areas include a living room, sunroom, reading nooks, and a room with a woodstove, TV, VCR, coffee and tea brewing area, and games table; guests share two and one-half baths; nearby attractions include Hells Canyon Recreation Area, Eagle Gap Wilderness Area, Wallowa Lake; llama trekking, horsepacking, and whitewater rafting trips arranged; snowmobiling and skiing (Alpine and Nordic) nearby; off-street parking; VISA cards; airport pickup (Joseph). Brochure available.

ROOM	BED	BATH	ENTRANCE	FLOOR	DAILY RATES S - D	(EP)
A	1K & 1T	Shd*	Sep	2	$35-$45	($10)
B	1K	Shd*	Sep	2	$35-$45	
C	1Q & 1T	Shd*	Sep	2	$35-$45	($10)
D	2T	Shd*	Sep	2	$35-$45	
E	1D	Shd*	Sep	2	$35-$45	

Pitcher Inn
608 "N" Avenue, LaGrande, Oregon 97850
(Central LaGrande)

(503) 963-9152

    Deanna and Carl Pitcher have taken great pains with the renovation of their 1925 Georgian home. Its fine, solid construction and elegant architectural details made it a natural for becoming the gracious haven of hospitality it is today. Beautiful roses in the front yard set the tone for the decor, which has a country Victorian flavor. A dramatic stairway leads to the second floor guest rooms. Each has its own charming color scheme and special decorator touches. Done in striking pink and black, the spacious Honeymoon Suite (D) is a vision of lace and roses. Here newlyweds may savor their breakfast in bed. Guests often gather around the fireplace in the lovely living room, in the solarium/sitting room amid white wicker and greenery, or in the formal dining room which displays some of Deanna's collection of pitchers ("Carl was the first!" she says.) These good-natured, friendly hosts provide a relaxing environment where genuine concern for their guests is paramount.

    No pets or smoking; children under twelve discouraged; full breakfast; coffee and tea service in each room; two full baths shared by three rooms; mountain and lake recreation nearby; street and off-street parking; major credit cards (V, MC); train or airport pickup. *Closed January 2-15*. Brochure available.

ROOM	BED	BATH	ENTRANCE	FLOOR	DAILY RATES S - D (EP)
A	1D	Shd*	Main	2	$40-$50
B	1D	Shd*	Main	2	$40-$50
C	2Q	Shd*	Main	2	$50-$60 ($10)
D	1D	Pvt	Main	2	$75

Secluded Bed & Breakfast   (503) 538-2635
19719 NE Williamson Road, Newberg, OR 97132
(Yamhill County wine region)

Oregon's growing stature as a wine-producing state is enhanced by a visit to its premier grape-growing region in Yamhill County. Whether you're making a quick stop between Portland and the coast or staying long enough to savor the fruits of the vine, Secluded Bed & Breakfast is an ideal stop. It's a woodsy retreat with quiet, natural surroundings and abundant seasonal wildlife. Del and Durell Belanger are long-time residents of the county. Among other things, Durell is a skilled violin maker and Del a fabulous cook. They know some excellent places to send you for dinner, and later you'll have a great sleep in wonderful country silence.

No pets; smoking outside only; full breakfast; living room with fireplace, TV, VCR; AC; off-street parking; airport pickup (Newberg, McMinnville). Master suite with queen bed, private bath, and balcony available on request at $50; Master suite with shared bath, $40 on request. Brochure available.

ROOM	BED	BATH	ENTRANCE	FLOOR	DAILY RATES	
					S - D	(EP)
A	1D	Shd*	Main	2	$35	
B	1D	Shd*	Main	2	$35	

The Highlands   (503) 756-0300
608 Ridge Road, North Bend, OR 97459
(Five miles east from U.S. 101)

Here's a stunning, architecturally designed cedar home situated at a high elevation with a dramatic perspective of Haynes Inlet and the Oregon coastal range. But that's just for starters. Guests of Marilyn and Jim Dow are given the entire lower floor which includes a large, fully equipped kitchen, a spacious family room with a wood-stove and a fantastic view, and two bedrooms with private baths (one with a whirlpool tub). Tasteful country furnishings have been well put together to impart a warm, homey, comforting feeling. The view alone might hold your attention, but there's also a TV and VCR for entertainment. Anglers shouldn't miss fishing for steelhead in the inlet below. The huge wrap-around deck is a fine place to sit and enjoy clean, fresh air and absolute serenity. Consider The Highlands a home base while you explore the area or a retreat to settle into for awhile. It's a winner either way.

No pets; no children under ten; smoking outside only; full breakfast; day bed extra in Room A; goldfish pond on property; off-street parking; major credit cards (V, MC).

ROOM	BED	BATH	ENTRANCE	FLOOR	DAILY RATES S - D (EP)
A	1D	Pvt	Sep	LL	$50-$55 ($10)
B	1D	Pvt	Sep	LL	$50-$55

Pringle House   **(503) 459-5038**
P.O. Box 578, Oakland, OR 97462
(One and one-half miles east of I-5; Seventh and Locust Streets)

Pringle House stands on a rise at one end of the main street of Oakland, a quaint little town of 850 people that is on the National Register of Historic Places. The 1893 Queen Anne Victorian has been lovingly restored and decorated with turn-of-the-century style. Each of the upstairs guest rooms has a unique personality. Public rooms include a front parlor, a living room with a fireplace and winged-back chairs, and a dining room where coffee, tea, and juices are always available. But those are only the basics. It's Jim and Demay Pringle themselves who make their B&B truly one of a kind. Imagination and hard work have transformed this old house into a home of distinction and warmth. It is literally packed with nostalgic treasures, each with a history (or at least a story). There are countless discoveries to be made without even leaving the house. Only in museums have I seen more collections; Demay's dolls fill an entire room, floor to ceiling. The friendliness, the sense of fun, and the generous hospitality at Pringle House make it a place you'll remember with a smile.

Two cats in residence; younger children by arrangement; no pets; smoking on porches; full breakfast; robes provided; historic walking tour, a museum, and Tolly's Dinner House, Ice Cream Parlor, Antique Store & Art Gallery nearby; also swimming, boating, fishing, picnicking, six wineries, an 18-hole golf course, summertime melodrama theater, and the noted Wildlife Safari nearby; off-street parking. 10% discount for five days or longer. Brochure available.

ROOM	BED	BATH	ENTRANCE	FLOOR	DAILY RATES S - D (EP)
A	1D & 1T	Shd*	Main	2	$30-$40 ($10)
B	1D & 1T	Shd*	Main	2	$30-$40 ($10)

Hilton House Bed & Breakfast　　　　　　　　(503) 929-3212
P.O. Box 267, Philomath, OR 97370
(1036 Main Street)

　　　Philomath is an old farming community neighboring Corvallis, a university town with all you'd expect in the way of restaurants, movies, cultural events, and places to shop. Whether you are looking for a destination or an overnight stop along your route, Hilton House is a shortcut to comfort and relaxation. There are intentionally few rules here; hosts Rodger and Ardis Hilton try in earnest to accommodate guests' needs and schedules. Hospitality is friendly and informal, the decor Native American/Western. Pine furnishings blend well with desert tones accented by shades of turquoise. Choose a front bedroom (A) with a skylight or a large master bedroom (B) with a deck and walk-in closet. A large sunny lounge, where guests are welcome, stretches across the back of the house. A woodstove, a TV, and a gorgeous view of the landscaped garden and patio area make you feel like putting your feet up. Go ahead; the Hiltons would take it as a compliment.

　　　No pets; children by prior arrangement; smoking permitted in lounge or outside; full breakfast, flexible timing; off-street parking; major credit cards (V, MC). 10% business traveler's discount Sunday-Thursday October-March. Brochure available.

ROOM	BED	BATH	ENTRANCE	FLOOR	DAILY RATES	
					S - D	(EP)
A	1Q	Shd	Main	2	$40-$45	
B	1Q	Pvt	Main	2	$50-$55	

Cape Cod Bed & Breakfast   (503) 246-1839
5733 SW Dickinson, Portland, OR 97219
(Seven miles south of downtown Portland)

Whether you have business in Portland or you're taking a quick break enroute to someplace else, Marcelle and John Tebos' lovely 1939 Cape Cod home can be a restful stopping place. It's in an older residential neighborhood with plenty of trees and very little traffic. The upstairs can be closed off for guests, affording the utmost privacy. There are two pleasant bedrooms and a newly renovated bath. Antiques and traditional furniture collected over a forty-year period are combined throughout the house. An outdoor spa enclosed in an ivy hedge relaxes you for the next day's activities. Marcelle tends a huge garden and serves delicious homemade jams and jellies with your full or Continental breakfast. This B&B home is an hour's drive from the beach or the mountains. It is just off the main route from Portland to the coast (Highways 99W and 18), which takes you through one of Oregon's major wine regions. It's a great place to begin or end a day of vineyard-hopping.

No pets or smoking; AC; public transportation (six blocks); off-street parking; some French spoken; bus, train, and airport shuttle pickup.

ROOM	BED	BATH	ENTRANCE	FLOOR	DAILY RATES S - D (EP)
A	1D	Shd*	Main	2	$35-$40
B	2T	Shd*	Main	2	$30-$40

The Clinkerbrick House   (503) 281-2533
2311 NE Schuyler, Portland, OR 97212
(Near Lloyd Center, Convention Center, and Coliseum)

In a quiet residential neighborhood just minutes from downtown Portland, discover the warm country comfort of The Clinkerbrick House. The 1908 Dutch Colonial offers all the pleasures of a welcoming, family environment, along with an extra measure of privacy for guests: a separate outside entrance, allowing one to come and go freely. The second-floor accommodations include a full kitchen/TV room and three spacious bedrooms. On the door of each room is a decoration hinting at the perfectly executed theme within. The Garden Room has a private bath, a small deck, and a botanical flavor. The Strawberry Room, with antiques and stenciled walls, shares a bath off the hallway with The Rose Room, a romantic haven done in pink roses and white wicker. Delicious full breakfasts are served in the bright, cheerful dining room or in your room. For the traveler who likes feeling independent and pampered at the same time, hosts Bob and Peggie Irvine have created the unique hospitality of The Clinkerbrick House.

No pets or smoking; full breakfast (special dietary needs accommodated); rollaway bed, $10; good area for walking or jogging; good public transportation and airport connections; street and off-street parking; major credit cards (V, MC). Brochure available.

ROOM	BED	BATH	ENTRANCE	FLOOR	DAILY RATES S - D (EP)
A	1Q	Pvt	Sep	2	$50-$55
B	1Q	Shd*	Sep	2	$40-$45
C	1Q & 1T	Shd*	Sep	2	$40-$45 ($10)

Georgian House Bed & Breakfast   (503) 281-2250
1828 NE Siskiyou, Portland, OR 97212
(Near Lloyd Center, Convention Center, and Coliseum)

Portland has only three true Georgian Colonial homes; one of them is Georgian House Bed & Breakfast. This authentic beauty, built in 1922, is red brick with white columns and green shutters. It stands on a double corner lot in a fine, old, northeast Portland neighborhood. Proud owners Willie and Mike Ackely have expertly restored the home in its every exquisite detail. The tasteful use of interior colors serves to enhance classic features such as leaded glass windows, built-in china cabinets, heavy mouldings, oak floors, a sunporch, and a fireplace. A graceful stairway leads to the second floor guest quarters. Each of the antique-furnished bedrooms, the East Lake and the Pettygrove, is a singularly charming creation. The romantic Lovejoy Suite is a light, spacious bedroom/sitting room with a canopy bed, French windows, a color TV, a ceiling fan, and a view of the lovely grounds. A wide deck overlooking the backyard gardens has been added; lingering over breakfast here is indeed a pleasure — one of many you'll experience at Georgian House.

No pets; children welcome; smoking outside only; full breakfast; TV/VCR in common area; robes provided; crib available; extra-long beds in Room B; guest rooms share one and one-half bath off hallway; good public transportation, train, and airport connections; street and off-street parking; major credit cards (V, MC). Brochure available.

ROOM	BED	BATH	ENTRANCE	FLOOR	DAILY RATES	
					S -D	(EP)
A	1D	Shd*	Main	2	$35-$40	
B	2T or 1K	Shd*	Main	2	$45-$50	
C	1Q	Shd*	Main	2	$45-$50	

Hartman's Hearth　　　　　　　　　　　　　　**(503) 281-2210**
2937 NE Twentieth Avenue, Portland, OR 97212
(Near Lloyd Center, Convention Center, and Coliseum)

Christopher and Katie Hartman make their home in a handsome 1911 arts and crafts period house. It's in one of Portland's prettiest and most convenient intown neighborhoods, marked by stately shade trees and well-cared-for yards that burgeon with flowers in the spring. In cooler months, guests succumb to the lure of the hearth, the focal point of the living room. Throughout the interior, fabrics, colors, and textures are combined with an eclectic mix of antiques, traditional pieces, and contemporary art. Two guest rooms on the second floor derive their color schemes from subtle floral motifs; wallpapers and window treatments seem especially appropriate. The suite comprising the third floor strikes a surprisingly different mood. Sleek and sophisticated, it has a muted art deco look. Tones of mauve and rose are used with grey and black in the huge space, which boasts a king-sized canopy bed, a black lacquered desk, and a bathroom with delightfully intricate tilework. Much thought has been given to the aesthetics of decor, lighting, music, and cuisine at Hartman's Hearth; it's a dream of a place to stay.

Three cats in residence; no pets; no children under eleven; no smoking on second or third floor; no RV parking; full breakfast (special dietary needs accommodated); TV room with VCR; color TV in Room C; fold-out loveseat in Room A; robes provided; sauna; spa; good area for walking or jogging; good public transportation and airport connections; off-street parking; major credit cards (V, MC). Brochure available.

ROOM	BED	BATH	ENTRANCE	FLOOR	DAILY RATES	
					S - D	(EP)
A	1T	Shd*	Main	2	$40-$45	
B	1Q	Shd*	Main	2	$40-$45	
C	1K	Pvt	Main	3	$65	($10)

The John Palmer House   (503) 284-5893, Ext. 400
4314 North Mississippi Avenue, Portland, OR 97217
(North Portland)

The John Palmer House is one of the West's finest examples of unrestrained Victorian elegance. Restoring the 1890 Queen Anne-style house has been a two-decade labor of love for the Sauter family. Each member contributes to the multifaceted hospitality that makes The Palmer House utterly extraordinary. Virtually anything a guest may desire can be arranged on an individual basis, and certain things are standard: High Tea, complimentary wine and hors d'oeuvres, leisurely breakfasts fit for a gourmet, and the modern Jacuzzi in the gazebo at "Grandma's Cottage." (Yes, there's a real Grandma!) Authentic Victorian-design wallpapers at their most elaborate are showcased in rooms featuring magnificent stained-glass windows, an abundance of intricate woodwork, gas-electric light fixtures, and comfortable period antiques. Accommodations range from a room with a shared bath to a suite consisting of a library, bedroom, and sitting room with a porch. To enter The John Palmer House is to leave the twentieth century for a while and "live the romance of the Victorian era."

No pets; smoking outside only; full breakfast; dinners by reservation; AC; hot tub; good public transportation and airport connections; off-street parking; major credit cards (V, MC). Rooms B and C may be reserved as a suite at $105. Three lovely rooms available in Grandma's Cottage on premises at $30 to $50. By arrangment: mystery weekends, weddings and receptions, group events, horse-drawn carriage rides, massage, Victorian sleepwear, chilled champagne, fruit or flower baskets, intimate dinners for two, you name it! Brochure available.

ROOM	BED	BATH	ENTRANCE	FLOOR	DAILY RATES S - D (EP)
A	1D	Pvt	Main	1	$70-$75
B	1D	Shd*	Main	2	$70-$75
C	1D	Shd*	Main	2	$50-$55

Gwendolyn's Bed & Breakfast
P.O. Box 913, Port Orford, OR 97465
(735 Oregon Street at Coast Highway 101)

(503) 332-4373

Gwendolyn's is a country-style guest house with three delightful bedrooms and lots of personality. There's a comfortable parlor with a fireplace and a Persian rug from the twenties, the same era as the house. Touches of brass, hand-crocheted lace accents, aged wooden paneling, and colorful braided rugs punctuate the decor. You'll be charmed by the springtime colors and watercolor flower pictures used throughout the house. A short stroll takes you to one of the loveliest unspoiled beaches on the south coast. Also close by are choice seafood restaurants. A stay in the Port Orford area would be enhanced by a tour in Lady Kathryn's Carriage, a sleek white French European model of Victorian vintage, pulled by Teddy, a retired logging horse of Belgian-Shire mix. Gwendolyn Guerin can take your tour reservation; she can also be your guide to the wealth of outdoor wonders and seasonal events close by.

Cable TV; telephone; crab or salmon tasting in season; off-street parking; wheelchair access; major credit cards (V, MC); airport pickup (Cape Blanco).

ROOM	BED	BATH	ENTRANCE	FLOOR	DAILY RATES	
					S - D	(EP)
A	1D	Pvt	Main	1	$40-$45	($10)
B	1D	Shd*	Main	2	$30-$35	($10)
C	2T	Shd*	Main	2	$30-$35	($10)

HOME by the SEA
P.O. Box 606-K, Port Orford, OR 97465
(444 Jackson Street)

(503) 332-2855

Alan and Brenda Mitchell built their contemporary wood home on a spit of land overlooking a stretch of Oregon coast that could take your breath away. The awesome view can be enjoyed from both lovely bedrooms and from the Sunspace where the Mitchells serve afternoon refreshments and get to know their guests. It's a short walk to restaurants, public beaches, historic Battle Rock Park, and the town's harbor — the home port of Oregon's only crane-launched commercial fishing fleet. Port Orford is a favorite of windsurfers as well as of whale, bird, and storm watchers. It's an enchanting discovery, and so is HOME by the SEA.

No pets, children, or smoking; full breakfast; cable TV; laundry privileges; phone jacks in rooms; off-street parking; major credit cards.

ROOM	BED	BATH	ENTRANCE	FLOOR	DAILY RATES S - D (EP)
A	1Q	Pvt	Main	2	$60 ($10)
B	1Q	Pvt	Main	2	$50

The Willows Bed & Breakfast (503) 638-3722
5025 SW Homesteader Road, Wilsonville, OR 97070
(Fifteen miles south of Portland, two miles east of I-5)

There's a gem of a bed and breakfast in the idyllic countryside just twenty minutes south of Portland. The historic Wilsonville area is marked by vast rolling hills, an assortment of crops and livestock, quaint old barns, and country roads. David and Shirlee Key have made their home on two gorgeous acres. The velvety lawn and luxuriant gardens are maintained to perfection, a creek crossed by two bridges meanders through the property, and one of the huge weeping willows supports a charming old wooden swing. This beauty is matched only by the gracious interior of the Keys' modern home. Guests have all to themselves a full garden-level suite with its own entrance. Like the rest of the house, it is furnished with utmost care. The larger bedroom features a brass bed, antiques, and an exquisite handmade quilt fashioned by Shirlee in aqua, cream, and burgundy. A smaller bedroom has two good twin beds. There is a spacious living/dining area with a TV, desk, and phone. A handy refrigerator and beverage-brewing area are included in the bathroom. The standards of quality, hospitality, and value found at The Willows are simply unsurpassed.

No pets; children over twelve welcome; smoking outside only; full breakfast; AC; hosts recommend side trip to historic Aurora Colony; off-street parking. Brochure available.

ROOM	BED	BATH	ENTRANCE	FLOOR	DAILY RATES
					S - D (EP)
A	1Q & 2T	Pvt	Sep	LL	$40-$45 ($10)

Please read "About Dining Highlights" on page *ix*.

BANDON

Bandon Boat Works, South Jetty; (503) 347-2111; seafood

Bandon Fish Market, Bandon Boat Basin; (503) 347-4282; seafood

BEND

Le Bistro Dinner House & Lounge, 1203 NE Third Street; (503) 389-7274; French

Pine Tavern Restaurant, 967 NW Brooks Street; (503) 382-5581; specializing in prime rib, beef, lamb, ribs, and sourdough scones

BROOKINGS

Mama's Authentic Italian Food, 703 Chetco Avenue (U.S. 101); (503) 469-7611; southern Italian

Plum Pudding, 1011 Chetco Avenue (U.S. 101); no phone; homemade lunches

COOS BAY

Blue Heron Bistro, 100 Commercial; (503) 267-3933; Continental

Benetti's, 260 South Broadway; (503) 267-6066; Italian

DUNDEE

Alfie's Wayside Country Inn, 1111 Highway 99W; (503) 538-9407; fresh seafood and fowl specialties

EUGENE

Café Central, 384 West Thirteenth Street; (503) 343-9510; innovative northwest cuisine

Chanterelle, 207 East Fifth Street; (503) 484-4065; fresh fish and pasta

Oregon Electric, 27 East Fifth Street; (503) 485-4444; specializing in prime rib and seafood

GOLD BEACH

The Nor'Wester, Harbor at the Port of Gold Beach; (503) 247-2333; seafood

Rod 'N Reel, west of U.S. 101 at end of bridge, Wedderburn; (503) 247-6823; seafood/Continental

GRANTS PASS

The Brewery Restaurant, 509 SW "G" Street; (503) 479-9850; American

Hamilton House, 344 NE Terry Lane; (503) 479-3938; fresh seafood, pasta, fowl, and beef

Matsukaze, 1675 NE Seventh Street; (503) 479-2961; Japanese

Morrison's Lodge, 8500 Galice Road, Merlin; (503) 476-3825; northwest regional specialties

Paradise Ranch Inn, 7000 Monument Drive; (503) 479-4333; Continental

HOOD RIVER

Stonehenge Inn, 3405 Cascade Drive; (503) 386-3940; Continental

JOSEPH

Gold Room Steak House, Main Street; (503) 432-2511

Pam's Country Inn Restaurant, 500 North Main Street; (503) 432-1195; steaks, seafood, etc. served in country French atmosphere

MC MINNVILLE

Nick's Italian Café, 521 East Third Street; (503) 434-4471

MOUNT HOOD AREA

Chalet Suisse, Highway 26 and Welches Road, Wemme; (503) 622-3600; unique Swiss specialties

OAKLAND

Tolly's, 115 Locust Street; (503) 459-3796; Continental

PORTLAND

Albertina's, 424 NE Twenty-second Avenue; (503) 231-0216; three-course luncheons

Alexis, 215 West Burnside Street; (503) 224-8577; Greek

Bread & Ink Café, 3610 SE Hawthorne Boulevard; (503) 239-4756; Continental

Café des Amis, 1987 NW Kearney Street; (503) 295-6487; light French/ Continental

Cassidy's, 1331 SW Washington; (503) 223-0054; seafood, pasta, and more

Genoa, 2832 SE Belmont Street; (503) 238-1464; Italian

The Heathman, Heathman Hotel, SW Broadway at Salmon Street; (503) 241-4100; creative northwest dishes

Indigine, 3723 SE Division Street; (503) 238-1470; Asian

Jake's Famous Crawfish, 401 SW Twelfth ; (503) 226-1419; northwest seafood

L'Auberge, 2601 NW Vaughn; (503) 223-3302; French/nouvelle northwest

Metropolis Café, 2015 NE Broadway; (503) 281-7701; European bistro

Modern Times Restaurant, NW Couch Street and First Avenue; (503) 223-0743; creative menu with French-influenced sauces

Perry's on Fremont, 2401 NE Fremont; (503) 287-3655; eclectic menu suitable for family dining

Piccolo Mondo, Water Tower at Johns Landing, 5331 SW Macadam; (503) 248-9300; northern Italian

PORT ORFORD

The Silver Door, Sixth and Jackson Streets on U.S. 101; (503) 332-9885; lunches and homemade pies

Whale Cove Restaurant, U.S. 101 opposite Battle Rock Park; (503) 332-7575; fresh seafood and Continental cuisine

WALLOWA LAKE

Vali's Alpine Deli & Restaurant, Upper Power House Road; (503) 432-5691; Hungarian, German, and American

Wallowa Lake Lodge, Route 1; (503) 432-9821; Continental

Washington

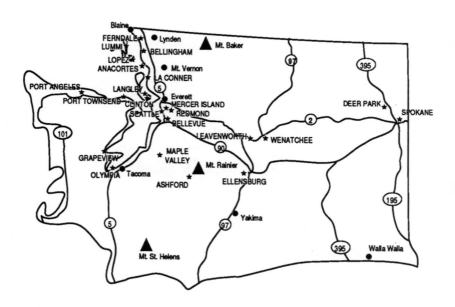

Washington wears two faces. On the west is a panorama of timbered mountains, deep canyons with rushing streams, fertile valleys, and shimmering, island-dotted bays. On the east lie black lava formations, the silver-green sagebrush plains, and rolling wheat country. The dividing line is the jagged snowy crest of the majestic Cascade Range, which separates the mild, wet climate from the drier east, where the mighty Columbia River carves a great arc, providing both water and power through its dam system.

Not far from the Interstate 5 mainline is Mount St. Helens, Washington's most famous performing mountain, which dominates the state's southern end of the Cascades. After losing 1,300 feet of its peak in the 1980 eruption, Mount St. Helens now stands at 8,300 feet. Visitors to this national monument can learn a lot about volcanos from the daily interpretive programs. You can even call ahead for an activity report — just in case Mount St. Helens decides to blow again.

Further north, Washington's most famous mountain, glacier-mantled Mount Rainier, towers nearly three miles above sea level. A network of state and forest roads and 300 miles of hiking trails provide access to this stately, pristine mountain. With thirty-four square miles of glaciers, it is the United States' largest single-peak glacier system outside of Alaska.

Travelers going north on Highway 101 will most likely be headed for the wild, wet, and wooded Olympic Peninsula. The Olympic Mountains rise 7,000 feet above the Pacific and overlook some of the last wilderness beaches in the country. The national park is comprised of nearly a million acres of untouched wilderness. Within it are 600 miles of hiking trails that take you from icy crags to driftwood-strewn beaches. Clamming, crabbing, and fishing are all rewarding along the impressive coastline. Hurricane Ridge, almost a mile high, provides the most accessible view along the Olympic Range. This knife-edged mountain ridge explodes with color when the wildflowers bloom in the summer. The Sol Duc Hot Springs testify to the region's volcanic origins.

Directly east is Puget Sound, a saltwater arm of the Pacific. Its hundreds of bays and inlets provide a total of no less than 1,800 miles of shoreline, much of it tree-lined and unspoiled. Getting around is sure to involve Washington's fleet of ferries, part of the state highway system.

The largest of Puget Sound's islands is Whidbey, approximately fifty miles long, where homes of the early settlers still dot the shore. Coupeville, one of the oldest towns in the state, has been restored and features Victorian buildings and picturesque shops. There are several parks on the island, including one of the state's finest at Deception Pass, where a bridge spans a gorge that is notorious for its unpredictable tidal currents.

215

From here it is a short distance to Mount Erie, about five miles south of Anacortes, on Fidalgo Island. Here you can get a good view of Mounts Baker and Rainier, the Olympic Peninsula, the Cascades, and the San Juan Islands. A paved road ascends its 1,300-foot summit.

A more intimate view of the San Juans can be had on a spectacular ferry ride, which leaves from Anacortes and weaves its way through this archipelago of 172 isles. The recreational opportunities in the San Juans are many — boating, water skiing, scuba diving, fishing, hiking, and bicycling.

Seattle, a city of hills and lakes, offers a number of attractions, including Pioneer Square, the Space Needle, the Pike Place Open-Air Market, and the waterfront. Southeast of Seattle is Snoqualmie Falls, which plunge a hundred feet farther than those of Niagara. A trail leads into the canyon. An antique steam engine chugs along a seven-mile loop, enabling railroad buffs to visit the falls by train.

Still further southeast, off Interstate 90, the college and cowboy town of Ellensburg projects a pleasant ease, with turn-of-the-century buildings and beautiful views of the Cascade Mountains. The Yakima River offers fine canoe and raft trips through deep gorges, as well as some of the finest trout fishing in the country.

If you stay eastbound on Interstate 90, you will eventually reach Spokane, a thriving, hospitable city stretching from the west plains to the Idaho border. With lakes and forests just minutes from its core, Spokane is known as the center of the great outdoors.

Returning west, perhaps along Highway 2, to the eastern boundary of the Wenatchee National Forest, you will encounter Leavenworth, a small community modeled after a Bavarian village. Here there are year-round festivals and much skiing activity in winter. Scenic Tumwater Canyon is about six miles to the west of Leavenworth, while glacier-fed Lake Chelan lies to the east. Surrounded by peaks of the Cascades, the lake's bottom drops to 400 feet below sea level.

Lake Chelan National Recreational Area, noted for its beauty and recreational opportunities, marks the southern boundary of the North Cascades National Park, one of the wildest and most rugged sections of the United States. There are 300 living glaciers in the park. Largely a backcountry wilderness area, the hardy will encounter breathtaking scenery and wildlife. The North Cascade Highway, which links the Puget Sound area to the North Cascades, offers some of the most astonishing vistas of mountains and alpine meadows anywhere. (The eastern section of the highway is closed in winter.)

If you're looking for unspoiled beauty, you're sure to find it in Washington. Here sea, mountain, and desert converge to provide enough natural diversity to satisfy the most restless of spirits.

Channel House

2902 Oakes Avenue, Anacortes, WA 98221
(Overlooking Guemes Channel, five minute

Channel House is a joyous discovery for anyone traveling to this corner of the country. It's a home of unusual character; every guest room is uniquely situated for gazing out at the Channel and the San Juan Islands. Shiny wood floors with Oriental rugs, fine antique furnishings, a library, and three fireplaces create an atmosphere of classic European elegance. Owners since 1986, Pat and Dennis McIntyre have preserved the flavor of the house while adding their own touches to make it their family home. The McIntyres, former restaurateurs, take pride in the quality and variety of the breakfasts they serve, usually before a crackling fire. Another treat for guests is outdoor hot-tubbing with a view of island sunsets. All in all, staying at Channel House is an experience to be savored.

No pets; children over twelve OK; no smoking; full breakfast; evening refreshments; off-street parking; major credit cards (V, MC); ferry pickup. Two additional rooms (at $85 each) available in Rose Cottage, adjacent to main house; individually decorated rooms have queen-sized beds, private baths with whirlpool tubs, and fireplaces. Off-season rates are $10 less. Brochure available.

ROOM	BED	BATH	ENTRANCE	FLOOR	DAILY RATES S - D (EP)
A	1D & 2T	Shd*	Main	2	$55-$65 ($10)
B	1Q	Shd*	Main	2	$55-$65
C	1D	Pvt	Main	1	$55-$75
D	1D	Pvt	Main	1	$55-$75

There's something very comforting about an older, stable neighborhood where people can stroll the sidewalks, picnic in a park, or visit the local museum. In this kind of setting, how appropriate to find a large, friendly looking home that welcomes bed and breakfast travelers. Mike and Melinda Hasty have devotedly restored each room in their turn-of-the-century home, building on its considerable character and adding tasteful antique pieces in just the right places. Melinda has quite an eye for color; she's created an interior imbued with the feeling of a warm spring day. The sunroom where you enter sets the tone for the rest of the house. It's like being in the prettiest of gardens — pure poetry, any time of year.

No pets; no children under eleven; no smoking; full breakfast; living room with fireplace; extra long bed in Room A; street and off-street parking; major credit cards; ferry and airport pickup (Anacortes). Information available on seven local day trips as well as hiking, kayaking, cycling, and fishing and boating charters.

ROOM	BED	BATH	ENTRANCE	FLOOR	DAILY RATES	
					S - D	(EP)
A	1D	Shd*	Main	2	$50	
B	2T	Shd*	Main	2	$50	
C	1Q	Pvt	Main	2	$65	($15)
D	1K	Pvt	Main	2	$65	($15)

Old Brook Inn   **(206) 293-4768**
530 Old Brook Lane, Anacortes, WA 98221
(Off Route 20 West, four miles south of Anacortes)

At the end of a quiet country lane you'll find this gem of a home set amidst an ancient orchard. Old Brook Inn is Cape Cod in style, constructed of cedar and stone. The lush, nine-acre setting is replete with verdant trees and flowering plants; a babbling brook through the property and a delightful trout pond enhance the feeling of peace and tranquility. The interior is endowed with natural colors, striking artwork, and comfy places to sit and sleep. A light-infused room with a bay window on the first floor commands a lovely view of Fidalgo Bay. A huge second floor bed/sitting room that can sleep up to five people overlooks the ever-changing color and beauty of the orchard. You're welcome to pick your own strawberries, raspberries, and blackberries in season, or host Dick Ash will do it for you. You will undoubtedly find his home a gracious haven in the magical freshness of the country.

Cat in residence; living room, fireplace, and TV available to guests; off-street parking; major credit cards (V, MC); airport pickup (Anacortes). Twin bed can be added to Room B.

ROOM	BED	BATH	ENTRANCE	FLOOR	DAILY RATES
					S - D (EP)
A	1Q	Pvt	Main	1	$50-$60
B	1Q & 2T	Pvt	Main	2	$55-$65 ($10)

Growly Bear Bed & Breakfast (206) 569-2339
37311 SR 706, Ashford, WA 98304
(One mile from entrance to Mount Rainier National Park)

Just before the entrance to Mount Rainier National Park, an old wooden homestead house stands hidden by a shield of mammoth cedars. Old-growth cedar was used in the original 1890 building, which has undergone recent renovations. Susan Jenny has made it her home for many years and calls it and her nearby bakery Growly Bear. As rustic as its surroundings, the house offers three B&B rooms on the second floor, named after the original homesteaders, a nearby mountain peak, and a local river. The first two are cozy and cheery, sharing a bath off the hallway. The third is an expansive space with lots of windows, a sitting area with sofas, a private bath, and Growly Bear slippers in the closet! In each room, stuffed bears form a welcoming committee and a snack basket satisfies the munchies. Be lulled to sleep by the sound of Goat Creek, awake to the aroma of fresh bread from the nearby bakery ovens, and then enjoy the breakfast of your choice up the road at the Wild Berry Restaurant where tasty and fortifying meals are served.

No pets; children negotiable; no smoking; full breakfast; off-street parking. Brochure available.

ROOM	BED	BATH	ENTRANCE	FLOOR	DAILY RATES	
					S - D	(EP)
A	2T	Shd*	Main	2	$50-$60	
B	1D	Shd*	Main	2	$50-$60	
C	1D	Pvt	Main	2	$60-$70	($10)

Mountain Meadows Inn   **(206) 569-2788**
P.O. Box 291, Ashford, WA 98304
(Six miles from entrance to Mount Rainier National Park)

The enchantment of Mountain Meadows Inn starts the minute you turn off the main highway to the clearing where this 1910 Craftsman-style home stands in a meadow encircled by forest and country quiet. It overlooks a stream-fed pond edged with cattails. The solid, character-filled house features a kaleidoscope of nostalgic images and artistic touches. Tanna Barney has taken familiar things recalled from childhood and put them together in refreshingly original ways. She collects art, literature, and memorabilia on Mount Rainier; partner Chad Darrah displays a lifetime of railroad paraphernalia — he's conductor on the Mount Rainier Scenic Railroad. Tanna prepares hearty breakfast fare on an old, wood-fired cookstove. Other old-fashioned pleasures include gathering 'round the campfire in the evening, visiting on the wide front porch, or reading hearthside in the living room. The property is a magical place to explore, and, of course, the mountain beckons.

Dog (Bo), cats, llama (Oscar), pig (Piglet), chickens, and ducks on property; no pets; children over ten welcome; no smoking in bedrooms; full breakfast; VCR in living room; pond has small dock, trout, and catfish; inquire about Scenic Railroad trips; off-street parking; major credit cards (V, MC). Brochure available.

ROOM	BED	BATH	ENTRANCE	FLOOR	DAILY RATES	
					S - D	(EP)
A	1Q	Pvt	Main	1	$65	($15)
B	1K & 2T	Shd*	Main	1	$60	($15)
C	1Q	Shd*	Main	1	$60	($15)

Bellevue Bed & Breakfast   **(206) 453-1048**
830 - 100th Avenue SE, Bellevue, WA 98004
(Overlooking downtown Bellevue)

Cy and Carol Garnett make their home at the end of a dead-end street on a hillside overlooking city and mountains. It's convenient to freeways, but very quiet, and just a short walk from the east shore of Lake Washington. Guests have their own entrance on the lower level of the house, offering extra privacy for a family, two couples, or a group. The 1200-square-foot suite consists of a spacious living room with wide picture windows all around and a large cable TV, a full kitchen, two bedrooms with private baths, and a laundry room. The Garnetts are gracious, caring hosts who want people to feel comfortable in their home. Whatever you desire — be it restful privacy, assistance with your plans, or conversation — it can be easily arranged at Bellevue Bed & Breakfast.

No pets or smoking; children over ten welcome; full breakfast; phone in guest quarters; good public transportation and airport connections; off-street parking; wheelchair access; major credit cards. Weekly and winter rates; seventh consecutive night free. Brochure available.

ROOM	BED	BATH	ENTRANCE	FLOOR	DAILY RATES S-D	(EP)
A	1D	Pvt	Main	LL	$45-$50	($15)
B	1D	Pvt	Main	LL	$45-$50	($15)

Petersen Bed & Breakfast   **(206) 454-9334**
10228 SE Eighth, Bellevue, WA 98004
(Fifteen minutes east of Seattle)

Though some think of Bellevue simply as part of suburban Seattle, it has come into its own in recent years as a major business and shopping area with its fair share of fine dining establishments and horticultural displays. In a quiet, established neighborhood, Eunice and Carl Petersen open their warm and inviting home to bed and breakfast guests. On the lower (daylight)level of the house you'll find two pretty, relaxing rooms with down comforters, plush carpeting, and tasteful decorator touches. Spend leisure moments on the large deck — perhaps in the steamy spa — that overlooks beautifully landscaped grounds. After a wonderful night's rest, enjoy a generous homestyle breakfast in the atrium kitchen. Then you should be able to face the day with a smile.

Smoking outside only; full breakfast; TV; VCR; hot tub; one mile from Bellevue Square shopping; good public transportation; off-street parking; airport pickup (Bellevue, Boeing, Sea-Tac). Waterbed in Room A.

ROOM	BED	BATH	ENTRANCE	FLOOR	DAILY RATES	
					S - D	(EP)
A	1Q	Shd*	Main	LL	$40-$45	
B	2T or 1K	Shd*	Main	LL	$40-$45	

Schnauzer Crossing (206) 733-0055
4421 Lakeway Drive, Bellingham, WA 98226
(Overlooking Lake Whatcom)

After visiting Schnauzer Crossing I began to view Bellingham as an ideal travel destination. A short getaway or a longer vacation could be happily spent in the quiet luxury of this beautiful home. There's plenty to do on the premises or nearby, and there are great day trips in every direction. Hosts Vermont and Donna McAllister have incorporated the best features of the lodgings they've stayed in abroad and added some of their own. The great room alone is a visual feast. Extensive woodwork, cathedral ceilings, lots of windows, and decking all around give it an open, close-to-nature feeling. The attractive iris motif in the fabric here is carried into the guest quarters which offer myriad special touches. The smaller of the two rooms has a view of the lake, while the master suite has a sunroom with a garden view, a fireplace, TV, telephone, desk, and a bath with a Jacuzzi tub and double shower. Fresh flowers and birdsong abound. Many repeat visitors hail the outstanding quality of the accommodations, the decor, the breakfast cuisine, and the amenities that put Schnauzer Crossing in a class by itself.

Two Standard Schnauzers and a canary in residence; bed and breakfast for your dog in an outdoor enclosed kennel, $10 (with advance notice); smoking outside only; full breakfast; robes provided; double futon in sunroom (B); outdoor hot tub and private tennis court; lake access for swimming and canoeing; blueberry and raspberry bushes for picking; off-street parking; major credit cards (V, MC). Brochure available.

ROOM	BED	BATH	ENTRANCE	FLOOR	DAILY RATES S - D (EP)
A	1Q	Pvt	Main	1	$65
B	2T or 1K	Pvt	Main	1	$95 ($15)

Bed & Breakfast With Love's (509) 276-6939
North 31317 Cedar Road, Deer Park, WA 99006
(Fourteen miles north of Spokane)

Using nineteenth-century plans, Bill and Leslie Love fashioned their three-story home, an authentic Victorian gray and mauve reproduction with white gingerbread trim. To encounter it in the woods set among tall pines is a dramatic surprise. One's initial delight is heightened upon entering the heartwarming interior. A stairway leads from the main floor to the guest quarters below; follow the trailing stenciled roses down to an ambiance of pure country Victoriana. There is a sitting room with a wood-burning stove, TV, and library. Two bedrooms of exceptional charm feature country antiques, handmade quilts, old-fashioned beds, lace curtains, and plush carpets. Both have French doors opening to a patio. This B&B is not only incredibly romantic — it's a family home filled with Love.

Dog and cats on premises; no pets; children by prior arrangement; smoking outside only; no alcoholic beverages; full breakfast; TV, VCR, and stereo in guest sitting room; AC; robes provided; private solarium/hot tub room; bicycles available; fishing, skiing (cross-country trails five minutes away), hiking, festivals, and museums nearby; off-street parking; inquire about birthday celebrations and garden weddings. Special rates: seventh consecutive night free; entire guest area $75 for honeymooners; after first night, $45 rate drops to $40. Brochure available.

ROOM	BED	BATH	ENTRANCE	FLOOR	DAILY RATES	
					S - D	(EP)
A	1Q	Shd*	Sep	1G	$40-$45	($10)
B	1Q	Shd*	Sep	1G	$40-$45	($10)

Murphy's Country Bed & Breakfast　　　　　　　**(509) 925-7986**
Route 1, Box 400, Ellensburg, WA 98926
(Near junction of I-90 and Highway 97)

Ellensburg, located in a wide, picturesque valley in central Washington, is cattle and horse country. The annual rodeo, western parade, and county fair draw folks from all over. Hiking in state parks, golfing, and cross-country skiing are also popular. Doris Murphy offers some of the area's most pleasant lodging in her stately home, situated on three rural acres. With a foundation of native stone, it is a house with a feeling of substance. From the lovely front porch, enter a commodious living room with high ceilings, an abundance of beautiful woodwork, and an inviting hearth. Also on the main floor are a formal dining room where Doris, a professional baker, serves breakfast, and a guest lounge with a TV. Second floor accommodations include two spacious bedrooms attractively decorated in peach and aqua. A large bathroom and a half-bath are shared by guests. Turn-of-the-century style combined with twentieth-century comfort make Murphy's Country Bed & Breakfast an altogether memorable place to stay.

Dog in residence; no pets or children; horses accommodated in corral, $15; no smoking on second floor; full breakfast; museums, art galleries, historical buildings, river rafting, cattle drives, berry-picking, and fishing nearby; off-street parking. Brochure available.

ROOM	BED	BATH	ENTRANCE	FLOOR	DAILY RATES S - D (EP)
A	1Q	Shd*	Main	2	$50-$55
B	1Q	Shd*	Main	2	$50-$55

Anderson House Bed & Breakfast   **(206) 384-3450**
P.O. Box 1547, Ferndale, WA 98248
(2140 Main Street)

David and Kelly Anderson's extensive renovations have brought out the best in this interesting old house, and the beautifully landscaped yard with its distinctive lampposts makes a welcoming impression. Inside, perfectly chosen furnishings strike just the right balance between comfort and aesthetics. Luxurious carpeting, wallcoverings, and fabrics, plus a stunning Bavarian crystal swan chandelier mark the decor. With humor and thoughtfulness, the Andersons make guests feel relaxed and pampered. Accommodations are of the highest quality, as is the cuisine. Each of the bedrooms is charming, but the Tower Suite (D) is especially unique; the huge space has a sloped ceiling, lots of angles, touches of wood and brick, an alcove with a day bed, a refrigerator, and a TV. It has one drawback: You may never come out to enjoy the rest of the Andersons' splendid hospitality.

No pets; children over twelve welcome; smoking outside only; extensive list of amenities; six restaurants in walking distance; forty-one minutes to downtown Vancouver, B.C.; thirty minutes to Victoria ferry; off-street parking; major credit cards. $10 for extra person in room. Brochure available.

ROOM	BED	BATH	ENTRANCE	FLOOR	DAILY RATES	
					S - D	(EP)
A	1D	Shd*	Main	2	$40	
B	2T	Shd*	Main	2	$40	
C	1Q	Pvt	Main	2	$49	
D	1K & 2T	Pvt	Main	2	$65	

Hill Top Bed & Breakfast   (206) 384-3619
5832 Church Road, Ferndale, WA 98248
(A mile west and one-third mile north of town center)

Doris and Paul Matz didn't skimp on windows when they built their sturdy brick home. It affords an expansive view out across the Nooksack River Valley to Mount Baker and the Cascades — truly one of the finest there is. Doris admits to an addiction to quiltmaking, and her museum-quality quilts appear throughout the house, enhancing the colonial theme. In addition to a guest room with a private bath on the main floor, the entire ground floor with its own patio entrance is available for guests. It's a nice, private place to come home to after a day of exploring Birch Bay, nearby islands, Lynden, or Mount Baker.

Families welcome; smoking outside only; TV, fireplace, and sofa bed in Fireside Room (B); bath on lower floor usually private; crib available in Room B; badminton, croquet, games, puzzles, and books available; off-street parking; major credit cards (V, MC); Norwegian spoken. 10% discount for three nights or more, or for seniors over 65. *Closed November-April.* Brochure available.

ROOM	BED	BATH	ENTRANCE	FLOOR	DAILY RATES	
					S - D	(EP)
A	1Q	Pvt	Main	1	$39-$44	
B	1Q	Shd*	Sep	LL	$44-$49	($10)
C	2T	Shd*	Sep	LL	$34-$39	($10)

Llewop Bed & Breakfast
(206) 275-2287
Box 97, Grapeview, WA 98546
(Southwest Puget Sound, off Highway 3)

This huge contemporary home rests on a wooded knoll over-looking an orchard, Case Inlet, and Stretch Island, with the summit of Mount Ranier showing on clear days. It is endowed with many windows, skylights, and decks, so it's easy to feel at one with the incredible beauty of the environment. There are three bedrooms for guests, all as lovely as can be. Room A has a spacious private deck with full view. Guests are welcome to sit around the living room fireplace, explore the property, swim, play pickleball, or unwind in the whirlpool spa   (tub in bathroom on main floor). Most of all, Llewop is a place for restoration and relaxation. The Powell family wants you to enjoy their home as much as they enjoy sharing it.

No pets; families welcome; smoking on decks; full breakfast; TV; extra beds; bathtub spa; pickleball court; golf course and restaurant four miles away; off-street parking. Clergy discount.

ROOM	BED	BATH	ENTRANCE	FLOOR	DAILY RATES S - D (EP)
A	1D	Shd*	Main	2	$35-$45 ($15)
B	2T	Shd*	Main	2	$35-$45 ($15)
C	2T	Pvt	Main	1	$35-$45 ($15)

Heather House   (206) 466-4675
P.O. Box 237, La Conner, WA 98257
(505 Maple, walking distance to town)

Walk through the rose hedge and down the brick pathway to Heather House. It was built in 1979 as an exact replica of a Cape Cod beach house (circa 1900) in Marblehead, Massachusetts. Bev and Wayne Everton made it their home for several years before moving into a cottage next door. Now the charming house is used exclusively for bed and breakfast. Guests appreciate the privacy and luxury of having the whole house to themselves while at the same time feeling pampered by caring hosts. Three bedrooms and two baths are on the second floor; a living room, dining room, and kitchen comprise the first floor. There's a full complement of amenities, including Four Seasons terry robes, bath sheets, early morning coffee, and an invitation to "raid the refrigerator." Views from Heather House are terrific. It overlooks a working farm with a vista of Skagit Valley, Mount Baker, and the Cascades. The historic waterfront village of La Conner is just blocks away.

No pets or children; no smoking upstairs; off-street parking; major credit cards. Room C is a suite with a sofa and a fireplace.

ROOM	BED	BATH	ENTRANCE	FLOOR	DAILY RATES	
					S - D	(EP)
A	1D	Shd*	Main	2	$45	
B	1Q	Shd*	Main	2	$55	
C	1Q	Shd*	Main	2	$65	

The White Swan Guest House   **(206) 445-6805**
1388 Moore Road, Mount Vernon, WA 98273
(Six miles from La Conner, on Skagit River)

A major shift in lifestyle was undertaken when Peter Goldfarb moved from New York City to the quiet countryside of the Pacific Northwest. (Observation: Hosting is definitely his forte.) He bought an essentially handsome Victorian home that was badly in need of attention and gave it his all. Keeping its charm and character intact, Peter's inspired renovations turned it into the jewel it is today. My favorite aspect of the decor is the bold use of color throughout the house. Vivid hues of a country garden create a cheerful environment, a lift to the spirit on dull days. Comfortable rooms are uniquely decorated, featuring Peter's large collection of antique samplers. Outside, English-style country gardens with seating areas and lots of flowers enhance the grounds. Mother Nature has richly endowed the surrounding landscape — it's great for walking along the river, cycling, and observing wildlife. Any way you look at it, The White Swan is a find.

Dogs in residence; smoking outside only (porch); homemade chocolate chip cookies all day; three rooms share two baths on second floor; off-street parking; major credit cards (V, MC).

ROOM	BED	BATH	ENTRANCE	FLOOR	DAILY RATES S - D (EP)
A	1K	Shd*	Main	2	$50-$55
B	1Q	Shd*	Main	2	$50-$55
C	1Q	Shd*	Main	2	$50-$55

Brown's Farm, A Bed & Breakfast Home Place   (509) 548-7863
11150 Highway 209, Leavenworth, WA 98826
(One and one-half miles north of town on road to Plain)

Leavenworth is a picturesque Bavarian village that overlooks the Wenatchee River and is outlined by snowcapped Icicle Ridge. Each season brings a celebration and thousands of visitors who are touched by the welcoming spirit that abides here. In the Chumstick Valley, you'll find Brown's Farm, A Bed & Breakfast Home Place. Wendi Krieg and her three children, along with the resident animals, make staying at this large, country farmhouse a rare experience in home-spun hospitality. The family worked together to build the house. It has exposed log beams, walls of local timber, a huge fireplace of stones from the Icicle Valley, multi-paned windows, and stained-glass accents created by Wendi and her family. Three bedrooms and a bath on the main floor make wonderfully cozy guest quarters. The simplicity of the decor is refreshing. Nothing about the ambiance is contrived; the charm is all natural. I can't imagine a healthier atmosphere for children growing up — or anyone else, for that matter.

Dogs, cats, horse, chickens, and ducks on premises; families welcome; children under five with sleeping bags at $5 each; no smoking in bedrooms; full country breakfast; sink in Room A; some cross-country skis and snowshoes available; hiking swimming, rafting, and sleigh rides nearby; off-street parking; major credit cards. Brochure available.

ROOM	BED	BATH	ENTRANCE	FLOOR	DAILY RATES S - D	(EP)
A	1Q & 1T	Shd*	Main	1	$65	($10)
B	1Q	Shd*	Main	1	$60	($10)
C	1D	Shd*	Main	1	$55	

Run of the River Bed & Breakfast (509)
P.O. Box 448, Leavenworth, WA 98826
(One mile off Highway 2 at 9308 East Leavenworth Road)

Situated just outside the pristine Bavarian village of Leavenworth is an unforgettably unique lodging discovery. Run of the River is the spacious log home of Monty and Karen Turner. Here they have created the perfect Cascades retreat, complete with every comfort imaginable to ensure a cozy and romantic escape from the ordinary. Inside, the fundamental warmth of log construction is enhanced by wood-burning stoves, handhewn log furniture, colorful quilts, and country decor. Each luxurious room or suite has a distinctive character and offers unusual privacy. Unwind in peaceful seclusion accompanied by spectacular, close-up views of the Icicle River, the towering mountains of Tumwater Canyon, and a huge variety of birds and other wildlife that find sanctuary here. If you're looking for that very special, year-round refuge, be forewarned: Run of the River could become the kind of habit you never want to break.

Two dogs in residence; no pets; no children under fifteen; no smoking; full country breakfast served riverside; color cable TV in each room; terry robes provided; decks; Jacuzzi tub in Rose Suite (A); outdoor hot tub; "menu" of thirty-seven things to do in area provided by hosts; off-street parking; Spanish spoken; major credit cards (V, MV, AE). Inquire about special getaway packages. Brochure available.

ROOM	BED	BATH	ENTRANCE	FLOOR	DAILY RATES S - D	(EP)
A	1Q	Pvt	Sep	2	$80-$90	($15)
B	1Q	Pvt	Sep	2	$69-$79	($15)
C	1Q	Pvt	Sep	2	$69-$79	($15)
D	2Q	Pvt	Main	1	$59-$69	($15)

z Island, WA 98261
lock on Port Stanley Road)

_opez Island can satisfy many tastes. It's the
the San Juans (be sure to wave!), so you'll feel
Cyclists and nature lovers consider it an ideal
ge̱   /ho appreciate luxury and superb cuisine will find
the. Inn ̱   , Bay much to their liking. The Tudor-style inn is
classy, stylish, a̱d oh, so comfortable. Hosts Christopher and Robert
provide every amenity a guest might need and then some. An
understated elegance marks the decor. When you're not out exploring the island, you'll find a choice of areas to relax that are just for
guests: your tastefully appointed bedroom, the living room by the
fireplace, the outdoor hot tub (sign up ahead for complete privacy),
or the sunning area. Mornings will find you at your very own table
enjoying a breakfast that is nothing short of sensational. Then take a
stroll down to the private beach across the road and let the day
unfold.

No pets, children, or smoking; full breakfast; TV/VCR with good
selection of movies (winter only); guest phone; hot tub; bicycles
available for rent in village nearby; off-street parking; Portuguese,
Spanish, and German spoken; pickup at ferry dock, airstrip, or sea-
plane dock. Brochure available.

ROOM	BED	BATH	ENTRANCE	FLOOR	DAILY RATES S - D (EP)
A	1Q	Shd*	Main	1	$65
B	1Q	Shd*	Main	1	$65
C	1Q	Pvt	Main	1	$80
D	1Q	Pvt	Main	2	$95

West Shore Farm Bed & Breakfast   (20█
2781 West Shore Drive, Lummi Island, WA 98262
(Sunset side of island)

A scenic, six-minute saltwater cruise across Hale Passage from the mainland (near Bellingham) takes you to Lummi Island, with quiet beaches, views of islands and sunsets, prolific wildlife, and scenic country roads for walking or cycling. It is truly a world unto itself, with Polly and Carl Hanson's West Shore Farm providing a great little hideaway. The handbuilt octagonal home is set into a slope, allowing sweeping views of sea, islands, sky, and trees from a series of large windows on three sides. Guests are housed on the lower level in total privacy and served delicious, home-produced meals upstairs by the unique twelve-sided, free-standing fireplace and the view windows. The cozy all-wood interior creates a habitat in perfect harmony with the surroundings. Guest rooms — one with a vanity sink, one with a reading corner and leather recliner chair, both with views — are named Heron and Eagle for birds in the area, which are featured in the decor. West Shore Farm is a perfect escape for romance, time alone, or a family outing.

Smoking outside only; full breakfast; other meals available; books, games, periodicals, and local interest publications in guest area; beach access; two bicycles available; arrangements made by hosts for private visits to local craftspeople, participation in island community events, and more; off-street parking; major credit cards (V, MC); ferry landing and airport pickup (island airstrip, free; Bellingham International, $15). Brochure available.

ROOM	BED	BATH	ENTRANCE	FLOOR	DAILY RATES S - D (EP)
A	2T or 1K	Pvt	Sep	LL	$50-$60
B	2T or 1K	Pvt	Sep	LL	$50-$60

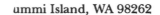

(206) **758-2620**

ummi Island, WA 98262

Victoria Flynn seized an opportunity few people have when she bought back the family home she'd grown up in on Lummi Island. It had been radically altered, so a great deal of work went into restoring it to its original beauty. Victoria and husband Gary now welcome guests to this elegant country inn. The Willows is rich in tradition but has fresh, lively touches in the decor. Extravagant floral arrangements from the garden, fine old linens used liberally throughout the house, heirloom furniture, and light, airy rooms make the ambiance at once cheerful and refined. Each beautifully decorated bedroom is named for the view from its window — Sunset, Sunrise, Rose, and Hillside. Above the inn on a flower-covered hillside is the Honeymoon Cottage, which also enjoys a beautiful view of the islands. Whether you're relaxing by the fireplace or on the expansive veranda, glorying in the cuisine presented by the Flynns, spotting a bald eagle overhead, or combing the beach below the inn, you'll be simply thrilled that you found this most romantic of retreats.

Cat in residence; no pets or children; smoking outside only; full three-course breakfast included; off-street parking; major credit cards (V, MC). Rate for Honeymoon Cottage is $100. Dinners available every night; special four-course candlelight dinners with wine on Saturday nights, by reservation only. Brochure available.

ROOM	BED	BATH	ENTRANCE	FLOOR	DAILY RATES S - D (E P)
A	2T or 1K	Shd*	Sep	2	$75
B	1Q	Shd*	Sep	2	$75
C	1D	Pvt	Sep	1	$75
D	1D	Pvt	Sep	1	$75

Maple Valley Bed & Breakfast   **(206) 432-1409**
20020 SE 228, Maple Valley, WA 98038
(Twenty-five miles due east of Sea-Tac International Airport)

After a demanding week at work or a day of hard traveling, how satisfying to find that perfect haven in the country for a few days of pampered relaxation — Maple Valley Bed & Breakfast. Jayne and Clarke Hurlbut have fashioned a rustic family home of outstanding warmth and charm. Built by Clarke, it sits in a clearing in the woods, surrounded by a carpet of neat green lawn. The later addition of an "eagles' aerie" lends a fairytale quality. Walls of warm cedar, a huge stone fireplace, open-beamed ceilings, and many interesting angles give the house its singular appeal, and two gabled guest rooms on the second floor couldn't be more endearing. The decor is country Americana, very well done. Each room has lacy curtains, antiques, and nostalgia pieces, as well as French doors that open to a large deck. Featured in Room A are a handhewn four-poster log bed and a pedestal sink; in Room B, beautiful heirloom quilts cover the twin beds. An upstairs sitting room and adjoining TV area are great for reading, playing games, working puzzles, and viewing the wildlife pond through binoculars. Attention to detail is the essence of what's so special at Maple Valley Bed & Breakfast. Far be it from me to spoil all the surprises.

Peacocks, chickens, cats, and dog live outside; no pets; smoking outside only; full breakfast; cots available; barbecue area; half basketball court; hiking and nature walks; available for outdoor weddings; off-street parking; airport pickup (Crest Airpark).

ROOM	BED	BATH	ENTRANCE	FLOOR	DAILY RATES S - D (EP)
A	1Q	Shd*	Main	2	$40-$45 ($15)
B	2T	Shd*	Main	2	$40-$45 ($15)

Mercer Island Hideaway   (206) 232-1092
8820 SE 63rd Street, Mercer Island, WA 98040
(Three miles south of I-90, off Island Crest Way)

It's only a fifteen minute drive from Seattle or Bellevue, but when you cross a bridge over Lake Washington to Mercer Island, it seems like another world. The Williams' home, Mercer Island Hideaway, is a place of quiet luxury. It is tucked into the lush green landscape that adjoins the wilderness of 113-acre Pioneer Park. No matter which of the attractive accommodations you stay in, it will be like "sleeping in a forest," as one guest put it. The home has been beautifully renovated throughout and is kept in immaculate condition. Anyone with an interest in music will be at home here. The spacious living room has tall windows and a cathedral ceiling. It holds two grand pianos, a reed organ, and a harpsichord, any of which Mary Williams will play on request. She and Bill excel in making every guest feel special. Their personal warmth enhances the outstanding hospitality at Mercer Island Hideaway.

No pets, smoking, or RV parking; full breakfast; TV; off-street parking. Room B is a suite with patio entrance. In high season, double rate is $55 if bath is shared; two-night minimum. *Closed November, January, and February.* Brochure available.

ROOM	BED	BATH	ENTRANCE	FLOOR	DAILY RATES	
					S - D	(EP)
A	1K or 1Q	Pvt	Main	1	$40-$65	($25)
B	2T or 1K	Pvt	Sep	LL	$40-$65	($25)

Mole House Bed & Breakfast   **(206) 232-1611**
3308 West Mercer Way, Mercer Island, WA 98040
(West shore of island)

It would take an album full of pictures to capture the many facets of Mole House. The rambling contemporary Northwest home overlooks Lake Washington, Seattle, and the Olympic Mountains. It is made up of several distinct sections that are harmoniously linked together by the hosts' collection of art, antiques, and family heirlooms. Don, a native of Seattle, and Petra, who emigrated from West Germany in 1986, extend caring hospitality in a refined atmosphere. Here you can have all the privacy you need, invite friends in for a visit, or enjoy the interesting company of Don and Petra. The three guest accommodations are on different levels of the house. The Eagle has its own sitting room, The Garden Suite has a sitting room and opens onto a patio, and The Apartment is a totally self-contained space with a deck and a panoramic view of the lake. Park-like surroundings, soft music, and elegant breakfasts contribute to the sensual delight of staying at Mole House. It is in every respect a rare find.

No pets; well-behaved children welcome; no smoking; full breakfast; sofa bed, telephone, TV, and kitchen with stocked refrigerator in Room C; patios, decks, and gardens; ten minutes to Seattle via bridge; twenty minutes to airport via freeway; good public transportation and airport connections; off-street parking; German and Spanish spoken. Brochure available.

ROOM	BED	BATH	ENTRANCE	FLOOR	DAILY RATES S - D	(EP)
A	1D	Pvt	Main	1	$45	
B	1D	Pvt	Main	LL	$45	
C	1D	Pvt	Main & Sep	2	$50	($5)

Pickerings' Landing　　　　　　　　　(206) 866-4537 (Keep trying!)
7825 Urquhart Street NW, Olympia, WA 98502
(Just outside Olympia, on lower Puget Sound)

After driving along unhurried, woodsy back roads, arriving at Pickerings' Landing is like finding the treasure at rainbow's end. The pristine white house is set in a commanding position with a view straight up Dana Passage. The home and landscaped grounds are a vision of stunning beauty. The front yard slopes down to a beach where you can dig for clams, hunt for agates and shells, and observe a variety of shorebirds. The home is extremely comfortable, with two lovely guest rooms and many windows to allow sweeping vistas of waterways and Mount Rainier. Jo and Chris Pickering feel that they have "something too good not to share," and I certainly agree. If you plan a visit to Pickerings' Landing, be sure to allow enough time to explore the area, enjoy the home and its surroundings, and get to know your genial hosts.

No pets; children over ten welcome; limited smoking; full breakfast; TV; AC; laundry privileges; boating; other meals (from the garden's bounty) by arrangement; off-street parking; Pacific Ocean is one hour west; Mount St. Helens National Park, one hour south; Seattle, an hour and a half north.

ROOM	BED	BATH	ENTRANCE	FLOOR	DAILY RATES S - D	(EP)
A	1D	Shd*	Main	1	$40-$45	
B	1D	Shd*	Main	LL	$40-$45	

Glen Mar by the Sea   **(206) 457-6110**
318 North Eunice, Port Angeles, WA 98362
(Overlooking Strait of San Juan de Fuca)

A glorious discovery on the Olympic Peninsula is Glen Mar by the Sea, a pristine house at the quiet end of a street that stops at the water. It has the look of a colonial home you might find in the Middle Atlantic states. Huge picture windows, elaborate mouldings, luxurious carpeting, and a few treasured antiques contribute to the ambiance of gracious elegance. Of the three lovely guest rooms on the second floor, two have sea views: one is a cozy room, and the other is a romantic suite with a whole wall of windows. The third room is pink with a mountain vista. Most secluded of all is the Hideaway on the main floor, with a whirlpool tub for two. Long-time residents Marvin and Glenndia Withrow pamper you with tea or coffee at any time, palate-pleasing full breakfasts, and any help you need to plan your stay. If you make Glen Mar by the Sea your home base, you can watch the activities of Port Angeles Harbor and the lights of Victoria. Best of all, you'll be poised for exploring the legendary and unsurpassed Olympic Peninsula.

No pets; children over ten welcome; smoking outside only; full breakfast; robes provided; TV in each room; VCR available; fireplace and piano in living room; walking distance from ferries, buses, restaurants, and shops; off-street parking; major credit cards (V, MC); ferry pickup; airport pickup (Fairchild). Inquire about commercial, off-season, and single rates. Brochure available.

ROOM	BED	BATH	ENTRANCE	FLOOR	DAILY RATES S - D (EP)
A	1D	Shd*	Main	2	$50
B	1Q	Shd*	Main	2	$50
C	1Q	Shd*	Main	2	$70
D	1K	Pvt	Sep	1	$70

Holly Hill House   **(206) 385-5619**
611 Polk Street, Port Townsend, WA 98368
(Historic Uptown District)

This Christmas-card-perfect 1872 Victorian stands on a corner lot with tall holly trees and other plantings from long ago, including an amazing Camperdown elm. Since Bill and Laurie Medlicott became the home's proud owners, they've been digging into its fascinating history and, with the slightest prompting, will entertain you with stories, the funniest of which center around Lizette and Billie. Two guest rooms are named in their honor, one with a view of the garden, the other with a view of Admiralty Inlet and the Cascades. Equally attractive newer rooms in the Carriage House include the Morning Glory and the Skyview. In the large country kitchen, Laurie creates sumptuous breakfasts that are served with a gracious air in the formal dining room. Both here and in the living room, notice the original stippled woodwork that was the rage in the house's heyday. Some furnishings are antiques, some reproductions, but the accent is on liveability. Hosts call it "a home, not a museum," and that's exactly how it feels.

No pets; children over twelve welcome; smoking outside only; no RV parking; full breakfast; historic buildings, Fort Worden State Park, interesting shops and restaurants nearby; off-street parking; major credit cards (V, MC); ferry pickup; airport pickup (Jefferson County). Brochure available.

ROOM	BED	BATH	ENTRANCE	FLOOR	DAILY RATES S - D	(EP)
A	1Q & 1T	Pvt	Main	2	$65	($25)
B	1Q	Pvt	Main	2	$70	
C	1Q	Pvt	Sep	1	$60	
D	1Q	Pvt	Sep	1	$65	

Cedarym, A Colonial Bed & Breakfast   (206) 868-4159
1011 - 240th Avenue NE, Redmond, WA 98053
(Twenty-five minutes from Seattle; East Sammamish Plateau)

It's a rarity on the West Coast to walk into a home and feel that you've stepped back in time, not one, but *two* centuries. Creating an authentic colonial-style home was a labor of love for Mary Ellen and Walt Brown. They have left out no detail — wide plank pine floors, wrought iron lift latches, stenciled walls, bullseye glass over the front door, hand-dipped candles — the list goes on and on. Guest quarters include two spacious bedrooms, each with an antique brass bed and a theme carried out by the stencil design, the Tulip and the Anchor. The exquisitely landscaped, cedar-encircled grounds add another dimension to a visit to Cedarym. There's a cottage garden of flowers and herbs, meditation paths to stroll, a large rose garden of both old and new varieties, and an irresistible gazebo-enclosed spa. A generous breakfast is served by the dining room fireplace each morning. A slice of colonial America awaits you at Cedarym. Try not to miss it!

No children or pets; smoking outside only; full breakfast; TV in each room; gazebo spa; Model T car for sightseeing jaunts; Gilman Village (Issaquah), antique malls, Carnation and Remlinger Farms, Snoqualmie Falls, and beautiful country drives nearby; off-street parking; major credit cards.

ROOM	BED	BATH	ENTRANCE	FLOOR	DAILY RATES S - D (EP)
A	1D	Shd*	Main	2	$45
B	1D	Shd*	Main	2	$45

Capitol Hill House Bed & Breakfast   **(206) 322-1752**
2215 East Prospect, Seattle, WA 98112
(Capitol Hill)

Mary Wolf's stately brick home is on a quiet, tree-lined street in one of Seattle's most prestigious older neighborhoods. Standing on a lovely corner lot, it is handsome indeed. Here you'll find luxurious accommodations with antiques, objects of art, tapestries, and Oriental rugs collected over the years. Two pretty guest rooms and an attractive master suite occupy the second floor. Mary keeps things just so for guests and enjoys setting a beautiful table where breakfast is graciously served. Refined comfort in a convenient location near the University of Washington, Volunteer Park, and downtown Seattle can be yours at Capitol Hill House Bed & Breakfast.

No pets; no smoking on second floor; nursery facilities for infants; older children by prior arrangement; full breakfast; TV in master suite (C); ample street parking; good public transportation and airport connections.

ROOM	BED	BATH	ENTRANCE	FLOOR	DAILY RATES S - D	(EP)
A	1D	Shd*	Main	2	$35	
B	2T	Shd*	Main	2	$40-$45	
C	2T or 1K	Pvt	Main	2	$50-$55	

Galer Place   (206) 282-5339
318 West Galer Street, Seattle, WA 98119
(South slope of Queen Anne Hill)

Galer Place has a British flavor that begins when you meet its owners. Chris is originally from England and ran a B&B in Sussex before moving to this country; her husband Terry hails from Philadelphia. They combine the best of those traditions with West Coast touches — relaxing informality, and freshly ground coffee with breakfast. Built in 1906 as a fine intown family residence, Galer Place is now a warm and inviting guest house in a most convenient location. Antiques of the period and other special features create a unique mood in each of four bedrooms: the Foxglove, the Wedgewood, the Sherwood, and the Crowsnest. The first floor parlor and dining room are natural places for guests to share that afternoon cuppa tea or the wonderful breakfasts that Chris prepares. Galer Place will not only charm you, it will put many of Seattle's highlights right at your doorstep.

Dog in residence; no large pets; older children negotiable; walking distance to Seattle Center; short bus ride to downtown Seattle; airport connections; ample street parking; major credit cards. Room B has a small deck; D has a private loft sitting room. 10% discount for five to seven days and midweek October-April; 10% discount for more than seven days. Brochure available.

ROOM	BED	BATH	ENTRANCE	FLOOR	DAILY RATES S - D (EP)
A	1K	Pvt	Main	2	$70-$80 ($15)
B	1D	Pvt	Main	2	$70-$80 ($15)
C	2D	Pvt	Main	2	$70-$80 ($15)
D	1Q	Pvt	Main	2	$70-$80 ($15)

Mildred's Bed & Breakfast   (206) 325-6072
1202 Fifteenth Avenue East, Seattle, WA 98112
(Capitol Hill, facing east side of Volunteer Park)

If ever a place could tug at your heartstrings, Mildred's would do it. It's the ultimate trip-to-Grandmother's fantasy come true. A large white Victorian possessed of a friendly charm, it's the perfect setting for Mildred Sarver's caring hospitality. Three guest rooms on the upper floor couldn't be prettier. Sitting alcoves, lace curtains, and antiques add to the ambiance of warmth and security. Off the hallway are a half bath and a very nice full bath with a skylight view. For longer stays, there's a self-contained apartment suite (D) on the ground floor with its own entrance, kitchen, bath, living room, and bedroom. Mildred's special touches and lavish breakfasts make her guests feel truly pampered.

No pets; smoking in restricted areas; full breakfast; TV available; fireplace in living room; sofa bed in living room of suite (D); park across street (site of Seattle Art Museum) good for walking or jogging; ample street parking; good public transportation and airport connections.

ROOM	BED	BATH	ENTRANCE	FLOOR	DAILY RATES S - D (EP)
A	1D	Shd*	Main	2	$45-$55 ($15)
B	1D	Shd*	Main	2	$45-$55 ($15)
C	2T or 1K	Shd*	Main	2	$45-$55 ($15)
D	1D	Pvt	Sep	1G	$75

Marit Nelson   **(206) 782-7900**
6208 Palatine Avenue North, Seattle, WA 98103
(Woodland Park area)

This cozy brick Tudor-style home is in a quiet north Seattle neighborhood with good access to freeways and public transportation. Here Marit Nelson offers her special version of Scandinavian hospitality. There's a very homey atmosphere, the kind that makes you feel like settling in for a while. A whimsical note is struck by the collection of stuffed bears flanking the stairs that lead to the three guest rooms (only two are used at any one time). Care has been taken to make each room comfy and attractive. Room B has a delightful view of water, mountains, and sunsets. A variety of guidebooks to Seattle and environs ensures that you'll find plenty to do, rain or shine. Breakfasts are delicious and beautifully served, a savory beginning to any day.

No pets, smoking, or RV parking; families welcome; full breakfast; walking distance to Green Lake and Woodland Park Zoo; ten minutes to downtown and Univesity of Washington; two blocks to bus stop; ample street parking; Norwegian spoken. Member Washington Bed & Breakfast Guild and Seattle Bed & Breakfast Inn Association. Brochure available.

ROOM	BED	BATH	ENTRANCE	FLOOR	DAILY RATES S - D (EP)
A	1Q	Shd	Main	2	$40-$50
B	1D	Shd	Main	2	$40-$50
C	2T	Shd	Main	2	$40-$50

Prince of Wales   **(206) 325-9692**
133 Thirteenth Avenue East, Seattle, WA 98102
(Capitol Hill)

From this handsome turn-of-the-century home you can easily walk or take public transportation to the city's conference sites and all the intown attractions you'll want to visit. Equally well-suited for convention, business, or vacation travelers, Prince of Wales has home-like comfort with a regal air. Interior colors hint at the owners' past on the eastern seaboard: navy, white, burgundy, and gray, with shades of pink added in the upstairs guest quarters. Conveniences such as a private telephone line and a laundry room with an iron can come in handy when you're on the road. Early morning coffee in your room and delicious full breakfasts round out the generous hospitality offered by hosts Naomi and Bert. But most impressive of all is the view — a stunning panorama of the city skyline, Olympic Mountains, and Puget Sound, with the Space Needle in the foreground. Two of the three guest rooms feature this ever-present reminder that you couldn't be anywhere but Seattle.

Two cats in residence; no pets or smoking; no RV parking; full breakfast; fireplace in living room; private garden; good public transportation and airport connections; off-street and street parking; major credit cards (V, MC).

ROOM	BED	BATH	ENTRANCE	FLOOR	DAILY RATES	
					S - D	(EP)
A	1D	Shd*	Main	2	$50	
B	2T	Shd*	Main	2	$50	
C	1Q	Pvt	Main	2	$65	($5)

Roberta's Bed & Breakfast (206) 329-3326
1147 Sixteenth Avenue East, Seattle, WA 98112
(Capitol Hill)

The friendly appeal of Roberta Barry's large old home is obvious at first glance. It fits comfortably into this quiet Capitol Hill neighborhood near the University of Washington and Volunteer Park and is convenient to downtown. And *you'll* fit comfortably into one of the lovely guest rooms on the second floor. Choose the romantic Peach Room (C) with its bay window and love seat. Or perhaps the Madrona (B), a cheery corner room where you can greet the morning sun. Every room is special at Roberta's. Her home is full of beautiful Oriental rugs, antiques, and good books. Add to these attributes the spice of her humor, and you've got a combination that's hard to beat.

Dog in residence; no pets; older children by prior arrangement; smoking outside only (porch); no RV parking; full breakfast; sleeping loft in Room A; Rooms A, C, and D share two baths; ample street parking; good public transportation and airport connections.

ROOM	BED	BATH	ENTRANCE	FLOOR	DAILY RATES	
					S - D	(EP)
A	1Q	Shd*	Main	2	$60-$65	($15)
B	1Q	Pvt	Main	2	$75-$80	
C	1Q	Shd*	Main	2	$65-$70	
D	1Q	Shd*	Main	2	$60-$65	

Blakely Estates   (509) 926-9426
East 7710 Hodin Drive, Spokane, WA 99212
(Seven miles northeast of city center)

In a park-like setting, right on the bank of the Spokane River, stands one of Spokane's original B&Bs. Experienced hosts John and Kathy Smith want guests to have just the kind of getaway they need. The atmosphere at Blakely Estates inspires relaxation and romance. Enjoy the luxuriant grounds and river view from a lounge chair or a park bench; take a rowboat out on the water; soak in the hot tub under the stars. When you settle in at night, you'll appreciate the privacy of the guest accommodations on the home's lower level. There's a living room with a woodstove, TV, VCR, and telephone; a craft corner and sitting alcove; two comfortable bedrooms; and a bath. Hikers, take note: The Smiths are proud that their property is adjacent to the Centennial Trail connecting Spokane and Coeur d'Alene, Idaho. Whether you take advantage of the wealth of outdoor recreation in the area or instead seek a holiday that is peaceful, restful, and utterly undemanding, Blakely Estates satisfies.

No pets, smoking, or alcoholic beverages; children ten or over welcome; full breakfast; extra-long bed in Room A; dock; off-street parking; airport pickup (Felts Field). Two-night minimum on weekends and holidays; inquire about extended stay and off-season discounts; complete guest suite with private bath, $53. Brochure available.

ROOM	BED	BATH	ENTRANCE	FLOOR	DAILY RATES	
					S - D	(EP)
A	1D	Shd*	Sep	LL	$38-$43	($10)
B	2T or 1K	Shd*	Sep	LL	$38-$43	($10)

The Georgian   **(509) 624-7107**
West 2118 Second Avenue, Spokane, WA 99204
(Historic Browne's Addition)

Grand homes inhabited by Spokane's most prosperous citizens at the turn of the century were concentrated in an area known as Browne's Addition. Overlooking historic Coeur d'Alene Park is one such home — The Georgian. Here Tex and Dottie Loosier offer warm hospitality in the southern tradition. The handsome home still has some of its original features: chandeliers, wallpaper, hardwood floors, mouldings, and copper wainscoting. Two deluxe guest suites occupy the second floor. The Lunette, with a view of the park and a charming fireplace, is done in blue and white; it's light, airy, and as pretty as a wedding cake. The spacious Americana-Lee has bay windows, a large, old-fashioned bathroom with tiny inlaid tiles, and early American charm. Within a few blocks of The Georgian, take a historic walking tour, visit the Cheney Cowles Museum, and have dinner at famous Patsy Clark's. Genteel lodging in the heart of Spokane awaits you at The Georgian.

No pets; no children under twelve; smoking outside only (veranda); full breakfast; TV on request; extra bedroom in Americana-Lee Suite; tennis court in park across street; public transportation and airport connections; ample street parking; major credit cards (V, MC). Special occasions catered to with special touches. Inquire about weekly rates. Brochure available.

ROOM	BED	BATH	ENTRANCE	FLOOR	DAILY RATES	
					S - D	(EP)
A	1Q & 1T	Pvt	Main	2	$75-$85	($15)
B	1D & 2T	Pvt	Main	2	$65-$75	($15)

Hillside House
East 1729 Eighteenth, Spokane, WA 99203
(South Hill)

(509) 535-1893
Days: 534-1426

There's something wonderful about a mature residential neighborhood with quiet, tree-shaded streets and houses of individual character. Hillside House graces such a setting, just three miles from downtown on Spokane's South Hill. While appearing deceptively small from the front, it is actually spacious inside. A large living room spanning the glassed-in back of the house overlooks the lush leafiness of a wooded hillside; it feels more like being outdoors on a terrace than enclosed in a room. Myriad artistic touches add to the vibrant interior. The use of fabrics, wallpapers, carpeting, and furnishings is both original and tasteful, lending a rich, textured look. A stairwell lined with art leads to the second floor guest rooms, which are as attractively appointed as the rest of the house. A guest once claimed to have slept on "the world's most comfortable bed" here. Hosts JoAnn and Bud cater to the needs of each guest, providing hospitality in the truest sense. In this spirit, they keep their B&B "small by intent."

Cat in residence; no pets; smoking outside only; full breakfast; common room with telephone and library; parks, museums, recreational and cultural attractions nearby; ample street parking. Brochure available.

ROOM	BED	BATH	ENTRANCE	FLOOR	DAILY RATES S - D (EP)
A	2T	Shd*	Main	2	$40-$45 ($10)
B	1D	Shd*	Main	2	$40-$45 ($10)

Marianna Stoltz House   (509) 483-4316
East 427 Indiana, Spokane, WA 99207
(Central Spokane, historic Gonzaga University area)

Phyllis Maguire and her family have the good fortune to live in the 1908 American foursquare classic home in which Phyllis grew up. She named it Marianna Stoltz in honor of her mother. Now one of Spokane's historic landmarks, it has the feel of a big, old-fashioned family home that's comfortable through and through. Period furnishings, handsome woodwork, leaded glass cabinets, and a lovely tile fireplace enhance the gracious interior. Accommodations are all on the second floor, and guests are welcome to come and go as they please; the front entrance is theirs alone. Beds are covered with the wonderful collection of old quilts that Phyllis so generously shares. Fond memories of Marianna Stoltz House might include visiting or reading on the wide, wrap-around porch, sipping a nightcap of home-made raspberry cordial, or breakfasting on cheese strada or Dutch babies. These and other pleasures await you at this popular intown B&B.

No pets; no children under twelve; smoking outside only; full breakfast; TV available; AC; choice of shower or clawfoot tub; good public transportation and airport connections; off-street parking; major credit cards (V, MC). Brochure available.

ROOM	BED	BATH	ENTRANCE	FLOOR	DAILY RATES S - D (EP)
A	1K	Shd*	Main	2	$40-$50 ($10)
B	2T	Shd*	Main	2	$40-$50
C	1Q	Pvt	Main	2	$40-$50
D	1Q	Pvt	Main	2	$40-$50

Town & Country Cottage Bed & Breakfast   (509) 466-7559
North 7620 Fox Point Drive, Spokane, WA 99208
(Five miles north of city center, near Whitworth College)

Wanda Johnson's Town & Country Cottage is an asset to its quiet, well-maintained neighborhood. The landscaped yard is studded with lovely flower gardens. Just out the back door, there's a covered patio with pretty wicker furniture and a garden-like atmosphere, a place of peaceful respite on mild days. The interior spaces have a soft elegance about them, a look enhanced by muted floral patterns in rose, lavender, and cream. A few treasured heirlooms catch the eye, such as the exquisite armoire that belonged to Wanda's grandmother. The liberal use of fresh flowers, thick towels, English soaps, and fine linens and lace add to the intimate Victorian ambiance. A comfortable night's sleep at Town & Country Cottage is followed by a breakfast that is creative, delicious, and beautifully presented. Indeed, Wanda's guests rate first-class treatment at every turn.

Cat in residence; no pets, children, or smoking; full breakfast; shared sitting room with fireplace and TV; shopping, golf, and Mount Spokane skiing nearby; public transportation; ample street parking. Brochure available.

ROOM	BED	BATH	ENTRANCE	FLOOR	DAILY RATES S - D (EP)
A	1D	Shd*	Main	1	$38
B	1T	Shd*	Main	1	$28

Whispering Pines Bed & Breakfast (509) 448-1433
East 7504 Forty-fourth, Spokane, WA 99223
(South Hill)

The Campbells designed their contemporary wood home to take full advantage of the magnificent view of the Spokane Valley and Mount Spokane. Nestled among pines in a commanding position, Whispering Pines Bed & Breakfast offers the happy contrast of luxurious accommodations in a rustic setting. Landscaped grounds harmonize with the wooded environment, which teems with wildlife that may be observed from the deck or from a vantage point inside. The commodious interior is elegant and meticulously kept. Going from room to room nourishes one's aesthetic senses through color, floral designs, varied textures, and the awesome panorama. Common rooms on the main floor include a living room with a fireplace and a southwest flavor, a country kitchen and den that open to a deck, and a strikingly beautiful dining room. Guest accommodations are on the lower level, view-side of the house: three guest rooms, private and shared baths, a living/dining area, a kitchen, and a separate entrance. Whispering Pines is just the place to unwind in the peaceful seclusion of the country.

No pets, children, or smoking; full breakfast; TV; AC; kitchen and laundry privileges at extra charge; off-street parking; twenty minutes to city center. Accommodations adaptable to self-contained guest suite at $85. Brochure available.

ROOM	BED	BATH	ENTRANCE	FLOOR	DAILY RATES S - D (EP)		
A	1Q	Shd*	Sep	LL	$43-$48
B	1Q	Shd*	Sep	LL	$43-$48
C	1K	Pvt	Sep	LL	$50-$55

Forget-Me-Not Bed & Breakfast   1-800-843-7552 or (509) 663-6114
1133 Washington Street, Wenatchee, WA 98801
(Central Wenatchee)

After concluding a chapter of their lives in Alaska, Frank and Juanita Young chose to settle in Wenatchee, a small town in central Washington with four distinct seasons. It is situated in a wide valley with majestic mountains in the distance and two rivers, the mighty Columbia and the Wenatchee, that converge. Their attractive 1904 home is cream colored, trimmed in dark green and rust. It occupies a large corner lot in a quiet residential neighborhood near a lovely park. The front porch swing looks inviting, as do the gazebo-covered hot tub and the sauna in the landscaped private yard. Inside, sloped ceilings add to the cozy appeal of the upstairs guest rooms. One has wood-paneled walls; another is decorated in dark green and white and spans the front of the house. In the two quaint, smaller bedrooms, hand-stenciled designs lend sweetness and warmth. The Youngs can share with guests a wealth of perennial activities in the area that make Wenatchee not just a great place to live, but an ideal vacation spot.

Dog and cat in residence; no pets; smoking outside only; full country breakfast; two baths available; piano, fireplace, and cable TV in living room; off-street parking; airport (Pangborn), train station, and bus depot pickup. Brochure available.

ROOM	BED	BATH	ENTRANCE	FLOOR	DAILY RATES S - D (EP)
A	1D	Shd*	Main	2	$47-$53
B	1D	Shd*	Main	2	$47-$53
C	1D	Shd*	Main	2	$47-$53
D	1D	Shd*	Main	2	$47-$53

Home By The Sea   **(206) 221-2964**
2388 East Sunlight Beach Road, Clinton, WA 98236
(Southwest end of island)

Few places so accessible to a metropolitan area possess the distant, get-away-from-it-all atmosphere of Home By The Sea. This year-round bed and breakfast retreat overlooks Useless Bay, a Puget Sound shipping channel, and the Olympic Mountains. Surrounding it is Deer Lagoon, a natural bird sanctuary and major Washington Wetlands area. The home is filled with art, antiques, and artifacts from around the world. Floor-to-ceiling windows in the dining area (binoculars provided) offer a mesmerizing view as you savor breakfast specialties that are not only luscious but original. There are two upstairs accommodations for guests, the Sunset Room and the Seabreeze Suite. White walls, fresh flowers, brass, antiques, and exquisite bedding — plus the view — create a dreamy, romantic ambiance. Most important to hosts Sharon Fritts-Drew and Helen Fritts is that you leave your cares behind and let this remote world of peace and tranquility enfold you. Simple pleasures like exploring the seashore, birdwatching, soaking in the beachside hot tub — hearing only the sounds of nature — can have a magical effect on your spirits, not to mention your relationship.

Dog and two cats in residence; no pets, children, or smoking; full breakfast; hot tub robes and towels provided; bonfire pit; hammock; off-street parking; major credit cards (V, MC). Five deluxe vacation cottages (families welcome) available at $95-$155; weekly rates. Brochure available.

ROOM	BED	BATH	ENTRANCE	FLOOR	DAILY RATES	
					S - D	(EP)
A	1Q	Pvt	Main	2	$90	
B	1D & 1T	Pvt	Main	2	$90	($5)

Blue House Inn   (206) 221-8392
513 Anthes, Langley, WA 98260
(Two blocks from village and water)

A short walk from the shops and restaurants of charming Langley is a traditional B&B of uncommon homeyness. It has an excellent view of Langley and Puget Sound, impressive gardens and decking in back, and a cozy brick fireplace in the living room where you may enjoy the company of hosts Mary and Rod Erickson. The two guest rooms have been lovingly outfitted with country antiques, lace curtains, nice linens, colorful rugs on polished wood floors, and alcoves with pedestal sinks. One has French doors leading to a private deck, while the other, slightly larger room has a window seat. Delectable full breakfasts are attractively served in the dining room, accompanied by the tantalizing vista. Your sojourn in Langley is sure to be enhanced by the comfort, convenience, and attentive care found at Blue House Inn.

Cat in residence; no pets; smoking outside only; full breakfast; no RV parking; TV; VCR; outdoor firepit; off-street parking; ferry pickup (Clinton); airport pickup (Porter Field).

ROOM	BED	BATH	ENTRANCE	FLOOR	DAILY RATES	
					S - D	(EP)
A	1D	Shd*	Main	1	$45-$55	
B	1Q	Shd*	Main	1	$45-$55	

Country Cottage of Langley   **(206) 221-8709**
P.O. Box 459, Langley, WA 98260
(215 Sixth Street, overlooking village and water)

"A Home Retreat in Country Elegance" accurately describes this fully renovated 1929 farmhouse. From the custom woodwork and cabinetry to the coordinated designer fabrics, wallpaper, and furnishings, the quality of workmanship and materials is meticulous in every detail. Cream and pale green combined with muted floral motifs create a soft, delicate look and a fresh, light atmosphere. Guests may curl up in front of the cozy fieldstone fireplace in their own living room and, in the morning, enjoy nourishing full breakfasts in the sunroom or dining room. A walkway with extensive decking and a gazebo connects the main house to a newer addition containing two guest suites. One has an extensive collection of old mirrors on display, the other has old tools and farm implements. Each of the four suites offers the utmost in comfort and country elegance in a tranquil, soothing environment. To top it all off, a stunning view of the Cascades, Saratoga Passage, and the village of Langley is your constant companion.

No pets; no children under twelve; smoking outside only; full breakfast; walking distance from village and water; off-street parking; wheelchair access; major credit cards (V, MC); ferry pickup (Clinton). Inquire about single rates and guest cottage on property. Brochure available.

ROOM	BED	BATH	ENTRANCE	FLOOR	DAILY RATES	
					S - D	(EP)
A	1Q	Pvt	Main	2	$75	
B	1Q	Pvt	Main	2	$75	
C	1Q	Pvt	Sep	1	$85	
D	1Q	Pvt	Sep	1	$85	

Eagles Nest Inn   **(206) 321-5331**
3236 East Saratoga Road, Langley, WA 98260
(One and one-half miles from village, overlooking Saratoga Passage)

Nancy and Dale Bowman's ingeniously designed home is set among tall firs and cedars with commanding views of Saratoga Passage, Camano Island, and Mount Baker. A pleasing contrast of contemporary and traditional elements give the interior an ambiance that is at once refined, comfortable, and aesthetically satisfying. Abundant windows and open space help to bring the outside in; you feel secluded and close to nature while you're being pampered beyond expectation. Each guest room is extra spacious, with a sitting area and view. The Saratoga Room has sweeping views of the Passage and triple French doors leading to a private balcony; The Forest Room has a large bay window with a water view through the trees, a skylight, and its own separate entrance; The Eagles Nest is perched at the top of the house with a private balcony and a dramatic 360-degree panorama. Each morning, selections from Nancy's wide-ranging breakfast repertoire start the day off right. Stroll about the grounds, paddle your own canoe, soak in the spa under the stars, savor the privacy of your romantic room — beautiful memories are yours for the making at Eagles Nest Inn.

No pets or children; smoking outside only; full breakfast; guest lounge with library/reading area and TV area; TV; VCR; woodstove in living room; robes provided; decks; outdoor spa; "bottomless" chocolate chip cookie jar; off-street parking; major credit cards (V, MC); ferry pickup (Clinton) and airport pickup (Porter Field) by prior arrangement. Brochure available.

ROOM	BED	BATH	ENTRANCE	FLOOR	DAILY RATES S-D	(EP)
A	1K	Pvt	Main	2	$65-$75	($25)
B	1K	Pvt	Sep	2	$65-$75	($25)
C	1Q	Pvt	Main	3	$65-$75	

Log Castle Bed & Breakfast   **(206) 321-5483**
3273 East Saratoga Road, Langley, WA 98260
(Beachside overlooking Saratoga Passage)

An authentic taste of the Northwest awaits you at this most unique of island homes. Far back from the road at water's edge, the fairytale log castle is full of family history. It was built of wood from the property and has evolved over the years into a rustic, homelike retreat for B&B guests. Aged, handhewn wood imbues the interior with a mellow warmth, and countless one-of-a-kind details delight you at every turn. A panorama of water, beach, mountains, and pasture are on view from a porch swing, your bedroom, or the living room with its huge stone fireplace and relaxing places to sit. Guest rooms are loaded with charm. One east-facing room has French glass doors to a private deck; the room above has a porch with a swing, a large bathroom, and a nifty woodstove. The second story turret room has two big windows overlooking the beach and mountains plus a porch with a swing. The third story turret room has windows on five of eight sides and is warmed by a 1912 woodstove. Breakfast is a multicourse feast. To work it off, you may want to walk the mile or so of beach to the village of Langley. At Log Castle, Norma and Jack Metcalf offer a peaceful, restorative atmosphere where your cares will slowly melt away.

Dog, ducks, and geese on property; no indoor pets; children over ten welcome; smoking outside only; no RV parking; full breakfast; TV in living room; canoe available; off-street parking; major credit cards (V, MC); ferry pickup (Clinton); airport pickup (Porter Field). Brochure available.

ROOM	BED	BATH	ENTRANCE	FLOOR	DAILY RATES S - D	(EP)
A	1Q	Pvt	Main	1	$60	
B	2T or 1K	Pvt	Main	2	$80	
C	2T or 1K	Pvt	Main	2	$70	($13)
D	1D	Pvt	Main	3	$80	($13)

DINING HIGHLIGHTS: WASHINGTON

Please read "About Dining Highlights" on page *ix*.

ANACORTES
Boomer's Landing, 209 "T" Avenue; (206) 293-5109; seafood

La Petite, 3401 Commercial Avenue; (206) 293-4644; European

ASHFORD
Alexander's Country Inn, Highway 706 E; (206) 569-2300; Continental

The Wild Berry, Highway 706 E; (206) 569-2628; hearty, mountain fare

BELLEVUE
Jake O'Shaughnessey's, Bellevue Square, NE Sixth and Bellevue Way; (206) 455-5559; peachwood broiled fresh seafood

Landau's, 500 - 108th Avenue NE; (206) 646-6644; Continental

BELLINGHAM
The Fairhaven Restaurant, 1114 Harris Avenue; (206) 676-1520; seafood, steak, and variety of other dishes

High Country Restaurant, 119 North Commercial Street; (206) 733-3443; steaks, seafood, chicken, and pasta

Il Fiasco, 1308 Railroad Avenue; (206) 676-9136; Italian

Wang's Garden, 1644 - 140th Avenue NE; (206) 641-6011; Chinese

BLAINE
Harbor Cafe, Fisherman's Wharf; (206) 332-5176; breakfast and lunch specials and seafood (noted for fish & chips)

BOW
Chuckanut Manor, 302 Chuckanut Drive; (206) 766-6191; seafood, steaks, and prime rib

The Oyster Bar, 240 Chuckanut Drive; (206) 766-6185; northwest seafood

Oyster Creek Inn, 190 Chuckanut Drive; (206) 766-6179; oysters and simple seafood dishes

The Rhododendron Café, 553 Chuckanut Drive; (206) 766-6667; seasonal fresh

CONWAY
Conway Tavern & Eatery, 1667 Spruce; (206) 445-4733; seafood, burgers, steaks

ELLENSBURG
The Blue Grouse, 1401 Dollar Way (Exit 106 off I-90); (509) 925-4808; American

Carriage House, 402 North Pearl; (509) 962-2260; lamb, beef, pasta, and seafood

Valley Café, 105 West Third; (509) 925-3050; seafood and pasta

ISSAQUAH
Harry O's, 719 North Gilman Boulevard; (206) 392-8614; northwest cuisine with a French flair

262

KIRKLAND

Café Juanita, 9702 NE 120th Place; (206) 823-1505; Italian

LA CONNER

Barkley's of La Conner, Second and Washington Streets; (206) 466-4133; northwest cuisine

Black Swan Café, 505 South First Street; (206) 466-3040; Mediterranean/northwest

Calico Cupboard, 720 South First Street; (206) 466-4451; bakery items, sandwiches, soups, desserts, all made from scratch

LANGLEY

Café Langley, 113 First Street; (206) 221-3090; Greek and Continental

Star Bistro Primavera, 210-1/2 First Street; (206) 221-2627; creative seafood and pasta dishes

LEAVENWORTH

Terrace Bistro, 200 Eighth Street; (509) 548-4193; Continental

LOPEZ ISLAND

Bay Café, Lopez Village; (206) 468-3700; eclectic menu

Gail's Restaurant, Lopez Village; (206) 468-2150; classic northwest cuisine

Jeanna's Seafood Gallery, Lopez Village; (206) 468-2114; fresh seafood

MOUNT VERNON

Longfellow Café, 120-B North First Street; (206) 336-3684; seasonal fresh

Wildflowers, 2001 East College Way; (206) 424-9724; international cuisine

PORT ANGELES

C'est Si Bon, 2300 U.S. 101; (206) 452-8888; French

PORT TOWNSEND

Fountain Café, 920 Washington Street; (206) 385-1364; seafood and pasta

Lanza's Ristorante, 1020 Lawrence; (206) 385-6221; Italian

Le Pavilion, 628 Water Street; (206) 385-4881; Continental

REDMOND

Kikuya, 8105 - 161st Avenue NE; (206) 881-8771; Japanese

Sweetwater, 7824 Leary Way; (206) 883-9090; homemade local dishes

SEATTLE

Apres Vous Café, 1530 Queen Anne Avenue North; (206) 284-9827; Continental and pasta dishes

Ayutthaya, 727 East Pike; (206) 324-8833; Thai

Bai Tong, 3423 South 160th Street; (206) 241-1122; Thai

Café Sabika, 315 East Pine; (206) 622-3272; neighborhood bistro

Café Sport, 2020 Western Avenue; (206) 443-6000; new American/Pacific Rim cuisine

Chez Shea, 94 Pike (Pike Place Market); (206) 467-9990; innovative French-inspired cuisine

Chinook's, 1735 West Thurman; (206) 283-4665; seafood

Il Bistro, 93-A Pike Street (Pike Place Market); (206) 682-3049; northern Italian

Julia's 14-Carrot Café, 2305 Eastlake Avenue East; (206) 324-1442; eclectic ethnic cooking

Le Tastevin, 19 West Harrison Street; (206) 283-0991; French

Olympia Pizza & Spaghetti, 1500 Queen Anne Avenue; (206) 285-5550

SNOQUALMIE

Old Honey Farm Inn Restaurant, 8910 - 384th Avenue SE; (206) 888-9899; northwest cuisine

SPOKANE

Aracelia's, South 111 Stevens; (509) 747-9361; Mexican

Café Roma, South 2727 Mount Vernon (Lincoln Heights Shopping Center); (509) 534-5540; Italian

Clinkerdagger, West 621 Mallon (Flour Mill); (509) 328-5965; seafood, fowl, and beef

Patsy Clark's, West 2208 Second Street; (509) 838-8300; Continental

Shenanigan's, 322 North Spokane Falls Court; (509) 455-5072; seafood and prime rib

WENATCHEE

Royal Palace Chinese Restaurant, North Wenatchee Avenue and Maple Street; (509) 663-1855

Sodbuster's Restaurant & Bakery, 731 Wenatchee Avenue; (509) 662-1118; family dining

Visconti's Italian Restaurant, 1737 North Wenatchee Avenue; (509) 662-5013

The Windmill, 1501 North Wenatchee Avenue; (509) 663-3478; steaks and seafood

British
Columbia

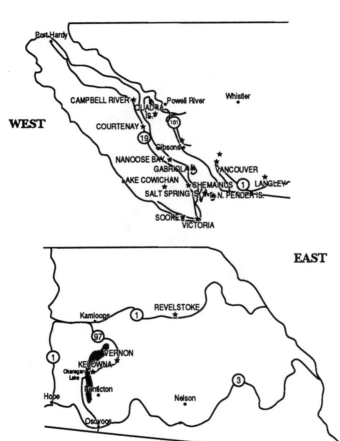

WEST

Port Hardy

CAMPBELL RIVER ★
QUADRA Is. ★
COURTENAY ★
(19)
Gibsons ●
NANOOSE BAY ★
GABRIOLA ★
LAKE COWICHAN ★
SALT SPRING IS. ★
SOOKE ★
VICTORIA

Powell River
(101)

Whistler ●

★
★ VANCOUVER
(1) LANGLEY ★
★ CHEMAINUS
★ N. PENDER IS.

EAST

REVELSTOKE ★
Kamloops ●
(1)
(97)
VERNON ★
KELOWNA ★
Okanagan Lake
Penticton ●
Nelson ●
(3)
Hope ●
Osoyoos ●

From Seattle the Princess Marguerite plys the Juan De Fuca Strait and eventually glides into the picturesque harbor of Victoria, a serene capital city steeped in British tradition. Treat yourself to high tea at the grand, ivy-covered Empress Hotel, tour the Provincial Parliament Buildings, and visit the intriguing Provincial Museum. After enjoying the magic of this lovely inner harbor, a drive west will take you to the quaint village of Sooke. Here you'll find excellent year-round salmon fishing. In the Sooke Region Museum you can trace the history of this pleasant coastal Salish settlement.

The picturesque Saanich Peninsula, north of Victoria, is home to the delicate perfumes so abundant in Butchart Gardens. At the peninsula's tip, you may embark on a ferry to the Gulf Islands.

Salt Spring, the largest of the islands, is blessed with a mild, sunny climate, peaceful tranquility, and breathtaking vistas — an artist's paradise. To experience the island's art, visit some galleries or artists' studios.

The idyllic, rustic character of Pender Island attracts visitors to its shores. Once you're there, the casual pace, friendliness, quiet country lanes, and fine beaches will make it difficult to leave.

Traveling north from Victoria on Highway 1, the east coast of Vancouver Island stretches some 300 miles. It is shaped by coal mines, native petroglyphs, and centuries of wind and waves. Small communities nestle in protected fishing coves. Nanaimo, supporting forestry, fishing, and agriculture, is the stepping stone to the cottage resort of Gabriola Island. Here you may cycle country roads, go scuba diving, relax on the beaches, and enjoy the view of mainland mountains across the water.

At Parksville, you may want to turn west and cross the island through some of British Columbia's most spectacular forest. Its delicate, subtle life epitomizes the very spirit of all seasons and seems never out of step with time. It provides a fine prelude to the robust Pacific with its sweeping storms, heavy mists, easterly leaning trees, and beaches that glisten whenever the sun peeks through.

North of Parksville in the Comox Valley, you will discover an unbelievable selection of things to do in any season. Comox, a bustling modern-day seaport, is the point at which to depart by ferry for Powell River and the numerous coves and inlets of the Sunshine Coast — paradise for scuba diver and beachcomber alike.

You may choose to continue north from Comox to Campbell River, famous for its salmon fishing and saltwater pier, with facilities that guarantee year-round use.

From downtown Campbell River, take the ten-minute ferry ride to

Quadra Island where you'll find all manner of fishing and boating activities. For land-lovers, there are scenic coastal trails and a panoramic view at the end of a hike up Chinese Mountain.

Shortly after leaving Campbell River, Highway 19 drifts from the coast and weaves through forest and frontier logging towns to Port Hardy's rugged headland. From here you may take the ferry that navigates the astonishing Inside Passage to Prince Rupert.

The cosmopolitan city of Vancouver boasts a Mediterranean climate and spectacular setting. It is easily accessible by ferry from Vancouver Island and has all the vacationer's necessities: parks, golf courses, museums, indoor and outdoor theaters, a domed stadium, fine stores, and myriad restaurants that offer a world of choice cuisines. Granville Island, set in the heart of False Creek, is a celebrated place to enjoy a succulent seafood dinner. Outdoor recreation abounds: Sunbathe and gaze at the vista while relaxing on splendid city beaches; take a leisurely stroll along the seawall surrounding the lush Stanley Park; skim the Pacific in a kayak, canoe, or power boat; ski the groomed slopes of Grouse and Seymour Mountains.

East of Vancouver lies the fertile Fraser Valley from which the Granville Island Market draws much of its bounty. The Fraser River meanders to the coast after carving a giant elbow at Hope, the gateway to craggy, forested mountains, deep canyons, shimmering mountain lakes, and the sun-drenched Okanagan.

Ookanawgan means "place of water." A valley of fruit trees — cherries, apricots, peaches, plums, apples, pears, and grapes — provides summer fare amidst sage brush, ponderosa pine, and glittering lakes. A pocket desert with cactus, horned lizards, and burrowing owls runs from Osoyoos on the east side north to Oliver. With the help of irrigation and ingenuity, the scorched desert gives way to rows of lush vines that produce some of the Okanagan's finest grapes. Many estate wineries in the area offer tours and tastings.

The valley narrows dramatically at McIntyre Bluff, a vertical cliff face north of Oliver. Past this point, the temperature changes as you approach the shallow, organically rich Vaseux Lake. Here, many species of birds, including the rare trumpeter swan, find sanctuary. In summer, the graceful California bighorn sheep can frequently be seen on the eastern slopes above the lake; in midwinter, they move to the lower areas and are a delightful sight for the traveler.

The three major Okanagan cities — Penticton, Kelowna, and Vernon — offer art galleries, museums, and stores. There is an abundance of recreational activities at beaches, parks, golf courses, summer festivals, and winter resorts. Summerland, tucked beside a volcanic plug called Giant's Head Mountain, presents a tranquil environment with a European flavor. Peachland, with its clean pebble beaches, is directly across Okanagan Lake from Okanagan Mountain Park, the only natural wilderness park in the valley. North of Kelowna, Winfield lies at the south end of Wood Lake, which drains into the blue-green waters of Kalamalka. Rattlesnake Point Park reaches into the lake. Dried bunch grass and sprawling ponderosa pines make hiking easy and add to the breathtaking beauty of the area.

On the north side of Vernon, the valley widens and fruit trees give way to field crops. Armstrong, a bountiful dairy community, is home to a fine cheese. Enderby is a sleepy, heritage-conscious town on the Shuswap River. It closes the valley with a rugged backdrop of cliffs.

Beyond the Okanagan Valley, the jagged, snow-crested Monashees converge with the Columbia River and the Selkirk Mountains in the region of Revelstoke, creating some of the world's most striking mountain vistas.

From Revelstoke, you can follow Highway 23 south along the Upper Arrow Lake and be swept into the unspoiled magnificence of the Kootenays, where avalanche-scarred, timbered mountains drop steeply into narrow, lake-filled valleys. Travelers to this area enjoy some of the finest rainbow trout found anywhere, spelunk in mysterious caves, and relax in soothing hot springs. The past lives on in the ghost town of Sandon and dwells in the artisan city of Nelson.

The soaring Rockies form a natural eastern boundary of British Columbia. Whether you are hiking an alpine meadow, hang-gliding over a ridge, or simply gazing at snowy peaks, you'll be inspired by their beauty, as others have been before you.

The Yellowhead (Tête Jaune) trail takes you west from the Rockies to the dynamic city of Prince George. Traveling north, fortune seekers full of pioneer spirit abide in a land of vast horizons, jade green mountain lakes, icy streams, and Northern Lights that shimmer their way south.

From Prince George the Yellowhead continues west to the lakes and rivers near Burns Lake, a sport fishing haven and fall foliage spectacle. Still farther west, the Skeena River surges toward the ocean city of Prince Rupert. From there, you may cross Hecate Strait and enter a world of timeless beauty, the Queen Charlotte Islands. On the west side of this emerald forested gem lies the powerful Pacific, and beyond, well...that is another story.

The Grey Mouse Tea House and Bed & Breakfast (604) 337-5795
Site 110, Unit 9, R.R.#1, Campbell River, B.C. V9W 3S4
(Saratoga Beach, between Courtenay and Campbell River)

For many, The Grey Mouse is a regular stop on the route north to Port Hardy. If you arrive around tea time, you're in for a treat. Tasty delicacies prepared and served by Cecille Dreger may be enjoyed by the fireplace in the delightful tea room by the sea. Painted wall murals, handcrafted mouse characters and tea cosies, and the warm ambiance provide a cheerful setting for lunch, tea, or the scrumptious breakfast that is cooked to order for each B&B guest. The guest area has its own separate entrance. It includes three well-appointed bedrooms, a bath, and a guest lounge with a refrigerator and television. From The Grey Mouse you can walk for miles along wide, secluded Saratoga Beach where you're likely to spot eagles, seals, killer whales, and other wildlife. Hospitable lodgings, first-rate cuisine, and an environment of peaceful tranquility make this seaside B&B an ideal overnight stop or destination in itself.

No pets; children welcome; smoking in designated areas; full breakfast; sport court for tennis, volleyball, basketball, shuffleboard, etc. on premises; salmon fishing and skiing (Alpine and Nordic) nearby; street and off-street parking. Tea House open to public Thursday-Sunday 1:00 to 4:00 April-September; B&B open all year. Brochure available.

ROOM	BED	BATH	ENTRANCE	FLOOR	DAILY RATES	
					S - D	(EP)
A	2T	Shd*	Sep	1	$40-$50	($10)
B	1Q	Shd*	Sep	1	$40-$50	($10)
C	1D	Shd*	Sep	1	$40-$05	($10)

Rates stated in Canadian funds.

Willow Point Guest House   **(604) 923-1086**
2460 South Island Highway, Campbell River, B.C. V9W 1C6
(On left when heading north, south of town center)

This contemporary home offers not only easy access to the fishing activities of the "Salmon Capital of the World," but shipshape accommodations and top-notch hosts. Valerie and George Bright extend a style of hospitality that is friendly, courteous, and tailored to each guest's requirements. If you need to make a fishing charter, you'll find a 4:00 a.m. breakfast and a packed lunch waiting (if required). Later, you'll return to a warm, clean place for some civilized comfort. Guests seeking a less demanding regimen should inquire about the enticing mini-vacation package the Brights have devised; it offers great value and requires no work to plan — all you have to do is show up! You'll sleep in one of three impeccably furnished bedrooms on the home's upper level. All front windows face a breathtaking view of mountains and Discovery Passage. A full English breakfast or a lighter breakfast is served in a manner befitting the refined ambiance of Willow Point Guest House.

Two cats in residence; no pets; no children under twelve; no smoking; no RV parking; full or light breakfast; afternoon tea and other extras included in mini-vacations; extra charge for packed lunch; TV and fireplace available to guests; fishing charters arranged; off-street parking; airport pickup (Campbell River). Brochure available.

ROOM	BED	BATH	ENTRANCE	FLOOR	DAILY RATES	
					S - D	(EP)
A	1D	Shd*	Main	2	$30-$40	($15)
B	2T	Shd*	Main	2	$30-$40	($15)
C	2T or 1K	Pvt	Main	2	$40-$50	($15)

Rates stated in Canadian funds.

Laughing Gull Guest House   **(604) 246-4068**
P.O. Box 83, Chemainus, B.C. V0R 1K0
(Downtown with sea view at 9836 Willow Street)

Although I usually avoid tourist attractions, Chemainus is an exception to my rule. It's a town with a dual focus: lumbering and art. The history of Chemainus, one of B.C.'s oldest towns, is told in a series of murals — twenty-six so far — on the sides of the buildings throughout the town. They were done by a number of visiting artists and are part of a master plan for an artisans' village, a major center for working artists and art education. The town is proud of its heritage and the murals that portray it. While exploring Chemainus, make your home base the Laughing Gull Guest House. The delightful stuffed characters who sit on the bench in the front yard will make you smile, and you'll still be smiling when you leave. Guest quarters in this comfortable New England-style home include three cheerful, immaculate bedrooms with private baths. From the Laughing Gull you can easily walk to the waterfront or to the shops, restaurants, pubs, and tearooms of downtown. The murals may bring you to Chemainus, but it's the friendly hospitality of Lloyd and Yvonne Rasmussen that will make you want to come back.

Small dog in residence; no pets or children; smoking outside in designated area; no RV parking; full breakfast; off-street parking; some German spoken; VISA cards. Brochure available.

ROOM	BED	BATH	ENTRANCE	FLOOR	DAILY RATES	
					S - D	(EP)
A	1Q	Pvt	Main	2	$40-$50	
B	2T	Pvt	Main	2	$40-$50	
C	1Q	Pvt	Main	1	$40-$50	

Rates stated in Canadian funds.

The Dahlia Patch   **(604) 336-8345**

R.R.#6, Courtenay, B.C. V9N 8H9

(3675 Minto Road, enroute to Cumberland)

Former educators Betty and Ivan Drew emigrated from England, via Saskatchewan, to British Columbia. Courtenay, where they raised their family, is definitely home to them. Nowadays they share their simple, ivy-clad house on ten acres with passing travelers who appreciate its quiet, off-the-beaten-track location. A colorful dahlia patch is set into the velvety front lawn, and a well-tended garden is on one side of the house. Accommodations on ground level are snug and compact. They include two bedrooms, a bath, and a sitting room with a color TV and VCR. On the main level, there is a larger guest room with an extra-long bed and a private bath. Guests often sit and visit on the veranda while enjoying the peacefulness and beauty of the countryside. In the morning, you may choose a light breakfast or a full English breakfast prepared by Ivan. The Dahlia Patch is your ticket to B&B in the best British tradition.

Children and pets welcome; smoking outside only (veranda); ten minutes from shops and restaurants; hiking trails, ski slopes, and Hornby and Denman Islands ferries nearby; off-street parking. Brochure available.

ROOM	BED	BATH	ENTRANCE	FLOOR	DAILY RATES S - D (EP)
A	2T	Shd*	Sep	1G	$30-$40
B	1D	Shd*	Sep	1G	$30-$40
C	1D	Pvt	Main	1	$35-$45

Rates stated in Canadian funds.

Greystone Manor   **(604) 338-1422**
Site 384, Comp. 2, R.R.#3, Courtenay, B.C. V9N 5M8
(On Comox Bay, across from mainland Powell River)

You can reach this outdoor recreation mecca, the Comox Valley, via the Sunshine Coast or the highway from Nanaimo. A perfect place to stay here is Greystone Manor, a big, solid house surrounded by old trees overlooking Comox Bay. It has all the homey comfort of Grandma's house and then some. Mary Nelson is a pharmacist who came to the area to slow down the pace of her life. She's been exploring, little by little, and has collected many informational books, brochures, maps, and menus to help her guests choose among the exciting things to experience close by — winter skiing at two resorts, summer salmon fishing, and hiking have proven to be popular activities. Whale-watching is a comfortable day's outing to the more northerly parts of the island.

Smoking outside only; full breakfast; fireplace; small collection of handcrafted items for sale; off-street parking; bus, train, or plane pickup by prior arrangement.

ROOM	BED	BATH	ENTRANCE	FLOOR	DAILY RATES S - D (EP)
A	2T	Shd*	Main	2	$40-$50
B	1D	Shd*	Main	2	$40-$50
C	1D	Shd*	Main	2	$40-$50
D	1D	Shd*	Main	2	$40-$50

Rates stated in Canadian funds.

Kiftsgate Inn   **(604) 338-7712**
3205 South Island Highway, Courtenay, B.C. V9N 2L9
(On left when heading north, just south of town center)

A beautiful front door of beveled glass offers a hint of the gracious welcome you can expect at Kiftsgate Inn, named for a favorite rose of hosts Patty and Ernie Daley. Set well back from the highway, the stately pioneer home is situated on 3.8 lovely acres. Inside, large, light-bathed rooms are done in florals and pastels. Polished wood floors add to the clean, crisp feel of the interior. The Daleys' attentive hospitality includes providing fine, line-dried linens, freshly aired pillows, and plenty of big, fluffy towels. Prettily papered bedrooms are a pleasure to look at and a comfort to sleep in. Each morning, individually prepared breakfasts are served in the delightful dining room overlooking the garden. Country elegance in a warm, casual atmosphere is in store for you at Kiftsgate Inn.

No pets; families welcome; smoking outside only (veranda); full breakfast; trundle bed in Room A or B; fishing, skiing, sailing, windsurfing, hiking, museums, theater, golfing, and tennis in vicinity of Courtenay; off-street parking; some French spoken. Brochure available.

ROOM	BED	BATH	ENTRANCE	FLOOR	DAILY RATES S - D (EP)
A	2T	Shd*	Main	2	$35-$45 ($10)
B	1D	Shd*	Main	2	$35-$45 ($10)
C	1Q	Pvt	Main	1	$55

Rates stated in Canadian funds.

Sahtlam Lodge & Cabins   **(604) 748-7738**
5720 Riverbottom Road, R.R.#2, Cowichan Valley, B.C. V9L 1N9
(One and one-half hours from Victoria)

Picture a fine old 1920s fishing lodge in a remote setting alongside a river with overhanging trees and small beaches. The ambiance of the quintessential lodge retreat prevails inside and out. Three rooms with private baths and a study accommodate guests on the second floor. Furnishings are colorful, eclectic, and very homey. An open living area on the main floor has inviting sofas and a big stone fireplace. Full or Continental breakfasts, lunches, and dinners (by reservation) are served in the pleasant lodge dining area. A wide, wrap-around veranda overlooking the Cowichan River is an irresistible place to relax or dine. Walking paths with vine-entwined arches lead the way to a variety of other accommodations — camp cabins, family cabins, honeymoon cabins, and unique tent bedrooms (right by the river, with lodge dining). Whether you come to fish, swim, hike, cycle, observe wildlife, or just curl up with a book by the fire, Sahtlam Lodge is the perfect spot for anything from a family vacation to a romantic interlude — any time of year.

No pets; children welcome in cabins; smoking outside only (veranda); extra charge for full breakfast; four golf courses, Chemainus murals, Gulf Island ferries, and regional museums nearby; excellent fishing fall through late spring; off-street parking; VISA cards. Inquire about cabins. Brochure available.

ROOM	BED	BATH	ENTRANCE	FLOOR	DAILY RATES S - D (EP)
A	1D & 1T	Pvt	Main	2	$80 ($10)
B	1D	Pvt	Main	2	$80
C	1D	Pvt	Main	2	$70

Rates stated in Canadian funds.

Bayside Manor   **(604) 247-8048**
Box 31, Gossip Corner, Gabriola Island, B.C. V0R 1X0
(On Degnen Bay, just off Gabriola Pass)

This contemporary, architecturally designed home is as multifaceted as gorgeous Gabriola, the most northerly of the Gulf Islands. The rambling wooden structure, built mostly of natural materials, was intended to blend in with and complement its surroundings — and this it does to perfection. Rooms of interesting shapes and on different levels are characterized by vaulted ceilings and wide expanses of glass that allow one to experience the changing environment firsthand. Bayside Manor is just thirty feet from the water, with a private deep water dock (bed, breakfast, and moorage available to the yachtsman). An entire guest wing that is open to only one party at a time includes two bedrooms (A and B), a bath, and a games room with a fireplace, sink, and small refrigerator. There is also a guest room (C) on the main floor. For the adventurous, hosts Dave and Liz Palmer operate charters and will arrange cruising excursions and scuba diving, plus fishing and day sailing trips. Other options include beachcombing, clamming, golfing, cycling, and visiting arts and crafts studios on the island. The Palmers' home and their style of hospitality are full of originality. Bayside Manor is indeed a one-of-a-kind island experience!

Dog in residence; no pets; children over twelve welcome; smoking outside only; full breakfast; waterfront deck; garden patio; fireplaces; hot tub; pool table; shuffleboard; off-street parking; ferry, float plane, or airport pickup at extra charge.

ROOM	BED	BATH	ENTRANCE	FLOOR	DAILY RATES S - D (EP)
A	1Q	Pvt	Sep	2	$45-$55
B	2T			2	$45-$55
C	1D	Pvt	Main	1	$45-$55

Rates stated in Canadian funds.   277

View to Remember   **(604) 769-4028**
1090 Trevor Drive, Kelowna, B.C. V1Z 2J8
(Central Okanagan Valley, west side of Kelowna)

     Views just don't get much better than this one. Robin and Celia Jarman, originally from Australia, chose this particular spot to raise their family because of the setting. Not a day goes by that they don't marvel at the wide vista of beautiful Okanagan Lake and the mountains beyond. Their sundeck is in constant use during the summer. Being very people-oriented, the Jarmans enjoy having guests and want to offer them the best. A large suite on ground level has a pretty bedroom with a canopy bed and antiques. The second bedroom has two beds, cable TV, and a cozy fireplace. There is also a comfortable family room with a baby grand piano and a fireplace available to guests. With the vast array of things to see and do nearby, it helps to have an insider's point of view. Enjoy the best the area has to offer with the assistance of your well-versed hosts.

     No pets or smoking; winter Jacuzzi; Alpine and Nordic skiing, golfing, swimming, water skiing (rental boats available), wineries, hiking, and much more nearby; off-street parking; some German spoken; airport pickup (Kelowna).

ROOM	BED	BATH	ENTRANCE	FLOOR	DAILY RATES	
					S - D	(EP)
A	1D	Pvt	Sep	LL	$45-$50	($15)
B	1D & 1T	Pvt	Sep	LL	$35-$40	($15)

Rates stated in Canadian funds.

Muench's Bed & Breakfast   (604) 888-8102
21333 Allard Crescent, R.R.#10, Langley, B.C. V3A 6X5
(Thirty minutes southeast of Vancouver on Fraser River)

In a quiet, rural setting near historic Fort Langley, Bernie and Mina Muench live on the original homestead that the Muenches settled in the 1860s. Guests may fish from a bar in the Fraser River or share the catch from the hosts' fish packer. Beautiful mountains loom in the background as you look out over the river from this exceptionally lovely home. Among its many assets are an indoor pool, spa, and sauna, a fireplace, a piano, and the warmth that natural wood imparts to the interior. You'll find walnut, cedar, oak, teak, and birch in the various rooms. The tasteful decor and physical comfort of the home are appealing indeed, but it's the heartwarming hospitality experienced at the hands of Bernie and Mina that you'll remember most.

No pets; no smoking in bedroom area or living room; rates include Continental breakfast and are $2 less without breakfast, $2 more with full breakfast; other meals optional; Room C is a two-section family unit; crib available; good area for walking; three museums at Fort Langley; off-street parking.

ROOM	BED	BATH	ENTRANCE	FLOOR	DAILY RATES	
					S - D	(EP)
A	2T	Shd	Main	1	$30-$39	
B	1D	Shd	Main	1	$30-$39	
C	2D & 1T	Shd	Main	LL	$25-$34	

Rates stated in Canadian funds.

Oceanside   **(604) 468-9241**
Box 26, Blueback, R.R.#2, Nanoose Bay, B.C. V0R 2R0
(Between Nanaimo and Parksville)

In a secluded spot far removed from any main highway, Oceanside is set among tall trees overlooking the sandy beach of Schooner Cove. The beach feels as if it could be yours alone. The well-protected setting is enhanced by beautiful, mature landscaping. The home is as carefully tended as the grounds, creating a neat and inviting environment. Two clean, pleasant B&B rooms are located on the main floor. One has a private half-bath, a deck, and a view of the water; the other overlooks the garden. On the lower level is a large, self-contained vacation suite with all the conveniences one could hope for, a private deck, and easy access to the beach. A favorite activity of nature lovers is watching the myriad wildlife that visit the bay — whales, eagles, otters, and seals are spotted regularly. Hosts Lee and Leone Chapman can suggest a variety of interesting sights, restaurants, and things to do close by. They are sold on their location, and you will be, too.

No pets; smoking outside only (decks); no RV parking; reasonably priced fishing charters offered by host; off-street parking; ferry pickup (Nanaimo) and airport pickup (Qualicum Beach or Nanaimo) by prior arrangement. Vacation suite with full kitchen, fireplace, and color TV sleeps up to five at $70 to $110; weekly rates. Brochure available.

ROOM	BED	BATH	ENTRANCE	FLOOR	DAILY RATES S - D	(EP)
A	1Q	Shd*	Main	1	$50	
B	1K	Pvt 1/2	Main	1	$60	

Rates stated in Canadian funds.

Prospect Bed & Breakfast   (604) 980-5800
4388 Prospect Road, North Vancouver, B.C. V7N 3L7
(In foothills of Grouse Mountain, overlooking Vancouver)

The comfortable modern home of Allan and Dorothy Evers is in a quiet, secluded setting. The grounds, which are floodlit at night, are rather like those of an English country estate. Tall evergreens encircle the house without blocking the vast panorama of city and water below. A guest suite with a private bath is a choice accommodation whether you're in Vancouver on business or on holiday. For your convenience, the suite has a TV, alarm clock-radio, and telephone. A full English breakfast, customized to your taste, is served each morning. After you phone for reservations you'll be sent a good map of the area, explicit directions on how to find the home, and pertinent details about the accommodations. There's even a tip on how to pronounce the hosts' last name: It rhymes with fevers. (Surprise them and get it right the first time!)

Cat in residence; no pets or children; no smoking preferred; full breakfast; laundry privileges by arrangement; off-street parking; near busline, Seabus, and Airporter pickup point; shops and pub within one mile; Grouse Mountain Skyride and Capilano Suspension Bridge within fifteen minutes' drive; Vancouver and Stanley Park, about thirty. 15% discount October-March; seventh consecutive night free.

ROOM	BED	BATH	ENTRANCE	FLOOR	DAILY RATES
					S - D (EP)
A	1D	Pvt	Main	1	$50-$55

Rates stated in Canadian funds.

Corbett House   **(604) 629-6305**
Corbett Road, Pender Island, B.C. V0N 2M0
(Five-minute drive from ferry dock at Otter Bay)

An escape to Pender Island is a heavenly antidote to the strains of modern life. This heritage farmhouse of pale golden yellow is a place to thoroughly unwind, slow down your pace, and let the pleasures of the country restore your well-being. Built in 1904 by the Corbett who ran the general store, the house has a comforting, well-lived-in feeling. Period antiques, lively watercolors, vases of fresh flowers, a crackling fire when it's nippy, and soothing music contribute to the rustic charm of the interior. Three cleverly papered bedrooms are enhanced by delightful combinations of colors and patterns. From every window, sample a different view of rural beauty, including the idyllic backyard scene: grazing sheep, an old split-rail fence, visiting ducks on the pond, ancient apple trees, a hammock, and birds galore. Hosts John Eckfeldt and Linda Wolfe invite you to give in to laziness or get to know the island a bit by walking or cycling on country roads, playing golf or tennis, ambling along the shoreline, or shopping for arts and crafts. It's all here — and more — on beautiful Pender.

No smoking; full country breakfast (choice of entrees); off-street parking; major credit cards (V, MC); ferry pickup. Rooms A and B have private two-piece baths and share a separate shower; C is a honeymoon suite with full bath and private balcony. Brochure available.

ROOM	BED	BATH	ENTRANCE	FLOOR	DAILY RATES	
					S - D	(EP)
A	1D & 1T	Pvt	Main	2	$45-$70	($25)
B	1D	Pvt	Main	2	$45-$70	
C	1Q	Pvt	Main	2	$45-$85	

Rates stated in Canadian funds.

Bonnie Bell Bed & Breakfast   (604) 285-3578
Box 331, Campbell River, B.C. V9W 5B6
(On West Road, two and one-half miles from ferry dock)

When John and Trudy Parkyn designed the home of their dreams, respect for the natural setting was their prime concern. Entirely hidden from other houses and the road, this B&B is set in the leafy privacy of alder and fir overlooking Gowlland Harbour, where loons and seals may be sighted. In every aspect, the ambiance is simple and pure, clean and uncluttered. The traditionally styled home combines country freshness with handcrafted construction. The living and dining area has an open-beamed ceiling and high windows all around. White walls, a brick hearth, and an array of fine woodwork are enhanced by a few well-chosen antiques and heirlooms. Second floor guest quarters with tree and water views consist of two wonderful bedrooms, a large, old-fashioned bathroom, a reading nook, and an enclosed porch. If you choose, you may charter a boat, the Bonnie Bell, skippered by John. And after a tranquil night's sleep, arise to an ample breakfast prepared by Trudy on the wood-fired cookstove; it can be plain or fancy, depending on your appetite. I suggest you let Trudy use her imagination — you won't be sorry.

Dog in residence; children and pets welcome; smoking on porch; full breakfast; off-street parking. Brochure available.

ROOM	BED	BATH	ENTRANCE	FLOOR	DAILY RATES	
					S - D	(EP)
A	2T	Shd*	Main	2	$20-$40	
B	1D	Shd*	Main	2	$20-$40	

Rates stated in Canadian funds.

283

Hyacinthe Bay Bed & Breakfast   (604) 285-2126
Box 343, Heriot Bay, B.C. V0P 1H0
(East coast of island, seven miles from ferry dock)

The contemporary home of Janice Kenyon and Ross Henry features dramatic open-beam cedar construction, a wide, wrap-around deck with a hot tub, and huge windows that frame a spectacular view of Hyacinthe Bay. Light bathes the interior, where traditional furnishings, family heirlooms, and Oriental rugs on polished wood floors create a most appealing contrast of old and new. A guest bedroom and bath on the main floor have been outfitted for maximum comfort and ease; there's extra sleeping space in the loft. The deck is a great place for sunbathing, stargazing from the hot tub, or enjoying a leisurely breakfast. Janice, a cookbook author, prepares a delectable specialty each morning and can provide a thermos of coffee to take over to the beach. You may wish to share the good company of Janice and Ross, a physician; bask in the serene beauty of Hyacinthe Bay; take a hike up Chinese Mountain; spend time in quiet repose; or all of the above. A time of relaxation and renewal awaits you at this Quadra Island retreat.

No pets; children over two welcome; no smoking; full breakfast; picnic lunches or suppers on request; TV and VCR for movies (rentals nearby); barbecue; hot tub; fishing charters arranged; off-street parking; French and German spoken. Brochure available.

ROOM	BED	BATH	ENTRANCE	FLOOR	DAILY RATES S - D (EP)
A	2T	Pvt	Main	1	$30-$50 ($10)

Rates stated in Canadian funds.

Joha House   **(604) 285-2247**
Box 668, Quathiaski Cove, Quadra Island, B.C. V0P 1N0
(Less than one mile from ferry dock)

After spending ten summers on beautiful Quadra Island, Joyce and Harold Johnson moved from California to take up full-time residency. Their unbridled enthusiasm is justified, as any visitor quickly learns. The contemporary wood home is oriented toward a breathtaking view of Quathiaski Cove, tiny Grouse Island, and the Inside Passage. Watch occasional cruise ships and regular ferries, or spot eagles and herons. Accommodations at Joha House include a self-contained, private garden suite and two B&B rooms on the upper level. Bedrooms are full of country charm, with attractive quilts providing each color scheme. The living/dining area features custom-designed stained-glass windows and a fireplace of smooth local stones with hand-hewn yellow cedar trim. It's a splendid setting for enjoying a tasty breakfast in full view of nature's glory. With the Johnsons' help, discover the many joys of Quadra Island.

No pets; children welcome in suite; smoking permitted in family room and on deck; full breakfast; robes provided; woodstove and sofa bed in suite; dock for guest boats; good collection of literature on hiking, whale-watching trips (July-September), and other local activities; fishing charters arranged; off-street parking; ferry pickup for walkers. Three-night minimum in suite; inquire about weekly beach house rentals. Brochure available.

ROOM	BED	BATH	ENTRANCE	FLOOR	DAILY RATES	
					S - D	(EP)
A	1D	Shd*	Main	2	$40-$45	
B	1Q	Shd*	Main	2	$45-$50	
C	1Q	Pvt	Sep	LL	$60	($10)

Rates stated in Canadian funds.

L&R Nelles Ranch   **(604) 837-3800**
P.O. Box 430, Revelstoke, B.C. V0E 2S0
(Highway 23 South)

Set amid the majesty of the Selkirk Mountains is L&R Nelles Ranch, located just a few miles out of delightfully refurbished downtown Revelstoke. Just being in this spectacular area affords a sense of wonder and exhilaration, and no one could love it more than Larry and Rosalyne Nelles. B&B guests are greeted with a warm, open, down-to-earth reception that makes them feel like members of the family. You'll find no urban cowboys here; what you will find is a realistic picture of life on a working horse ranch. For those so inclined, Larry offers wilderness trail rides of varying lengths at reasonable prices. Many photos and trophies displayed in the house attest to his expertise as a horseman. An expert skier as well, he knows intimately the area's variety of skiing opportunities. Rosalyne's full ranch breakfasts are sure to satisfy the most powerful of appetites. An enjoyable family atmosphere, comfortable accommodations, and breathtaking natural beauty are in store for you at L&R Nelles Ranch.

Small dog in residence; dog, cats, and horses on property; overnight horse accommodation; no smoking in bedrooms; full breakfast; TV, VCR, and stereo available; crib and rollaway available; information on numerous outdoor activities provided by hosts; off-street parking; airport pickup (Revelstoke). EP rate for adults is $15. Brochure available.

ROOM	BED	BATH	ENTRANCE	FLOOR	DAILY RATES	
					S - D	(EP)
A	1D	Shd*	Main	2	$30-$40	($10)
B	2T	Shd*	Main	2	$30-$40	($10)
C	2D	Pvt	Main	1G	$30-$40	($10)
D	1D	Shd*	Main	1G	$30-$40	($10)

Rates stated in Canadian funds.

Country Cottage Bed & Breakfast   **(604) 885-7448**
General Delivery, Roberts Creek, B.C. V0N 2W0
(On Sunshine Coast, off Highway 101 above Gibsons)

You'll find Country Cottage Bed & Breakfast in the tiny hamlet of Roberts Creek. The heart warms at the first glimpse of this small, butterscotch-colored farmhouse, trimmed in red, with flower gardens flanking the walkway. To the left of the house are fruit trees, a vegetable garden, sheep grazing contentedly, and chickens roaming about. The interior was lovingly created by hosts Loragene and Philip Gaulin. The look of warm wood, colorful handloomed rugs, nostalgic collectibles, and family heirlooms brings to mind the simple pleasures of an earlier time. Upstairs, the Rose Room evokes in every detail a Victorian rose garden, and a delightfully original solarium/half-bath is attached. Loragene's legendary breakfasts, prepared on a wood-burning cookstove, are served with exquisite care in the old-fashioned country kitchen. Honeymooners and other romantics like to escape to their own little world in the sweetest cottage imaginable, just to the right of the farmhouse. It has an iron bed, a pull-out sofa, a fully equipped kitchen, cable TV, a woodstove, wood floors with colorful rugs, and decor in blues and reds. The extraordinary charm of Country Cottage Bed & Breakfast is the obvious result of a clear vision perfectly executed.

Dog and two cats in residence (main house); no pets; children ten and over welcome; no smoking; full breakfast; afternoon tea; for bathing, Rose Room shares full bath on main floor; fifteen-minute walk to beach and the excellent Creekhouse Restaurant; off-street parking; French spoken. Brochure available.

ROOM	BED	BATH	ENTRANCE	FLOOR	DAILY RATES S - D	(EP)
A	1D	Pvt 1/2	Main	2	$40-$50	
B	1D	Pvt	Sep	1	$55-$65	($15)

Rates stated in Canadian funds.

Southdown Farm   **(604) 653-4322**
R.R.#1, Fulford Harbour, B.C. V0S 1C0
(Four miles from ferry at 1121 Beaver Point Road)

In the tradition of the English countryside, here's a vintage farmhouse on a working farm — a bucolic, peaceful setting. Architect/host Jonathan Yardley has fashioned two unique spaces for guests, each with its own allure. The Vinehouse is a private apartment on the lower level of the farmhouse. It has a modern kitchen, a comfortably appointed living room, a bedroom, a bath, and a vine-covered solarium. Antiques from Sue Yardley's native England, artwork, and fresh flowers enhance the interior while scenes of rolling farmland with old barns and fences, fruit trees, and distant tall evergreens comprise the view. The silence is broken only by tinkling windchimes, singing birds, and humming bees. In a woodsy setting with its own driveway, The Cottage is totally private. It has white walls enlivened by Northwest art, extensive cedar woodwork and glass, and French doors to a wrap-around deck. In this romantic haven, you'll feel at one with nature but ensconced in total comfort. Guest books overflowing with praise confirm my conviction: A getaway to Southdown Farm gives new meaning to the word *retreat.*

Sheep, chickens, dogs, and cats on farm; children welcome; smoking outside only; full breakfast (choice local ingredients including farm fresh eggs and home-cured bacon are left for guests to prepare at their leisure); kitchenette in Cottage; sofa beds; woodstoves; whirlpool tubs (double in Cottage); off-street parking; wheelchair access in Vinehouse; major credit cards (V, MC, AE); ferry pickup. Off-season rates. Brochure available.

ROOM	BED	BATH	ENTRANCE	FLOOR	DAILY RATES	
					S - D	(EP)
A	1Q	Pvt	Sep	LL	$65	($20)
B	1D & 2T	Pvt	Sep	1	$95	($20)

Rates stated in Canadian funds.

Burnside House   **(604) 642-4403**
1890 Maple Avenue, Box 881, Sooke, B.C. V0S 1N0
(Off Route 14, just past Sooke Village)

A glimpse of the Sooke region's pioneer heritage can be yours at Burnside House, circa 1870. The renovated Georgian farmhouse originally belonged to Michael Muir, fourth son of John Muir, Sr., who initiated Sooke's lumbering industry. It is ideally located for exploring historical sites, arts and crafts stores, and the area's exceptional parks. Hosts Gisela and Heinz Kappler are proud of the fact that the renovation and decoration of Burnisde House received a Hallmark Society Award of Merit. They offer guests a choice of five generously proportioned bedrooms sharing two full baths on the second floor, some with water and mountain views. On the main floor, there is an attractive living/dining room exclusively for guests. The Kapplers' style of hospitality is summed up in their irresistible slogan: "We'd love to spoil you."

Children six and older welcome; no smoking preferred; full country breakfast; antique shop on property; golfing, swimming, hiking trails, salt and and fresh water fishing nearby; seal and whale watching from beaches; picnic lunches available; complimentary bicycles; off-street parking; German spoken; major credit cards (V, MC). Brochure available.

ROOM	BED	BATH	ENTRANCE	FLOOR	DAILY RATES S - D (EP)
A	2T	Shd*	Main	2	$50
B	1Q	Shd*	Main	2	$60
C	1D	Shd*	Main	2	$60
D	1Q	Shd*	Main	2	$65
E	1D	Shd*	Main	2	$50

Rates stated in Canadian funds.

Malahat Farm
(604) 642-6868

Anderson Road, R.R. #2, Sooke, B.C. V0S 1N0
(Eight miles west of Sooke)

A genuine Canadian farm vacation awaits you at a fully restored heritage house near Sooke. Surrounded by acres of farmland and quiet bucolic scenery, two lovely homes on the property offer accommodations. The larger one where hosts George and Diana Clare live has its guest quarters on the second floor. Here there is a guest lounge, along with two of the most inviting bedrooms imaginable. These commodious rooms, each with a private keyed entrance, are outfitted with antiques, down comforters, and ruffled curtains; private bathrooms have whiter-than-white clawfoot tubs. Next door, Malahat Cottage has a cozy living room with a fireplace, three attractive bedrooms, a bath, and a country kitchen. Up to six people can vacation together in their own private space. Have your delicious farm breakfast delivered to the door or join the folks in the main house for this meal, which is a major event featuring ingredients fresh from the farm and everything homemade. Visitors love the tranquility of the countryside. They thrill to see how bright stars can be in an ink-black sky. But most of all, they're touched by the caring hospitality at the very heart of Malahat Farm.

Dogs, cat, cows, geese, chickens on property; no pets; children welcome in cottage; full country breakfast; guest lounge has refrigerator, beverage brewing facilities, and sitting area; nearby parks offer beachcombing, birdwatching, hiking, and picnicking; salmon charters arranged; off-street parking. Brochure available.

ROOM	BED	BATH	ENTRANCE	FLOOR	DAILY RATE	
					S - D	(EP)
A	1Q	Pvt	Main	2	$65	($15)
B	1Q	Pvt	Main	2	$65	($15)
C	1Q & 2D	Pvt	Sep	1 & 2	$95	($15)

Rates stated in Canadian funds.

White Heather Guest House   (604) 581-9797
12571 - 98 Avenue, Surrey, B.C. V3V 2K6
(Twenty minutes from U.S. – Canada border at Blaine)

A sincere welcome awaits you at White Heather Guest House, home of Glad and Chuck Bury. The quiet southeast suburb of Vancouver offers good bus service, as well as a fun and easy trip downtown by Sky Train. At afternoon tea time, you may wish to enlist the help of your seasoned hosts in planning your stay. They consistently search out cream-of-the-crop experiences to share with guests. Whether you're looking for the perfect restaurant — ethnic, family, or special occasion — or for attractions that are most worth visiting, the Burys offer sound advice. Full English breakfasts, cooked to perfection by Chuck, are served in a sunny, garden-like room with a dramatic view of snow-capped mountains. Spend leisure moments relaxing or visiting on the patio overlooking the back yard. All this, plus a good night's sleep, makes White Heather Guest House a most hospitable place to stay.

No pets; family accommodation by arrangement; no smoking; no RV parking; full breakfast; fireplace and TV available; games room with toys and piano; licensed chauffeur available; off-street parking; pickup from airport or cruise ships. Inquire about EP rates.

ROOM	BED	BATH	ENTRANCE	FLOOR	DAILY RATES S - D (EP)
A	1Q	Pvt 1/2	Main	1	$35-$40
B	1D	Shd*	Main	1	$30-$35

Rates stated in Canadian funds.

Connie's Place   (604) 263-9661, FAX: (604) 263-2250
6730 Oak Street, Vancouver, B.C. V6P 3Z2
(Near West Forty-ninth Avenue)

Connie Buchanan is the former owner of The Windmill House in Vernon; guests who stayed there may wish to visit her when they need a friendly and convenient place to stay in Vancouver. Located on the main north-south route into the city (99), Connie's Place is easy to find and is only fifteen minutes from downtown and from the airport. It's a white, blocky, 1950s-style house built on various levels. The cheery front entrance takes you into a blonde wood interior. The spacious living and dining area has a velvety carpet, and the ceiling imparts an Oriental flavor. There is a den with a TV and library, a sundeck, and two bedrooms for guests. The informality of Connie's Place makes you feel comfortable using the whole house. Connie offers a choice of breakfasts at flexible serving times. It's good to know that her hospitable manner is alive and well in metropolitan Vancouver.

No pets or smoking; laundry and kitchen privileges by arrangement; good public transportation and airport connections; off-street parking.

ROOM	BED	BATH	ENTRANCE	FLOOR	DAILY RATES	
					S - D	(EP)
A	2T	Shd*	Main	1	$45-$55	
B	1Q	Shd*	Main	1	$45-$55	

Rates stated in Canadian funds.

Kenya Court Guest House   (604) 738-7085

2230 Cornwall Avenue, Vancouver, B.C. V6K 1B5
(Overlooking Kitsilano Beach, English Bay, and downtown)

Here's a place with the best location you could hope for and just the right balance of privacy and attentive care. Kenya Court is a three-story heritage building with gracious antique furnishings, a music room with grand piano, and a penthouse solarium where breakfast is beautifully served each morning. Accommodations consist of a single guest bedroom with a shared bath (A), a guest bedroom with a private bath (B), a two-bedroom suite (C), and a two-bedroom suite with a kitchen (D). From the solarium and the suites there is an unobstructed view of the beach, ocean, mountains, and city. Downtown is just minutes away by direct busline. Across the street there are tennis courts and a large, heated, outdoor saltwater swimming pool; Granville Island and the Planetarium are within walking distance. Dr. and Mrs. Williams respond to the individual needs of guests, ensuring that their stay in Vancouver is a memorable one.

No pets or smoking; choice of full or Continental breakfast; TV in each room; VCR available; fireplaces in B & C; private garden with picnic table; jogging trail at water's edge; good public transportation and airport connections; inquire about off-street parking; French, German, and Italian spoken. Suite D also has a queen sofa bed and can sleep up to six. Brochure available.

ROOM	BED	BATH	ENTRANCE	FLOOR	DAILY RATES S - D	(EP)
A	1T	Shd	Main	3	$60	
B	2T or 1K	Pvt	Sep	3	$85	($25)
C	3T or 1K	Pvt	Sep	2	$85	($25)
D	1K & 1Q	Pvt	Sep	1	$8	($25)

Rates stated in Canadian funds.

Laburnum Cottage
(604) 988-4877

1388 Terrace Avenue, North Vancouver, B.C. V7R 1B4
(Off Capilano Road, enroute to Grouse Mountain)

The home of Alex and Delphine Masterton is tucked away in a quiet corner of a gracious older neighborhood that is wonderful for walking. Despite its feeling of seclusion, it's convenient to downtown Vancouver, Horseshoe Bay, Grouse Mountain, and other attractions. Laburnum Cottage is set in a half-acre English garden so breathtaking that one feels privileged to experience its serene beauty. A meandering stream crossed by a little red bridge, an exquisite array of pampered plants, and a pond with a rippling fountain delight the senses and the soul. The enchantment of the garden permeates the guest quarters. A refined English charm marks the interior of the main house, where three lovely bedrooms on the second floor overlook the garden. Set in its midst is the Summerhouse Cottage (pictured), a self-contained haven with a romantic brass bed and a fresh, light atmosphere. Laburnum Cottage offers not only lodging for most any occasion, but first-rate hospitality to match its magnificent setting.

Cat in residence; no pets; smoking outside only (deck); full breakfast; robes provided; good public transportation; off-street parking; French and German spoken; major credit cards (V, MC). Brochure available. A larger cottage sleeping up to six is available at $100, EP $25.

ROOM	BED	BATH	ENTRANCE	FLOOR	DAILY RATES S - D	(EP)
A	1Q	Shd*	Main	2	$65	
B	2T	Shd*	Main	2	$65	
C	1Q	Pvt	Main	2	$75	
D	1D	Pvt	Sep	1	$95	

Rates stated in Canadian funds.

Castle on the Mountain   (604) 542-4593
Site 10, Comp. 12, R.R.#8, Vernon, B.C. V1T 8L6
(Upper Okanagan Valley on Silver Star Road)

This large Tudor-style home is located on the southern exposure of Silver Star Mountain, seven miles from city center. The elevation not only allows a sweeping view of valley, lakes, and the lights of Vernon, but gives you a head start in getting to the ski slopes at Silver Star (seven miles away). In this choice setting, Castle on the Mountain offers a unique lodging experience. Hosts Sharon and Eskil Larson are artists/craftspeople; they have an ever-changing collection in their in-home gallery studio where guests enjoy browsing. Tea is served on the adjacent deck. The entire ground floor is provides accommodations: There's a living room with comfortable places to relax by the fire, two bedrooms, one bath with a Jacuzzi tub and one with a shower, and a kitchen area for light meals. Views are phenomenal, especially from the huge turret-shaped and multiwindowed bedroom (B). The second floor has two comfortable guest rooms, a shared bath with a large shower, and a private "crow's nest" balcony. All in all, Castle on the Mountain is spectacular.

Smoking outside only; TV; phone; bunk beds also in Room B; camp/picnic area with bonfire pit; hiking, beaches, fruit-picking in summer; skiing (Alpine and Nordic) and snowmobiling in winter; off-street parking; good wheelchair access; major credit cards (V, MC); airport pickup (Vernon). Brochure available.

ROOM	BED	BATH	ENTRANCE	FLOOR	DAILY RATES S - D	(EP)
A	1D	Pvt	Sep	LL	$40-$50	
B	2T or 1K	Pvt	Sep	LL	$50-$60	($10)
C	1D & 1T	Shd*	Main	2	$40-$50	
D	1D & 1T	Shd*	Main	2	$40-$50	

Rates stated in Canadian funds.

The Falcon Nest (604) 545-1759
R.R.#8, Site 7A, Comp.1, Vernon, B.C. V1T 8L6
(Upper Okanagan Valley, enroute to Silver Star Ski Hill)

Exceptional comfort, attentive hospitality, and international cuisine can be yours at a vantage point high above the Okanagan Valley, Lake Okanagan, and the city of Vernon. The Falcon Nest is Emmy Kennedy's winning creation — a large, contemporary wood home with a variety of accommodations to suit most any travel need, from a family outing to a romantic escape. The interior is in perfect keeping with the magnificent view. Rooms are spacious, open, and beautifully appointed. Generous breakfasts with a European flair are served in three areas, so that different groups can gather as they wish. The living room has a fireplace and inviting places to sit, relax, visit, or read, while an adjoining room has a carpeted conversation pit in front of another fireplace. Accommodations, which are well spread out in this rambling home, are quite varied, yet Emmy's high standards of comfort and aesthetics remain constant. She is an artist and an adventurer; she takes no shortcuts where her guests are concerned.

Smoking outside only; full breakfast; games room; solarium with hot tub; TV in living room; Room D is a family accommodation for up to four people; hot springs, skiing, hiking, fishing, golfing, and horseback riding nearby; German and Italian spoken; off-street parking; VISA Cards. Honeymoon suite with Jacuzzi tub also available at $85-$100. Brochure available.

ROOM	BED	BATH	ENTRANCE	FLOOR	DAILY RATES	
					S - D	(EP)
A	1D	Shd*	Main	1	$30-$50	($10)
B	2T	Shd*	Main	1	$30-$55	($10)
C	1D	Shd*	Main	LL	$30-$50	($10)
D	1D & 2T	Pvt	Main	LL	$65	

Rates stated in Canadian funds.

The Schroth Farm　　　　　　　　　　　　　　(604) 545-0010
Site 6, Comp. 25, R.R.#8, Vernon, B.C. V1T 8L6
(One and one-half miles east of Vernon)

    A memorable vacation can be yours at this warm and cozy vintage home on a family farm just outside Vernon. A self-contained, ground-level guest accommodation has plenty of room for a family. There's a bedroom, bath, kitchen, laundry room, and a living room with two sofa beds. The Schroths have been welcoming people from around the world into their home for years. They find that some people appreciate the boundless recreational activities close by, while others are satisfied to do nothing more than watch contented livestock grazing in bright green pastures against a mountain backdrop. However relaxed or busy you want to be, you'll be touched by the genuine welcome you'll receive. And when the time comes to leave, it will be like leaving old friends.

    Children welcome (inquire about special rates); no smoking preferred; cable TV; game room; twin and double sofa beds in guest quarters; beaches, ski slopes and trails, hot springs, and mountain lakes with good fishing nearby; off-street parking.

ROOM	BED	BATH	ENTRANCE	FLOOR	DAILY RATES S - D	(EP)
A	2T	Pvt	Sep	LL	$29-$35	($10)

Rates stated in Canadian funds.

Twin Willows by the Lake (604) 542-8293
Site 10, Comp. 16, R.R.#4, Vernon, B.C. V1T 6L7
(Five miles west of Vernon on Okanagan Lake)

Picture yourself in a rope hammock suspended between two giant weeping willows just steps from water's edge. The setting is perfect and with it, the view. The Pringles offer guests a spacious lakefront suite, which is wood paneled and has a bedroom, a bath, and a family room with two sofa beds, fridge, and TV. You'll have plenty of privacy, a patio, and easy access to the dock for swimming and boating. While the suite is perfect for either couples or families, one or two people might prefer the main floor lake view bedroom (B). Enjoy a hearty breakfast on the deck overlooking the lake, and then give in to the lure of the water — or maybe that hammock.

Children welcome (inquire about EP rates); smoking outside only; full breakfast from choice of menus (including homemade jams and muffins); crib available; off-street parking.

ROOM	BED	BATH	ENTRANCE	FLOOR	DAILY RATES S - D (EP)
A	1Q	Pvt	Sep	LL	$45-$50
B	1D	Pvt	Sep	1	$40-$45

Rates stated in Canadian funds.

The Windmill House   **(604) 549-2804**
Site 19A, Comp. 2, R.R.#1, Vernon, B.C. V1T 6L4
(Nine miles east of Vernon)

Want something totally unique in a bed and breakfast home? Well, this is *IT*. In the rural beauty of the Coldstream Valley east of Vernon, you can experience sleeping in a replica of an authentic windmill. It was built by a Dutchman for his family and later turned into a B&B. The construction is fascinating. The four-story home is wood paneled throughout and has many angles and stairways and a wrap-around deck. Outside, you may enjoy the lovely garden with lawn chairs, barbecue, and picnic table. After you've stayed at The Windmill House, wonderfully hosted by Rosemary and Jeremy Dyde, chances are you'll be talking about it for years.

Pets in residence; smoking outside only; full breakfast with choice of tempting entrees; other meals by arrangement; TV; VCR; fireplace; rollaway bed; off-street parking; bus depot or airport pickup (Vernon). Room D is a family room that can accommodate up to five people. Child and senior rates negotiable; inquire about winter rates. Brochure available.

ROOM	BED	BATH	ENTRANCE	FLOOR	DAILY RATES S - D (EP)
A	2T	Shd*	Main	2	$35-$45
B	1D	Shd*	Main	2	$35-$40
C	1T	Shd*	Main	2	$35
D	1Q & 1D	Pvt	Main	3	$50

Rates stated in Canadian funds.

Carriage Stop Bed & Breakfast   **(604) 383-6240**
117 Menzies Street, Victoria, B.C. V8V 2G4
(Short walk from beach and downtown)

Close proximity to the heart of Victoria is just one of the assets of Carriage Stop Bed & Breakfast. It's an older blue house with a gabled roof, interesting angles, and lots of character. The charm of its age comes through, while renovations have given the interior a clean, new feeling of light and openness. With this background, the well-chosen artwork shows up to good advantage. Other elements of the decor that I found most attractive include the tulip wallpaper and curtains in the dining room. One of the guest rooms is on the first floor; two rooms and a bath on the second floor make ideal quarters for several people traveling together. Besides the convenient location and agreeable atmosphere, you'll get expert advice on picking that special restaurant to suit your mood, your palate, and your purse. At Carriage Stop, the best of old and new come together in an ambiance of casual comfort.

Two cats in residence; no pets; no children under twelve; smoking outside only; no RV parking; Continental or full breakfast; common room with fireplace and TV; patio in summer; major credit cards (V, MC); good public transportation and airport connections. Off-season rates. Brochure available.

ROOM	BED	BATH	ENTRANCE	FLOOR	DAILY RATES	
					S - D	(EP)
A	1D & 1T	Shd	Main	1	$45-$60	($10)
B	1D	Shd*	Main	2	$45-$60	
C	1D & 1T	Shd*	Main	2	$45-$60	($10)

Rates stated in Canadian funds.

Laird House   (604) 384-3177
134 St. Andrews Street, Victoria, B.C. V8V 2M5
(James Bay area, near Beacon Hill Park)

An exceptional place to stay in the quiet and lovely James Bay section of Victoria is the inviting 1912 heritage-style home of Ruth Laird. It has been restored and decorated with the utmost attention to detail. In fact, one gets the feeling that every square inch of Laird House was fashioned to offer visual delight and comfort to its inhabitants. On the main floor, a guest living room and parlor exude quality; coffered ceilings and impressive woodwork are enhanced by beautiful floral motifs in rose, green, and cream. Tea and sherry are available to sip by the fireplace as soft music soothes the senses. On the second floor, three most attractive bedrooms (one with a fireplace and balcony) are full of special touches including fresh flowers and fruit. Two shared bathrooms are stocked with amenities while another room contains a guest refrigerator, sink, coffee, tea, and cookies. Elegant three-course breakfasts are served in the prettiest dining room imaginable — a sterling way to start your glorious day in Victoria!

Small dog in residence; no pets, children, or smoking; no RV parking; full breakfast; robes and hair dryers provided; fifteen-minute walk to heart of downtown; shorter walk to ocean front and Beacon Hill Park; good public transportation and airport connections; off-street parking; major credit cards (V, MC). Brochure available.

ROOM	BED	BATH	ENTRANCE	FLOOR	DAILY RATES S - D	(EP)
A	1D	Shd*	Main	2	$65	
B	1Q	Shd*	Main	2	$65	
C	2T	Shd*	Main	2	$45-$60	

Rates stated in Canadian funds.

Olympic View Guest House   (604) 370-1931
1563 Richardson Street, Victoria, B.C. V8S 1R2
(Two blocks from ocean, across street from Government House)

Staying at Olympic View Guest House puts you close to Craigdarroch Castle, the Art Gallery, Government House, city buses, and the beach. A great view of the Olympics is a definite plus. English floral motifs set a pleasing tone in the common rooms and the bright, immaculate bedrooms where shades of peach, pink, and blue predominate. The largest of the guest rooms boasts a sweeping view. For your leisure moments, there is a lovely back yard with well-tended gardens. Wanda Nunan takes pride in serving full English breakfasts of the most civilized sort, using her finest china, silver, and table settings. Accommodating the needs and schedules of guests is a top priority at this comfortable guest house.

No pets; no children under fourteen; no smoking; full breakfast; robes provided; good public transportation, airport and ferry connections; off-street parking. Brochure available.

ROOM	BED	BATH	ENTRANCE	FLOOR	DAILY RATES	
					S - D	(EP)
A	1 D	Shd	Main	1	$50	
B	1 D	Shd	Main	2	$40-$50	
C	2T or 1K	Shd	Main	2	$55	

Rates stated in Canadian funds.

Rose Cottage   **(604) 381-5985**
3059 Washington Avenue, Victoria, B.C. V9A 1P7
(One and one-half miles northwest of inner harbor)

A stay at this charming 1912 guest house takes you into the world of Victorian England. Experience traditional bed and breakfast at its finest, surrounded by antiques, collectibles, and memorabilia of the period. Spend a cozy evening visiting or reading in the guest parlor by the oak-manteled fireplace. Tempting four-course breakfasts are served in the formal dining room on fine English china; heart-shaped scones and homemade jams and marmalade are specialties of the house. Four bright, cheery guest rooms with high ceilings are decorated in pastels and floral prints. The Blue Room (A) even has a small "mother-in-law" room adjacent. Shared split baths offer the choice of shower or clawfoot tub. On display in the sewing room are London Cockney costumes that Vicky Smith fashions for her husband Bob, a musician/comedian at a local pub. To top off your English experience, you may want to stop there for a pint and a jolly good time.

Cat in residence; no pets; children eight and over welcome; smoking outside only (veranda); full breakfast; ample street parking; major credit cards (V, MC); good public transportation and airport connections. Brochure available.

ROOM	BED	BATH	ENTRANCE	FLOOR	DAILY RATES	
					S - D	(EP)
A	2D	Shd*	Main	2	$45-$58	($18)
B	1Q	Shd*	Main	2	$45-$58	
C	1D	Shd*	Main	2	$45-$58	
D	1Q	Shd*	Main	1	$45-$58	

Rates stated in Canadian funds.

Seaview Bed & Breakfast   (604) 383-7098, FAX: (604) 385-1962
1144 Dallas Road, Victoria, B.C. V8V 1C1
(On sea front near Beacon Hill Park)

Think back to your most satisfying bed and breakfast experience in England — or imagine what it would be like. In other words, think of the very *essence* of bed and breakfast: warm, lively hosts, a comfortable bed, and a hearty breakfast. Add to this a breathtaking view of the Olympic Mountains and lights of Port Angeles across the Strait of San Juan de Fuca. From Pat and Alec Gordon's seaside home, stroll along the waterfront, explore adjacent Beacon Hill Park, or make the five-minute drive to city center (many people walk). These words from a former guest of the Gordons appeared in the *San Francisco Examiner:* "The hosts...provide comfortable beds and a superb breakfast, with congeniality, a rare sense of humor, and an unusual willingness to help out a tired or frustrated tourist." I couldn't have said it better myself.

Small dog in residence; no pets or smoking; full English breakfast; TV in each room; Room B has sun porch; ample street parking; ferry pickup at city harbor; bus from Swartz Bay ferry.

ROOM	BED	BATH	ENTRANCE	FLOOR	DAILY RATES S - D (EP)
A	1Q & 1T	Pvt	Main	1	$45-$70 ($10)
B	1Q	Pvt	Main	2	$45-$70

Rates stated in Canadian funds.

Scholefield House   (604) 385-2025
731 Vancouver Street, Victoria, B.C. V8V 3V4
(Four blocks behind the Empress Hotel)

Enjoy the privilege of staying in a designated Heritage Victorian Home, built in 1892 for Ethelbert Olaf Stuart Scholefield, provincial librarian and archivist. Randy and Janet Thompson offer the refinement and splendor of a bygone age in their handsome home. Guest rooms are individually decorated in antiques, beautiful old quilts, and fine linens and lace. Beds of various sizes are mostly of cast iron and brass. Two shared baths provide the choice of clawfoot tub or shower. Waking up at Scholefield House is a joy as you catch the aroma of fresh coffee and a luscious breakfast that includes homemade jams and fruit butters. Then take off on foot to explore Victoria's special charms, knowing that when you return you'll be greeted with a calming cuppa tea by the parlor fireplace. Round out a satisfying day with dinner at one of the choice restaurants in the area. Gracious comfort in historical surroundings awaits you at Scholefield House.

Two cats in residence; no pets; no children under twelve; no smoking; full breakfast; 3/4-size Victorian mahogany wall bed extra in Room A; public transportation; street and off-street parking; major credit cards (V, MC). Brochure available.

ROOM	BED	BATH	ENTRANCE	FLOOR	DAILY RATES S - D	(EP)
A	1Q	Shd*	Main	2	$65	($15)
B	1D	Shd*	Main	2	$60	
C	1D	Shd*	Main	2	$60	
D	2T	Shd*	Main	2	$60	
E	1D	Shd*	Main	2	$45	

Rates stated in Canadian funds.

Sunnymeade House Inn   **(604) 658-1414**
1002 Fenn Avenue, Victoria, B.C. V8Y 1P3
(At Cordova Bay; central to ferries, Butchart Gardens, and city)

The new colonial-style home of Nancy and Jack Thompson is, in a word, exceptional. The picture-perfect garden and patio are as well maintained as the house itself, and the Thompsons have clearly anticipated everything a guest might need or desire. A hallway leads from the foyer on the main floor up to the guest quarters. There is a lounge for guests, along with four bedrooms, a bed/sitting room (D), and three baths. Luxurious, tastefully appointed rooms have their own vanity/sinks, luggage racks, and other niceties. Luscious full breakfasts are served, with a choice of menu items. For a warm welcome, elegant accommodations, and first-rate hospitality, Sunnymeade House Inn is simply unsurpassed.

No pets; smoking outside only; full breakfast; extra-long bed in Room A; walking distance from beach and three fine restaurants; regular bus service to Victoria and Swartz Bay ferry; off-street parking; VISA cards. Single room with private bath on ground floor also available. Inquire about EP, weekly, and monthly rates. Brochure available.

ROOM	BED	BATH	ENTRANCE	FLOOR	DAILY RATES S - D (EP)
A	1Q	Shd*	Main	2	$69-$79
B	1D	Shd*	Main	2	$67-$79
C	1D & 1T	Shd*	Main	2	$69-$79
D	1D & 1T	Shd*	Main	2	$69-$79
E	1D	Pvt	Main	2	$69-$79

Rates stated in Canadian funds.

Top O'Triangle Mountain
(604) 478-7853

3442 Karger Terrace, Victoria, B.C. V9C 3K5
(Between Victoria and Sooke)

Staying out of the city has its advantages — peace and quiet, a slower pace, ease of parking — but this B&B offers much more. Top O'Triangle Mountain is just twenty-two minutes out of Victoria, but the view from this elevation is wondrous: the city and inner harbor, Port Angeles, the Olympic Mountains, and a spectacular light show at night. The house is built of interlocking cedar logs, and the warmth of wood permeates the interior. There are plenty of windows, decks all around, and a solarium where ample breakfasts are served. The three guest accommodations, all with private baths, include a room on the main floor and, on the ground floor, a mini-suite and a suite with a TV/sitting room. Comfort and silence ensure a sound sleep. Hosts Henry and Pat Hansen encourage unrestricted relaxation and sincerely want guests to think of their B&B as home.

No pets; families welcome; no smoking in bedrooms or dining area; full breakfast; off-street and street parking; major credit cards (V, MC). Brochure available.

ROOM	BED	BATH	ENTRANCE	FLOOR	DAILY RATES S - D	(EP)
A	1D	Pvt	Main	2	$60	
B	1Q	Pvt	Main	1G	$70	($15)
C	1Q	Pvt	Main	1G	$55	

Rates stated in Canadian funds.

307

The Vacationer   **(604) 382-9469 or 384-6553**
1143 Leonard Street, Victoria, B.C. V8V 2S3
(Two blocks from beach, bordering Beacon Hill Park)

One glance at this B&B and you feel the promise of something good inside. Pass the manicured front lawn and flower beds, enter the front door, and you'll receive the heartiest of welcomes from hosts Anne and Henry DeVries. They raised their family here and now keep their home in top shape for B&B guests. The spacious living room with a fireplace of stone is so comfortable that you might feel like inviting friends in for a visit — and you are welcome to do so. The adjacent dining area is the scene of beautifully presented, four-course breakfasts. Anne prides herself on coming up with a different specialty each morning, no matter how long you stay. Three pretty bedrooms with excellent mattresses and color TVs, along with two bathrooms, occupy the second floor. Hosts offer the use of their secluded back yard, bicycles, and a separate phone line. They have a wealth of budget-stretching tips that should help to maximize your resources while visiting lovely Victoria.

No pets, children, or smoking; full breakfast; robes provided; tennis courts nearby; walking distance from downtown; off-street parking; Dutch and German spoken; major credit cards (V, MC); free pickup from downtown, ferries, and bus depot. Off-season rates. Brochure available.

ROOM	BED	BATH	ENTRANCE	FLOOR	DAILY RATES	
					S - D	(EP)
A	1Q	Shd*	Main	2	$40-$60	($15)
B	1Q	Shd*	Main	2	$40-$60	
C	2T	Shd*	Main	2	$40-$55	

Rates stated in Canadian funds.

Please read "About Dining Highlights" on page *ix.*

CAMPBELL RIVER

Driftwood Restaurant, South Island Highway, Oyster Bay; (604) 923-5505 or 923-3833; Chinese and Western cuisines and seafood

Gourmet-by-the-Sea, 4378 South Island Highway, Oyster Bay; (604) 923-5234; fresh seafood and creative Continental cuisine

The Royal Coachman Inn, 84 Dogwood Street; (604) 286-0231; Continental cuisine in English pub atmosphere

CHEMAINUS

Horseshoe Bay Inn Dining Room, 9576 Chemainus Street; (604) 246-3425; varied menu

Saltair Neighborhood Pub, 10519 Knight Street; (604) 246-4942; pub fare

COURTENAY

Fifth Street Café, 384 Fifth Street; (604) 338-0354; breakfast and lunch specialties

The Homestead Restaurant, 932 Fitzgerald; (604) 338-6612; variety of homemade dishes

The Old House Restaurant, 1760 Riverside Lane; (604) 338-5406; Continental dining and pub fare

GANGES (Salt Spring Island)

Harbour House Hotel & Restaurant, 121 Upper Ganges; (604) 537-5571; Continental

KELOWNA

The Finer Choice, 237 Lawrence Avenue; (604) 763-0422; Continental

Hollywood on Top, 211 Bernard Avenue; (604) 763-2777; salads, burgers, fresh pastas and seafood, grilled beef and chicken

Vintage Room, Capri Hotel, 1171 Harvey Avenue (Highway 97); (604) 860-6060; Continental

NANOOSE BAY

Schooner Cove Resort, 3521 Dolphin Drive; (604) 468-7691; varied menu, fresh local seafood, pub fare

PARKSVILLE

Kalvas Restaurant, 180 Molliet; (604) 248-6933; seafood and European cuisine featuring all natural ingredients

PENDER ISLAND

Port Browning Marina Neighbourhood Pub & Cafe, Hamilton Road; (604) 629-3493; home-cooked meals, seafood, burgers, salads

Driftwood Café, Bedwell Harbour Road; (604) 629-6433; chicken specialties, seafood, chowders

Eagle Nest Restaurant, Pender Lodge, Mackinnon Road; (604) 629-3221; Continental

PENTICTON

Theo's, 687 Main Street; (604) 492-4019; Greek

REVELSTOKE

Black Forest Inn, TransCanada Highway West; (604) 837-3495; Bavarian dishes and seafood

The 112, Regent Inn, 112 East First Street; (604) 837-2107; Continental

ROBERTS CREEK

The Creekhouse, Roberts Creek Road and Beach Avenue; (604) 885-9321; Continental

SOOKE

Margison House, 6605 Sooke Road; (604) 642-3620; lunch and afternoon tea

Sooke Harbour House, 1528 Whiffen Spit Road; (604) 642-3421; Pacific northwest cuisine specializing in fresh local seafood

STEVESTON

Steveston Seafood House, 3951 Moncton Street (Richmond); (604) 271-5252; fresh seafood

SUMMERLAND

Shaugnessy's Cove, 12817 Lakeshore Drive; (604) 494-1212; seafood restaurant and pub

VANCOUVER

Chesa Seafood & Grill, 2168 Marine Drive, West Vancouver; (604) 922-3312; seafood and grilled meats

Chez Michel, 1373 Marine Drive, West Vancouver; (604) 926-4913; French

Delilah's, 1906 Haro Street; (604) 687-3424; Continental/northwest

Flamingo House, 7510 Cambie Street; (604) 325-4511; elegant Chinese and creative dim sum

The Harbour House Revolving Restaurant, Harbour Center, 555 West Hastings Street; (604) 669-2220; traditional favorites and West Coast specialties

Horseshoe Bay Boathouse Restaurant, 6695 Nelson Avenue, West Vancouver; (604) 921-8188; fresh seafood

Kettle of Fish, 900 Pacific Street; (604) 682-6661; fresh seafood

Pasparos Taverna, 132 West Third Street, North Vancouver; (604) 980-0331; Greek

The Prow Restaurant, Canada Place; (604) 684-1339; innovative West Coast Canadian cuisine

Salmon House on the Hill, 2229 Folkestone Way, West Vancouver; (604) 926-3212; specialty, barbecued salmon

The Ship of the Seven Seas, Marine Drive at foot of Lonsdale, North Vancouver; (604) 987-3344; seafood buffet

Snappers, 656 Leg-in-Boot Square; (604) 872-1242; seafood

Sprinklers, in the VanDusen Gardens, 5251 Oak Street; (604) 261-0011; Continental

VERNON

Demetri's Steak House, 2705 - 32nd Street; (604) 549-3442; Italian and Greek

Intermezzo Italian Restaurant, 3206 - 34th Avenue; (604) 542-3853

Swiss Hotel Silver Lode Inn, Silver Star Mountain Resort; (604) 549-5105; European and Canadian

Vernon Station Restaurant, 3112 Thirtieth Avenue; (604) 549-3112; burgers, sandwiches, Mexican, spaghetti, lasagne, etc.

VICTORIA

Adrienne's Tea Garden Restaurant, 5325 Cordova Bay Road; (604) 658-1515; Continental

Blethering Place, 2250 Oak Bay Avenue; (604) 598-1413; British

Café Francais, 1635 Fort Street; (604) 595-3441; French

Chantecler Restaurant, 4509 West Saanich Road; (604) 727-3344; Continental

Cordova Express, 5166 Cordova Bay Road; (604) 658-8668; steaks, chicken, fish

Cordova Seaview Inn, 5109 Cordova Bay Road; (604) 658-5227; steak and seafood

Da Tandoor, 1010 Fort Street; (604) 384-6333; Indian

The French Connection, 512 Simcoe Street; (604) 385-7014; French

Grand Central Café, 555 Johnson Street; (604) 386-4747; seafood, pasta, and more

Herald Street Caffé, 546 Herald Street; (604) 381-1441; Italian Continental

London Fish & Chip, 5142 Cordova Bay Road; (604) 658-1921

The Metropolitan Diner, 1715 Government Street; (604) 381-1512; California-style cuisine

Oak Bay Beach Hotel, 1175 Beach Road; (604) 598-4556; afternoon tea

Spinnakers Brew Pub, 308 Catherine Street; (604) 386-BREW; self-serve brew pub serving lunch, snacks, and dinner

Swan's Pub, 506 Pandora Avenue; (604) 361-3310; pub fare Yokohama, 980 Blanshard Street; (604) 384-5433; Japanese

How each friend represents a world in us, a world possibly not born until they arrive, and it is only by this meeting that a new world is born.

—Anaïs Nin

Do you know that conversation is one of the greatest pleasures in life? But it wants leisure.

—W. Somerset Maugham

CALIFORNIA

OREGON

WASHINGTON

BRITISH COLUMBIA

CALIFORNIA

OREGON

WASHINGTON

BRITISH COLUMBIA

B & B Home Locations

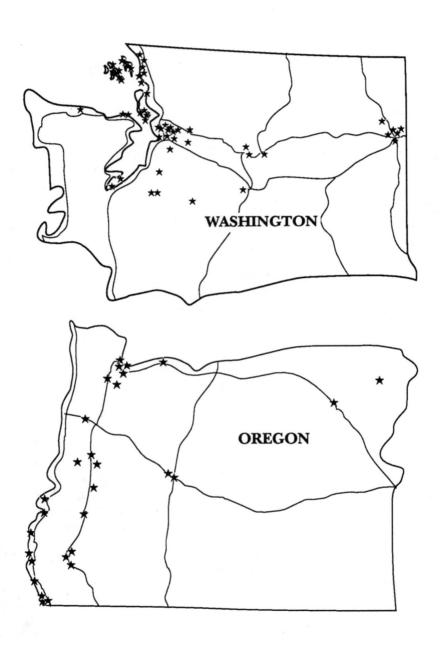